Expansion and Structural Change

Expansion and Structural Change

Higher Education in Germany, the United States, and Japan, 1870–1990

Paul Windolf

WestviewPress

A Division of HarperCollins*Publishers*

All rights reserved. Printed in the United States of America. No part of this publication may be reproduced or transmitted in any form or by any means, electronic or mechanical, including photocopy,
recording, or any information storage and retrieval system, without permission in writing from the
publisher.

Copyright © 1997 by Westview Press, A Division of HarperCollins Publishers, Inc.

Published in 1997 in the United States of America by Westview Press, 5500 Central Avenue, Boulder,
Colorado 80301-2877, and in the United Kingdom by Westview Press, 12 Hid's Copse Road,
Cumnor Hill, Oxford OX2 9JJ

A CIP catalog record for this book is available from the Library of Congress.
ISBN 0-8133-9008-7 (hc)

The paper used in this publication meets the requirements of the American National Standard for
Permanence of Paper for Printed Library Materials Z39.48-1984.

10   9   8   7   6   5   4   3   2   1

Contents

Preface

This volume explores the expansion and structural changes that universities in Germany, the United States, and Japan have experienced over the past century. The expansion began in the latter third of the 19th century and has continued more or less uninterrupted down to the present. This process of expansion has followed a simple rule: enrollment has been higher in virtually every year than in the year before it. Even when enrollment figures declined for a short period, they quickly regained their previous level, from which the expansion then continued. In Germany less than 0.5% of a cohort attended university in 1870, 2% in 1930, 5% in 1960, 21% in 1980, and 32% in 1992.

While the quantitative growth reflected in such figures is considerable, the expansion in educational institutions has consisted of not merely a continual increment in the number of students but also the demise of traditional institutional structures and their replacement by new ones (Chap. 4). In Germany the ever growing number of students transformed the elitist *Gymnasium* into a mass secondary institution, and the earlier, elitist "Humboldt" style of university has been replaced by institutions of mass higher education. Both the goals and the substance of education have also changed, as the abstract, general education of the past has given way to a practical, professionalized training oriented to the demands of the marketplace. University expansion and the process of institutional change are the twin themes of the research presented here. The rapid growth necessitated a structural change in universities, which in turn accelerated the process of expansion even further.

The social origin of students provides a third topic of analysis (Chap. 2). A university education bestows not only academic credentials but also a set of privileges and rights in society, which for groups excluded from economic and political power are indispensable for cultural and political emancipation. The social origin of students, analyzed here for the period 1887-1990, provides something of a mirror of the political struggle for access to university education. The driving force behind university expansion in Germany and other European countries are political struggles: first, that of the bourgeoisie against the aristocracy for political liberalization, second, that of the working class against the bourgeoisie, and, third, that of women for emancipation and equal rights. The introduction of admission quotas for ethnic minorities in the United States opened yet another round in this struggle for equal opportunity to university access.

This historical sequence of conflicts between social groups is reminiscent of Pareto's concept of the circulation of elites: "Because of the circulation of elites the ruling elite is constantly in a state of transformation. It flows like a river that today is never what it was yesterday. From time to time there occur sudden and violent eruptions. These revolutions always take place when in the ruling class – whether because of inadequate circulation or other causes – decadent elements collect which are no longer able to muster the force necessary to hold onto power. ... In the meantime, persons of particular ability have gained power within the lower class who command the forces needed to carry out government functions, and who are prepared to use violence."

To Pareto the circulation of elites is, as a rule, a violent and revolutionary process, and this explains the central role which the concept of violence plays in his theory. Because the ruling elites seek to hold onto their power and deny new elites of the lower classes access to higher status positions, the circulation process is usually enforced by violence and revolution.

Over the past century the "circulation of elites" has been tamed in modern industrial societies, and what previously occurred as "sudden and violent eruptions" appears today as processes of social reform and peaceful evolution. A continual process of circulation through institutionalized channels has replaced revolutionary upheavals. In modern democracies the educational institution, in particular the university, provides the most important avenue of upward mobility. The selection processes of the university and the government bureaucracy determine the rate of exchange mobility (circulation) in a given country. This can be accelerated or slowed by a relative "opening" or "closure" of educational institutions, changes in selection criteria, or the introduction of selection procedures (e.g., entrance examinations). From the point of view of the "circulation of elites" one can analyze a country in terms of whether an exchange is taking place, the extent to which government institutions regulate the exchange, and the role of universities in determining the rate of exchange.

The expansion of university education has not only had an impact upon the structure of the universities and social mobility but has also accelerated a process of modernization which Max Weber characterized as the bureaucratization and rationalization of Western nations (Schluchter 1989). As early as the 17th century Prussia introduced a system of eligibility for positions in the bureaucracy which led to a symbiosis between it and the university. As the basis for eligibility, and thus status, the new system substituted meritocratic principles for aristocratic birth or patronage (Rosenberg 1958). The meritocracy – the selection of personnel for higher status positions on the basis of formal education – became a model on which the management of large industrial firms subsequently came to orient themselves. Thus the university and the bureaucracy became allies in ascribing status in the modern industrial society.

On the part of the students there is the expectation that a university degree will provide them with a life-long entitlement to appropriate job and salary opportunities. On the other hand, the state bureaucracies in Germany and in France had been and are still obliged by law to fill the higher administrative positions with university graduates. This system stabilizes an exchange relationship between bureaucracy and university; the university recruits and socializes potential personnel in terms of the needs of the government bureaucracy. The academic education and culture of civil servants then represents a basis for the independence of the bureaucracy vis-à-vis the political parties and government. A large part of the university's power rests on this exchange. I illustrate the implementation of meritocratic selection principles here in administrative reforms carried out in Prussia and, from a comparative perspective, also in the United States, France, and Japan (Chap. 5).

Educational expansion, the structural reform of universities, the political struggle of different social groups for access to universities, and the meritocratic selection for higher status positions are mutually reinforcing processes. The growing number of students caused the collapse of the traditional elitist university and forced structural change and adaptation. However, the more important a university diploma became for obtaining access to higher positions, the more the political battle intensified between those who had gained access to higher education and those who had been excluded from it.

Although this analysis focuses principally on the expansion and structural change of German universities, I also try to take into account the historical development of universities in other countries, particularly in the United States and Japan and, as far as data are available, also in France and Italy. It is impossible to present a systematic comparison of several countries over such a long period of time. Nevertheless, the comparative view puts the specifically German or Japanese paths into perspective and demonstrates the extent to which patterns of university expansion, bureaucratization, and modernization have differed in various nation states.

Enrollment rates in higher education are an important indicator of modernization processes and are analyzed here over a period of 120 years. Success and stabilization of the nation state in one period, its failure and erosion in another, are reflected, respectively, in accelerated and slowed growth rates of enrollment in higher education. Participation in university education is also a valid indicator of the sociopolitical status of women in different societies, which becomes particularly evident when comparing enrollment rates for women in the United States with those in Japan (Sect. 6.1).

There are two basic dimensions of the analysis in this book: a comparative and an historical. To understand their "system" character educational institutions can be analyzed only from a comparative perspective (Archer 1979). Observing them over a long period of time allows one to identify long-term structural changes and their impact on other social systems. The historical and the comparative perspectives are combined here.

This analysis compares the development of higher education in different nation states. However, states may change or even lose their identity over time, and therefore become a "moving target" rather than a stable point of reference for the analysis. This is particularly true for Germany, which – as a nation state – changed its constitution and political regime four times during this period, altered its borders substantially, and with the partition into two separate states between 1949 and 1989 lost its "identity" as a single nation state.

"Germany" thus represents a different country at different times in this comparison. From 1871 to 1919 (the Imperial period) Germany experienced its greatest geographic extension in modern times. After the First World War "Germany" continued to exist as the Weimar Republic (1919-1933) but covering a reduced territory. From the Second World War until 1989 two "Germanies" existed, and since 1989 Germany has tried hard to become "one" Germany again. The analysis presented here refers to the territory and population of "Germany" during the respective periods under consideration. For the period 1950-1990 the analysis is limited to the Federal Republic of Germany (West Germany).

All data sources which have been used for Tables and Figures are given in Appendix I unless otherwise noted.

Paul Windolf

Acknowledgments

The beginnings of this book go back to 1984. At that time I was Visiting Scholar at Stanford University and was happy to enjoy the hospitality of my colleagues there. In discussions with John Meyer I came to appreciate the substantial differences between the educational systems of European countries and that of the United States.

In 1985 I was the guest of Robert Salais at INSEE in Paris, where I collected data on the French educational system. Two years later I was awarded the Jean Monnet Fellowship to the University Institute in Florence, Italy. As this Fellowship entailed no teaching responsibilities, I was able to devote myself while there to studying the Italian educational system. I am very indebted to the help of Alessandro Cavalli, in Pavia, who provided me valuable assistance in analyzing the Italian university system.

A stipend from the German Research Council allowed me to assemble an historical dataset on the university system of Germany. The State Library in Berlin has in its collection a unique archive that encompasses substantial historical statistics on the universities of Prussia in the 19th century, including information not only on students' subjects but also on their social backgrounds.

During my time as Visiting Professor at Columbia University in 1992-1993 I was able to carry out the spectral analysis in Chap. 7 on the cycles of educational expansion. Harrison White at the Center for the Social Sciences provided me the opportunity to discuss and develop my research there, and I am very indebted to him for his valuable suggestions.

While enjoying an extended stay in Japan in 1994 I was able to supplement the study further with data on the Japanese university system. I wish to thank Keiichi Yoshimoto, without whose help I would not have had access to rewarding sources of data.

I also extend my appreciation to Terry Barton in Heidelberg, who not only translated the text but helped me to overcome many "Teutonic" idiosyncracies.

P.W.

1

Educational Expansion as Secular Process

1.1 Time Series in Comparison

The concept of educational expansion refers generally to the substantial growth witnessed by universities during the period between 1960 and 1975. This period is often associated with the politicization of universities and with the student movement, which are popularly seen as a result of the expansion. During these 15 years the educational system of West Germany experienced much that had been going on gradually over many decades in other countries: universities lost their status as institutions for the elite and were opened to the masses. This phase of rapid expansion was of short duration; the increase in enrollment returned to more normal levels in the mid-1970's, after which the period of rapid expansion appeared as a unique event at a time of predominantly liberal educational policies.[1]

However, this expansion in educational institutions was in fact not an isolated event in the years after the Second World War but rather a phase in a longer, secular process. The educational systems of many industrializing countries have been expanding since the 19th century, and data are available to document this expansion, particularly that of universities, at least since the late 19th century. The curve of university expansion shows a long-term rise over the past century, and in fact hardly affected by the various economic cycles. From the time of German unification in 1870/1871 down to the First World War university enrollment grew in Germany at an annual rate of almost 2%, and during the interwar years the universities experienced a particularly rapid expansion, due in large part to the influx of the middle class and women.[2] Between 1925 and 1932 the number of students rose from 86,000 to almost 140,000. The expansionary curve of these years then underwent phases of stasis and decline, finally resuming its upward climb again in the mid-1960's.

Figures 1.1-1.4 present the curve of the enrollment rates[3] in Germany, the United States, and Japan between 1870 and 1990 for men and women separately; Fig. 1.5 shows the enrollment rates for women in the United States, France, and Germany. These data show clear differences in the rate of growth both between the countries and between various periods within each country. Growth in the years before the First World War was comparatively modest, with expansion in the three countries developing similarly (although the lead of the United States in higher education was visible already before the First World War). In the interwar period the expansion in the United States and Japan (men) accelerated, while the economic and political catastrophes that befell Germany during this era are reflected in steep, reversed, and broken segments of its curve (Fig. 1.1, men). It was only in the 1960's that German universities then attained the growth which the United States (and to some extent men in Japan) had experienced already before the Second World War. Since the beginning of the 1970's the rate of educational expansion in the United States has been declining, so that in the late 1970's the respective curves have met. The two "late comers" (Japan, Germany) have surpassed the "first new nation" (Lipset 1963), at least with respect to enrollment rates in higher education. This, however, is true only for men. For women, the "modernization gap" between the United States, on the one hand, and Japan and Germany, on the other, is still evident, even though German women narrowed the gap during the 1970's and 1980's (Fig. 1.4).

Whereas women were allowed admission to university in Prussia only in 1907, in the United States they already made up 15% of university students in 1870. As in the case of their male counterparts, American women attended university in continually growing numbers from 1890 until the depression of the 1930's, when a leveling off is seen about 1932-1934. However, also in the United States the depression was unable to substantially hinder the educational expansion. Despite the nearly 13 million unemployed in 1933 (some 25% of the work force) the expansion continued with only a short stasis phase until the Second World War (Fig. 1.1).

1.2 Competing Theories of Educational Expansion

Why is it that ever growing numbers of students spend an ever longer period at universities, in spite of the fact that students' de facto expectations regarding professional careers have worsened with these growing numbers?[4] What are the reasons for the constant growth in university enrollment?

The simplest explanation for this growth lies in a self-perpetuation of university education over several generations (inheritance effect). Once a liberal education policy has set in motion the expansion of universities, this expansion accelerates automatically over generations. It is an "iron law" of educational research that the children of university graduates attain on average a higher educational level than do children of those who did not attend university.[5] Children of the working class who obtain a university education, then, no longer belong to the working class. Their children, in turn, without roots in the working class, enjoy a higher likelihood of obtaining a university education than do working class children. This multiplier effect in the proportion of university students is evident as early as the second generation. From one generation to the next, the educational level attained climbs continually, albeit with decreasing speed.[6]

This sort of growth can be seen as *endogenous*, as it derives from forces set in motion by the educational expansion itself. However, such endogenous growth cannot, by itself, explain the growth pattern as shown in Figs. 1.1-1.5. In the case of Germany, for instance, one can distinguish three periods: (a) that before the First World War, with a low growth rate; (b) that between the World Wars, with zero growth and extreme cyclical variations; and (c) that after the Second World War, with a high growth rate. The expansion in university enrollment is not maintained solely by endogenous forces, but is influenced by economic and political circumstances which, in terms of the educational system, can be termed exogenous.

There are many general theories about educational expansion, however, only few systematic efforts to explain the long-term growth which has characterized the history of the institution. Among the range of theories in the social scientific literature one finds at least three competing models of educational expansion: functionalist theories, theories of status competition, and a third model which will be termed here as "conflict theory" (Collins 1971, 1979). The central theses of these theories are summarized below, followed by an examination of the extent to which each is supported by historical data.

Functionalist Theories (Human Capital)
Functionalist theories are in agreement that educational expansion meets a

4

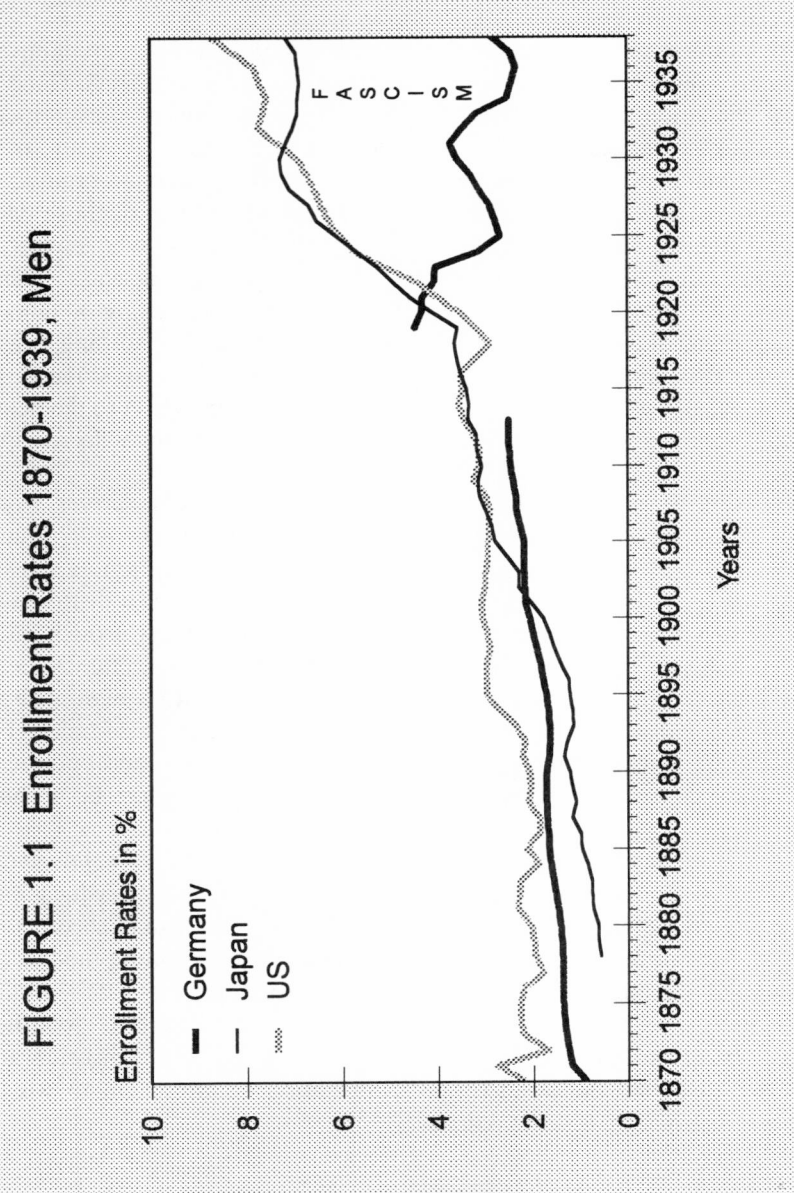

FIGURE 1.1 Enrollment Rates 1870-1939, Men

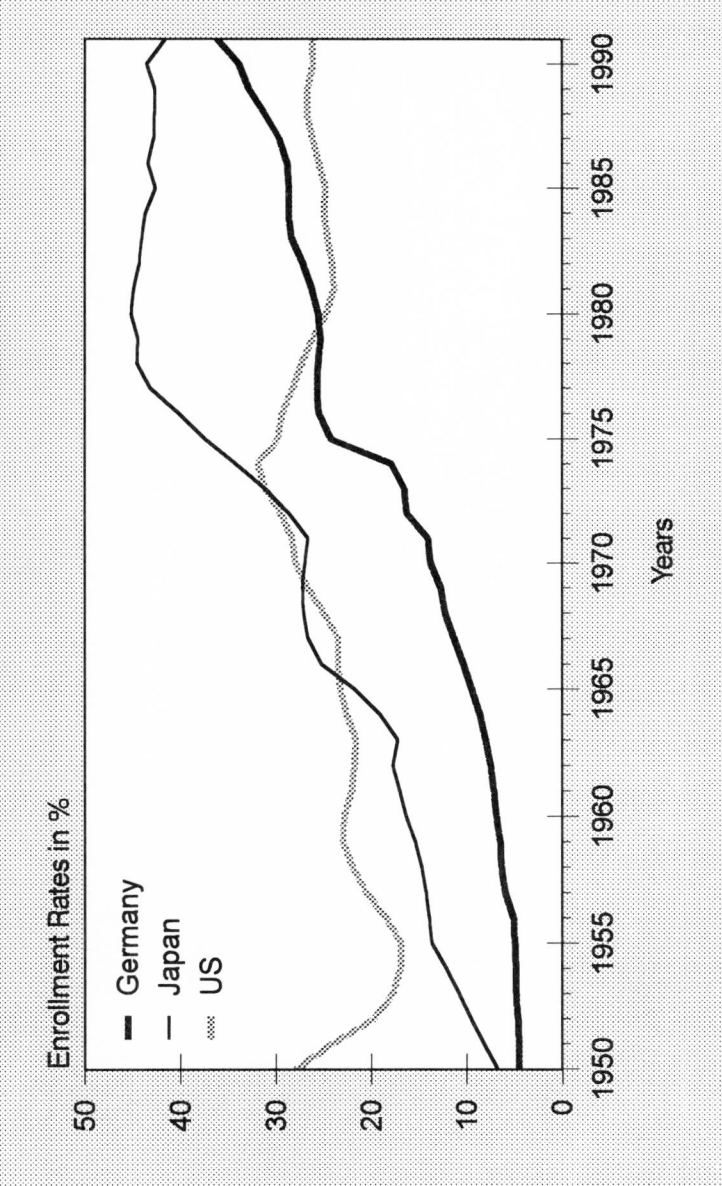

FIGURE 1.2 Enrollment Rates 1950-1991, Men

6

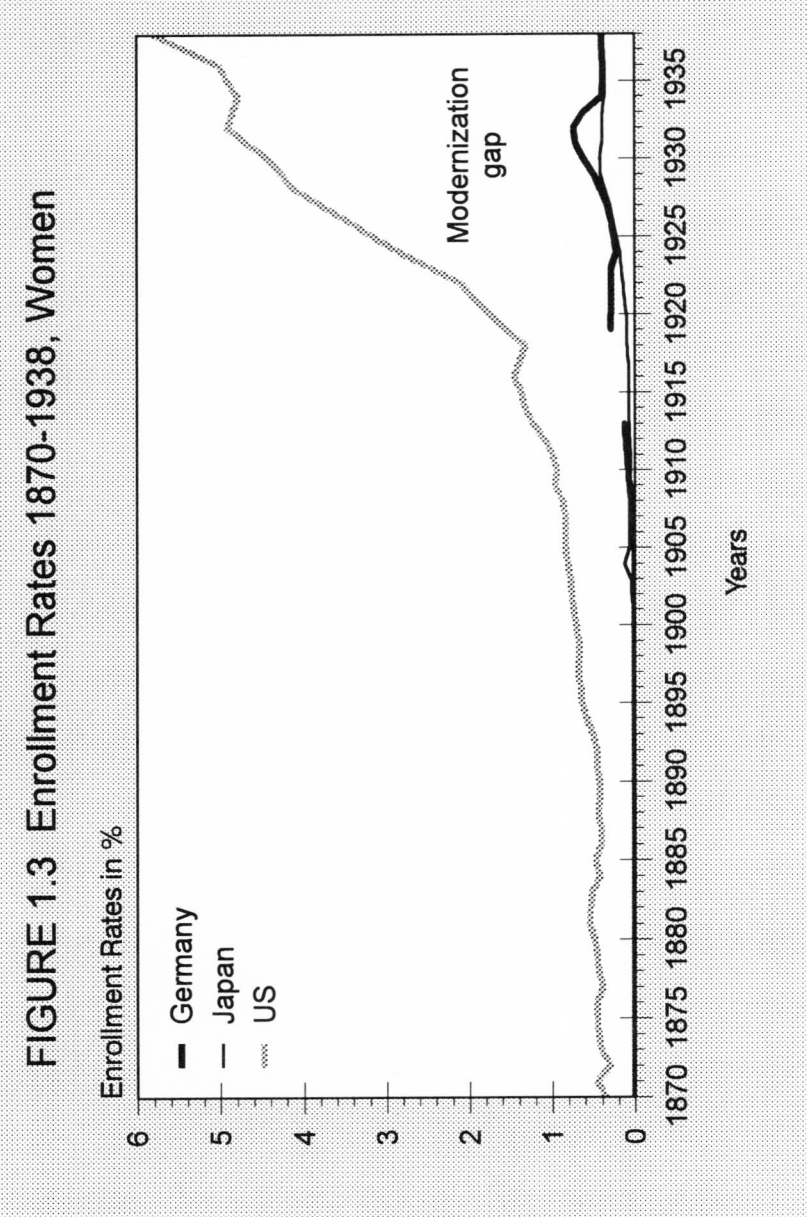

FIGURE 1.3 Enrollment Rates 1870-1938, Women

FIGURE 1.4 Enrollment Rates 1950-1991, Women

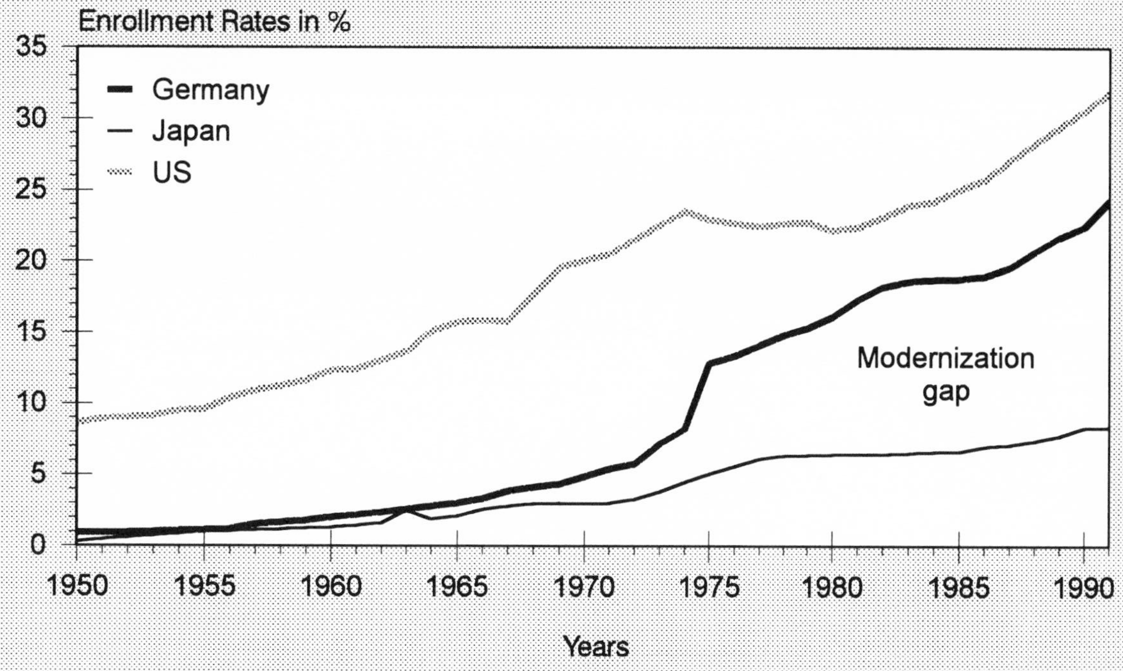

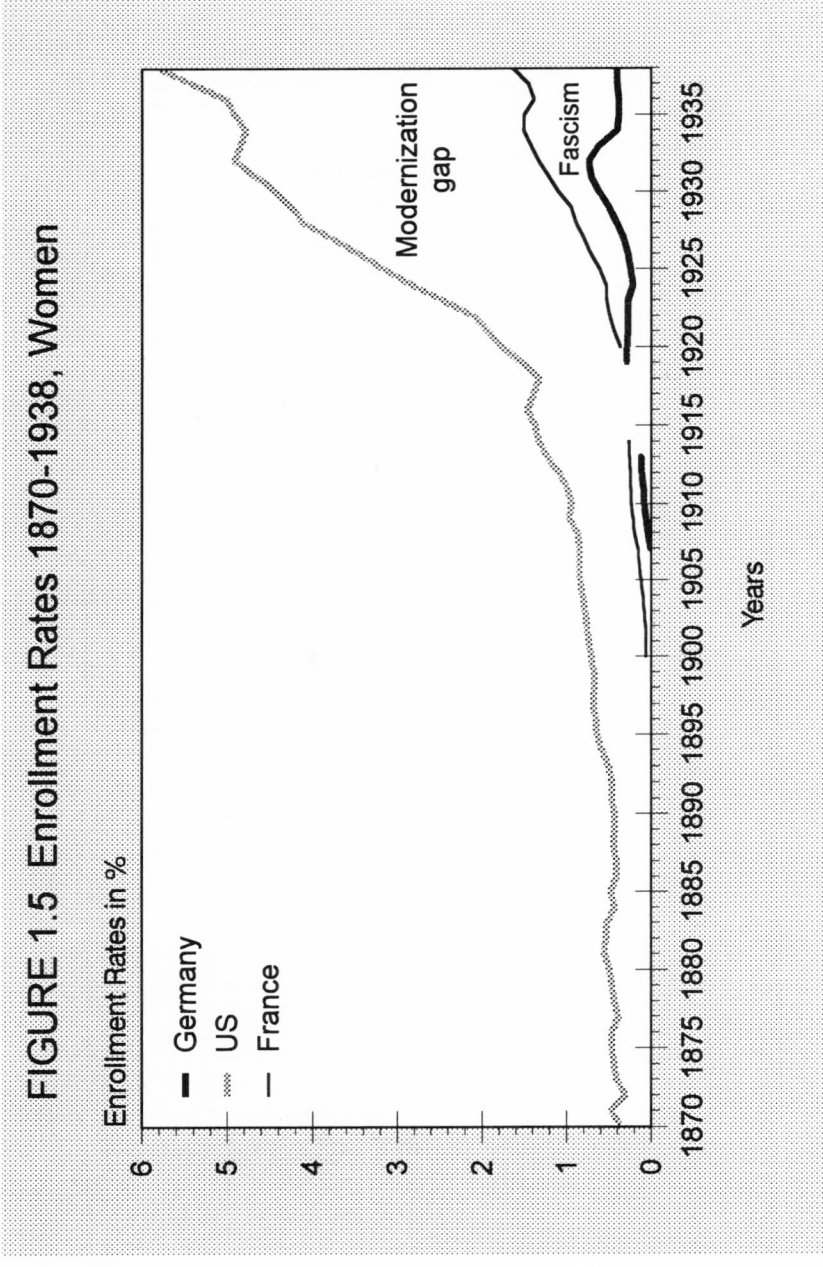

FIGURE 1.5 Enrollment Rates 1870-1938, Women

societal need; disagreement arises among them, however, regarding the definition of what this societal need is. The theory of human capital maintains that education raises labor productivity: highly trained personnel are more innovative, productive, and flexible than unskilled workers. Thus, seen from the perspective of society, education is an investment for future growth and modernization.[7] In addition, the theory of human capital postulates a straightforward market relationship between the demand for trained personnel and university enrollment levels: times of economic growth are accompanied by university expansion while economic recessions are marked by declining numbers of university students. This view regards the labor market and the university as mutually regulating systems: university expansion does not continue endlessly but is limited by the demand for specialized qualifications. Although there are periods of over- or undersupply, this model regards the relationship between educational system and labor market as one approaching equilibrium.[8]

A second form of the functionalist explanation emphasizes the educational responsibility of the educational system. Universities as well as schools are seen principally not as conveying occupationally oriented knowledge but as socializing the young for the demands that their future occupation will put upon them. Bowles and Gintis (1978, p. 37), for example, stress the stabilizing effect of the educational system for capitalist production: "Since its inception in the United States, the public-school system has been seen as a method of disciplining children in the interest of producing a properly subordinate adult population. Sometimes conscious and explicit, and at other times a natural emanation from the conditions of dominance and subordinacy prevalent in the economic sphere, the theme of social control pervades educational thought and policy." Taking over from the family, educational institutions instill orientations toward the world that are necessary for the person's acclimatization to the working world.[9] For instance, it is not a body of technical knowledge that is to be expected from a university education but a professional ethos, discipline, perseverance, and flexibility in responding to quickly changing conditions. Thus, the educational institutions produce the personality structure which is accommodated to different job demands: high school drop-outs for the monotonous assembly line, community college graduates for respectable administrative work, and university graduates for professional jobs.

The assumption that economic growth and modernization are the motor behind the expansion of educational institutions was questioned as early as the turn of this century by the Prussian economist and educational researcher Franz Eulenberg, who pointed out a paradoxical relationship between university and labor market (1904, p. 256): "Favorable economic conditions tend to limit university enrollment and unfavorable conditions to expand it." Eulenberg's observation represented an assault on modernization theories, which had traced university expansion to the rising demand by industry for technically trained personnel.[10] Thus, even a century ago the integration of the university in the labor market did not seem to function as hypothesized by the theory of human capital, and as was still maintained by its proponents 60 years later.

Eulenberg supported his position with empirical data: the number of students at German universities had increased every year since 1866, even during the depression that severely affected economic conditions after 1875. Later, during the depression of the 1930's, it was estimated that between 80,000 and 100,000 university graduates were unemployed or had taken positions for which they were overtrained; despite this, however, the universities were experiencing a hitherto unprecedented flood of students.[11]

Aside from the periods of the two World Wars there have been only two periods in the history of German universities since 1866 during which the absolute number of students declined; one was at the time of the 1922-1923 hyperinflation which wiped out the savings of many middle class families, and the other was after the introduction in 1933 by the new Nazi regime of statutory ceilings for the number of university admissions in specific subjects. Data on university enrollments in France and the United States show that the expansionary curve in these countries continued to rise during these periods and was eventually brought to a halt only by the outbreak of the Second World War.

Figure 1.6 presents the enrollment levels at Italian universities between 1888 and 1912. The curve here offers further support for Eulenberg's view: despite the economic recession there from 1888 to 1902 the number of students increased dramatically, whereas matriculations declined over the subsequent years of economic upswing.[12] These data provide an early indication of the "anti-cyclical" relationship between cycles of economic and of educational expansion (see Chap. 7).

Comparable data from the United Kingdom also confirm Eulenberg's view, as is shown by Stone's (1974) historical analysis of expansion in universities there. Enrollment levels at British universities witnessed avirtually unbroken expansion throughout the second half of the 19th century and continuing up to the Second World War. The number of new students (only men) rose from 1323 in 1870 to 2507 in 1903 – an average annual increase of 1.9%.[13] The United Kingdom was also subject to the

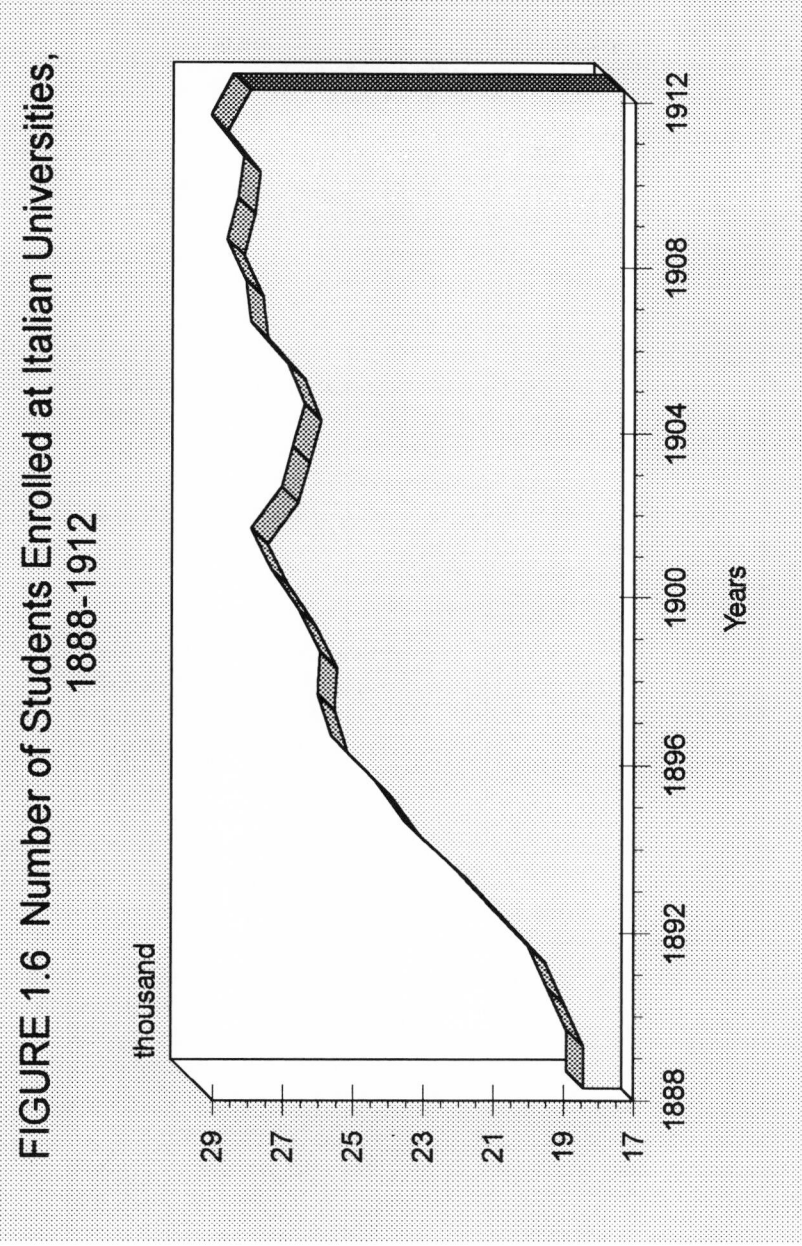

FIGURE 1.6 Number of Students Enrolled at Italian Universities, 1888-1912

depression of the third quarter of the 19th century; however, student numbers did not decline. "In 1879 there began a profound depression that hit agriculture particularly hard, and especially those areas devoted exclusively to arable farming. Rents fell dramatically, and many tenants and rural landlords found themselves in severe difficulties. Not only were the landed gentry very hard hit, but the finances of the colleges suffered a crippling blow, from which they did not recover until after the First World War. The graph of admissions continued to soar triumphantly past this economic watershed as if it never existed..."[14] The upward course of university expansion in the United Kingdom also continued unabated during the depression of 1928-1932.

These data show that it is not economic upswing but precisely economic downturn which accelerates educational expansion – in apparent contrast to all the laws of economic rationality. Why is it that students flock to the universities at times when the career opportunities offered by a university education seem to be in decline? If the expansion of universities is independent of the business cycle, economic theories of market regulation mechanisms cannot be expected to contribute much to explaining the causes of the expansion.

Individual Status Competition

With the chronic overproduction of university graduates since, at the latest, the early 1970's this question has again become a central issue in the area of educational sociology. The French sociologist Boudon (1977) has argued that the educational decision of individual actors can have undesired long-term side effects for the overall society. The educational expansion is not, in this view, limited by a societal need, as maintained by theorists of the human capital approach; rather, *a competition for status* develops among individuals attempting to outbid one another for a scarce number of positions. With educational certificates serving as an important condition for the opportunity to pursue a professional career and to climb the social ladder in meritocratic society, individuals take an attitude resembling that in an arms race: "The more, the better."[15] In this way, that which for the individual appears entirely rational becomes for society in general increasingly irrational. The unrestricted aspirations of individuals for educational qualification accumulate throughout the society to a chronic market oversupply of university graduates – and the hypothesized equilibrium between the economic and educational systems becomes ever less tenable.

In contrast to proponents of the human capital theory, Boudon (1977) maintains that no such natural limit acts as a brake on educational expansion: it is neither the market demand for technical qualifications nor the societal need for accommodated personality structures that drives educational expansion but *individual* status competition. This competition for status does not diminish in the face of hard times – indeed, if anything, it becomes more intense due to the scarcity of positions on offer. The greater the number of unemployed seeking a given number of jobs, the more individually rational it becomes to prolong one's education to be able to compete with greater prospect of success and thus escape the fate of those who – irrationally – broke off their education earlier.

The only external limit to such educational competition that is envisaged by this theory is the cut in public funding to the universities, which is an important subsidy to the upwardly aspiring student, especially in countries such as Germany, France, and Italy where the individual student contributes little directly to the cost of his or her university education.

The two theories of educational expansion discussed here – the functionalist and that of status competition – can also be contrasted from another angle, that of integration/decoupling regarding the relationship between university and labor market. *Integration* here refers to the increasing accommodation of the university to the demands of an expanding labor market; *decoupling*, on the other hand, is the opposite trend – the increasing autonomy of the two systems and their independence from one another (Lutz 1979). Functionalist theories assume the integration of the two, grounded in the mechanisms of market forces, whereas theories of status competition see them as undergoing a decoupling.

Integration and decoupling do not only characterize the problematic relationship between university and labor market but also delimit respective historical phases in the expansion of educational institutions. The expansion of the universities that began after German unification (1871), the establishment of natural science institutes, and the rapid success of polytechnics were responses to opportunities in the labor market that had opened up in the late 19th century.[16] The university thus measured its educational ideal not only against academic standards but also against certain recognized needs of the labor market as a legitimate basis of university education. However, by the end of the Weimar Republic the expansion of German universities had become a process effectively independent of the economic needs of society. Even during this time a relationship certainly existed between the business cycle and university expansion – which reached crisis proportions in 1929-1931 –

but this relationship was by no means a positive response to conditions in the labor market. By this time students attending universities were seeking less the qualifications required for pursuing an occupation in the future than the (state-subsidized) refuge from the otherwise very probable unemployment.[17]

Functionalist theories and theories of status competition, however, are not necessarily mutually exclusive in all points, for individuals who attempt to improve their competitive position by obtaining supplementary qualifications and degrees can thereby be fulfilling society's need for well-trained personnel. Nevertheless the two models do generate contrary prognoses in times of economic recession and high unemployment. Whereas the human capital view would predict declining enrollment rates due to the lack of demand in the labor market, proponents of the status competition theory would foresee stable, if not in fact expanding, enrollment levels, for it is precisely at such times that a university degree can offer the greatest comparative advantage due to the intensified struggle over a declining number of available jobs.

Over the past century there have been several serious economic downturns, characterized by relatively long duration and a decline in economic activity to the extent that living standards were reduced. Each of these recessions reached beyond the borders of individual nations and seriously affected all Western capitalist countries. These were the depressions of 1878-1890[18] and 1928-1935 and a more recent economic recession which began in Germany in 1975 and lasted almost a decade. What were the enrollment rates at universities in these periods? Did they show a downturn in parallel with the level of economic activity, as the human capital theory would predict, or continue to rise, as would be expected by the status competition school? Time series of university enrollment and economic activity (gross national product) are analyzed below to answer these questions.[19]

Collective Conflict Theory

The third theory of university expansion, that referred to here as "conflict theory" (Collins 1971, 1979), points to differences in prestige and power of the various status groups struggling for social mobility. Max Weber, who originally developed this concept, emphasized differences in religion, ethnicity, sex, educational and cultural resources to explain stratification processes and social inequality in modern societies. This approach also begins with competition, but not that of individuals competing for social status, rather that of *social groups* struggling for political and cultural emancipation and for the right of participation in political decision-making processes. According to this approach the expansion in higher education cannot be explained by the business cycle, but is propelled by political struggles of the working class against the bourgeoisie, of women against men and of ethnic minorities against "White Anglo-Saxon Protestants." Access to higher education is an instrument for emancipation and equal rights of different status groups in modern societies.

Turner (1960, p. 856) introduced the term *"sponsored mobility"* to characterize institutionalized channels of social mobility and national differences in the selective access to higher education. He compares mobility processes in the United States and United Kingdom and argues that "under sponsored mobility elite recruits are chosen by the established elite or their agents, and elite status is *given* on the basis of some criterion of supposed merit and cannot be *taken* by any amount of effort or strategy." *"Contest mobility"* which characterizes the predominant mode of mobility in the United States, "is a system in which elite status is the prize in an open contest and is taken by the aspirants' own efforts." Under "sponsored mobility ... individuals do not win or seize elite status; mobility is rather a process of sponsored induction into the elite" (Turner 1960, p. 857).

With some modifications Turner's concept of *"sponsored mobility"* may be used to analyze the highly institutionalized mobility chains in Germany and other European countries which are under *state* control; here, individual competition plays only a secondary role in obtaining access to university and, subsequently, to an elite position. There is only limited status competition in an open market, but rather a controlled selection process which begins at the age of 12 when parents decide whether their children will attend the academic tracks of secondary education or pursue vocationally oriented training.

German universities are not controlled by market forces but by a centralized state bureaucracy which may apply different instruments to reinforce its authority over the educational system. First, the state bureaucracy has the exclusive power to entitle secondary schools to award the *Abitur* diploma, without which no student can gain access to a university. At the turn of the century there was a bitter dispute whether secondary schools which did not teach the classical languages (Latin and Greek) or did so for only a few years should be licensed to grant the *Abitur*. A nine-year curriculum of classical languages proved a formidable barrier to university admission for students from lower social classes. When technical secondary schools were authorized to award the

Abitur the number of university students grew rapidly.

Secondly, German universities are funded exclusively by the state and are not allowed to charge fees. Thus, the universities are totally dependent upon state grants and are unable to raise their budget with the rising number of students. Flooded by the growing number of students, the universities themselves ask for a *Numerus clausus*, which is the third instrument that the state bureaucracy may use to control the university system. For many academic subjects a ceiling of first-year students is stipulated beyond which universities do not enroll students. Since the number of applicants for such subjects as medicine, biology, architecture, psychology, management science, and chemistry is always higher than the number of university places, students are selected according to their grades at high school, but military service or service in a hospital (for medical students) may also be helpful. Because of the *Numerus clausus* many students who want to study architecture, psychology, or chemistry are forced to enroll in other subjects.

Status competition is not enough to overcome these politically defined barriers to entrance. Periods of rapid university expansion (e.g., 1925-1930, 1967-1975) were also periods of strong collective movements and political liberalization, the first during the Weimar Republic in Germany and the second during the student movement of the late 1960's.

At the turn of the century women were granted the right of equal opportunity in applying for university admission in Germany, and the subsequent throng of female university students between 1925 and 1930 was a principal contributor to the continued expansion in university enrollment rates. Following the Second World War the increase in the numbers of students with working class background and women attending university led to a further rise in enrollment levels.

If mobility chains are "sponsored" and the selection process for elite positions is controlled by the state and bureaucratic selection criteria, access to universities cannot be obtained by individual status competition but only by a collective struggle to overcome political barriers. In Germany, phases of accelerated university expansion can probably not be explained solely by reference to the business cycle. Rather, they are seen as the result of a "political cycle" in which periods of liberal "openness" alternate with periods of conservative "closure" regarding university admissions. Phases of accelerated growth of universities do not correspond to periods of economic expansion but rather reflect times of particular liberalism in educational policies. The outcome of political class conflicts and the relative balance of political power among competing social groups which led to liberalism in education policies seems to have more explanatory power for the secular university expansion in Germany.

A similar observation can be made for *Japan*. During the interwar-years Japan experienced a period of "liberalization" similar to that of the Weimar Republic in Germany. The Taisho period (1912-1926) was characterized by a number of democratic reforms, such as a labor exchange bill, a tenancy dispute arbitration law, and, most importantly, the universal manhood suffrage law (1925) that enfranchised Japanese adult males aged over 25 (Takayoshi 1966). During this period the number of labor disputes increased, the Japan Federation of Labor (Sodomei) was founded (1921), and a number of left-wing and even communist student associations became active at Japanese universities. The Taisho years mark the period of a strong expansion of higher education in Japan (for men; see Fig. 1.1). However, most observers have characterized the Taisho period as "ambiguous": It was a period of relative political liberalization, but – as in Germany – also of political confrontation between left- and right-wing parties. After 1930 Japan became more and more reactionary, nationalistic, and authoritarian – a political climate which provoked a stasis and decline of higher education after 1930.

Theories of status competition and "conflict theories" of expansion in higher education are not mutually exclusive, but differ in their emphasis on market competition and collective action. Both stress competition for high-status positions as the driving force behind the expansion. However, whereas status competition models emphasize the competition of *individuals*, the expansion of universities is seen from the point of view of "conflict theories" as a *collective* battle of social groups for emancipation and equal rights. Women try to attend universities regardless of whether the unemployment rate is low or high precisely because they regard their university degree as part of a political (collective) struggle for the emancipation of women in a male-dominated society. In the status competition model individual actors compete in the market place for higher status positions. "Conflict theories" stress the role of collective actors such as the state bureaucracy, the political parties and interest groups in providing access to university.

In this section, three models have been outlined to explain the secular process of expansion in higher education: The human capital theory sees the university and the labor market as mutually regulating systems; university expansion is stimulated by job opportunities but also limited by high unemployment. The model of status competition stresses the individual competition for high status position as the driving force behind the expansion, and this competition may be more intensive in times of high unemployment. Finally, if mobility chains are "sponsored" and controlled by a state bureaucracy, individual competition is not sufficient to gain access to the university; a collective conflict strategy for a liberal and "open" educational policy may be a more promising avenue to higher status positions.

The competing hypotheses of these three theories are examined in the following chapters. Since only those of the human capital and status competition approaches lend themselves to quantified data analysis, the discussion in Sect. 1.3 restricts itself to consideration of these two theories. The "conflict theory" is tested in subsequent chapters by means of an analysis of the social backgrounds of university students and the political struggles for university admission (see Chap. 3).

To anticipate an overall conclusion of the analyses, we can note that none of the three theories is clearly falsified; each can find considerable support in the available data. However, considering the somewhat conflicting empirical results generally, educational expansion seems to be explained by a combination of collective struggle for political emancipation and power (in particular on the part of women and lower socioeconomic groups) and individual status competition. The aspiration of individuals for social status remains an indispensable factor, setting in motion the somewhat self-perpetuating process of expansion. Factors relating to the economic cycle, finally, appear important insofar as they limit the range of actors' freedom, particularly in times of economic recession. Even if in times of high unemployment status competition becomes intensified, individuals' educational aspirations must often be modified, because of reduced resources both of the individuals and of the government.

1.3 Expansion as a Cyclical Process

In Germany, as in other countries, educational expansion has not been a continual process of growth over the past century. Economic depressions and both World Wars have stalled the expansion, and the totalitarian measures of the Nazi regime attempted to return university enrollment to a preindustrial level. Periods of rapid expansion have almost always been followed by times of stasis, albeit seldom involving the decline in absolute numbers of those enrolled.

The time series presented in Fig. 1.1 can be separated into three different components: a trend, a cycle, and what one can refer to as "chance" or "disturbance" (Borchardt 1977). The trend refers to a long-term, often secular development which underlies the individual observation points. In this case the trend represents the forces that have held university expansion on course fairly continuously for over a century – despite occasionally massive "disturbance" and short-term stasis. In Germany, for instance, the development in university enrollment rates was disrupted momentarily by the two World Wars and the chaos of the interwar period; however, the course of its development was, in the long-term, only postponed by these events and was eventually resumed.

The cycle describes a regular, wavelike variation along the curve of the trend. The introduction of the cycle component makes evident that educational institutions do not grow monotonically, with the various waves representing circumscribed periods of expansion, followed by stasis, followed by renewed expansion. It can be seen that these variations have a certain *regularity* and thus constancy and, to some extent, measurable cyclical variation (period). When we observe the short-term, wavelike variations in Fig. 1.1, the question is: do these in fact show such a regular, cyclical structure, or do they reflect mere chance disturbance along the long-term course?

The relationship between cycle and disturbance can be illustrated in the data from the *Weimar Republic era*. The waves in the curve for university enrollment reflects the course of political and economic crises which Germany experienced between the World Wars. The abrupt decline in enrollment rates after 1921 is largely due to the postwar hyperinflation that decimated the savings of the middle class. The later downturn of 1933 reflects the policy of the new Nazi regime aimed explicitly at limiting the overall number of university admissions. As regards the long-term course of university enrollment rates, the fact that an economic factor such as hyperinflation or a political factor such as totalitarian education policy could reverse the long-term trend is a matter of "chance." This by no means labels such events, of course, as inexplicable but recognizes merely that they are singular events that can be explained only by means of historical reconstruction of specific, nonrecurring causes and as such merely "disturb" the course of developments which, on the other hand, do grow out of forces at work over the long term.

Such obvious "disturbances" play little or no role in the data from before the First World War or those from after the Second. Constructing a straight line in Fig. 1.1 from beginning to end of the respective curves for these periods would show the variations to be cyclical waves above and below the imaginative linear development. These wavelike cycles are fairly regular and are probably influenced by the business cycle (I return to this relationship below).

The differences between trend, cycle, and chance (disturbance) components can be illustrated not only when one looks back into the past but also when gazing into the future. Since the trend and cycle represent long-term, regular, recurrent forces, their extrapolation onward from the present would permit predictions about future levels of university enrollment levels (regardless of how nearly correct they might prove to be). Such prognoses, however, cannot be derived from the disturbance component.

If, in the year 1913, one had looked backed over the period since 1870, an annual increment of 1.7% would have been evident in university enrollment rates in Germany, and this long-term average (trend) could have served for predictions into the future. Had not the First World War, postwar hyperinflation, and Nazi totalitarianism (massive disturbances) intervened, these predictions may well have proven fairly accurate. In contrast to Germany, however, where these historically singular events led repeatedly to steep declines in university attendance, enrollment in the United States continued over this period to increase, and in fact at an ever faster pace.

On the basis of the above distinctions we can now specify more precisely what is meant by "explanation" of the time-series data in Figs. 1.1-1.5. First of all, it means clarifying what forces underlie the trend – the long-term secular growth in university enrollment rates. Secondly, the reasons must be sought for short-term but regular and recurrent wavelike variations around this trend, which theoretically can also be ascribed to a general law. There then remain the "residual" variations, or "chance disturbances," for the explanation of which only historical reconstruction suffices.

A model is presented in this section which simplifies the historical course of educational expansion. Periods of growth can be divided into three phases: after a slow "take-off" phase comes a period of rapid growth followed by a "leveling off" or plateau phase. A logistic growth curve describes a diffusion process that characterizes not only the awarding of degrees in secondary or tertiary education but also the spread of innovations through the technologically developed industrial society (e.g., social changes and consumer habits). The curve rises until it reaches a ceiling level – which is either not crossed (saturation threshold) or shows stasis or even decline. Characteristic of this sort of diffusion process is the long initial phase, during which the goods or behavior pattern is the province of an elite, followed by a phase of accelerated growth as the object becomes diffused among the masses of the population, and finally a phase when the diffusion comes to an end and the growth ends. If in the third phase the absolute saturation threshold is not reached, the diffusion may be continued through further social strata, or such further diffusion is not possible due to the relative underdevelopment of the society.

The process of educational expansion over the past century can be seen as a series of such growth cycles. Barring the outbreak of war or the intervention of other political calamities, the phase of stasis proceeds imperceptibly to the beginning of the next growth cycle. Thus periods of zero growth follow, and are followed by, periods of rapid growth; the ceiling level of one cycle becomes the take-off level of the next.

When several growth cycles follow one another, the logistic curve has the appearance of a harmonic oscillation along the trend line. Figure 1.7 illustrates an expansion process with consecutive periods of growth and stasis or temporary decline, while the overall system continues its long-term expansion. A number of analyses have shown that such a model of cyclical variations along a rising trend line best describes the historical process of university expansion.[20]

The expansion of universities in terms of cycles along an overall expanding trend can be seen as a form of "ratchet effect." In the absence of severe interventions (wars, totalitarianism), the curve never falls below an enrollment level that has once been attained. It is by no means the case that phases of stasis in university expansion coincide with periods of economic depression. At the end of the Weimar era, as unemployment reached almost 6 million, university enrollment levels climbed to previously unprecedented heights. While the educational system is not immune to the effects of economic cycles, these effects are often felt only after a time lag and do not express themselves directly in the form of an increase or a decrease in the number of those enrolled at university. Once a social group has achieved access to university education, it attempts to guarantee this privilege for its next generation. This inheritance effect leads to a growth process that continues over time, and that is impervious to the effects of economic depression.

This can be illustrated by the time series for enrollment rates in *Germany* between 1870 to 1939.[21] In Germany enrollment expanded continually and without significant disruptions until the First World War; only in 1890-1894 was there a relative slowing in the growth rate. After the First World War university enrollment stood at more than 30,000 above the prewar level. University enrollment generally increases after wars and is accelerated by a "backlogged" demand. Such a tendency is found in the statistics on Prussian students as far back as the 17th century and may be explained as a reaction of the younger generation to cope with

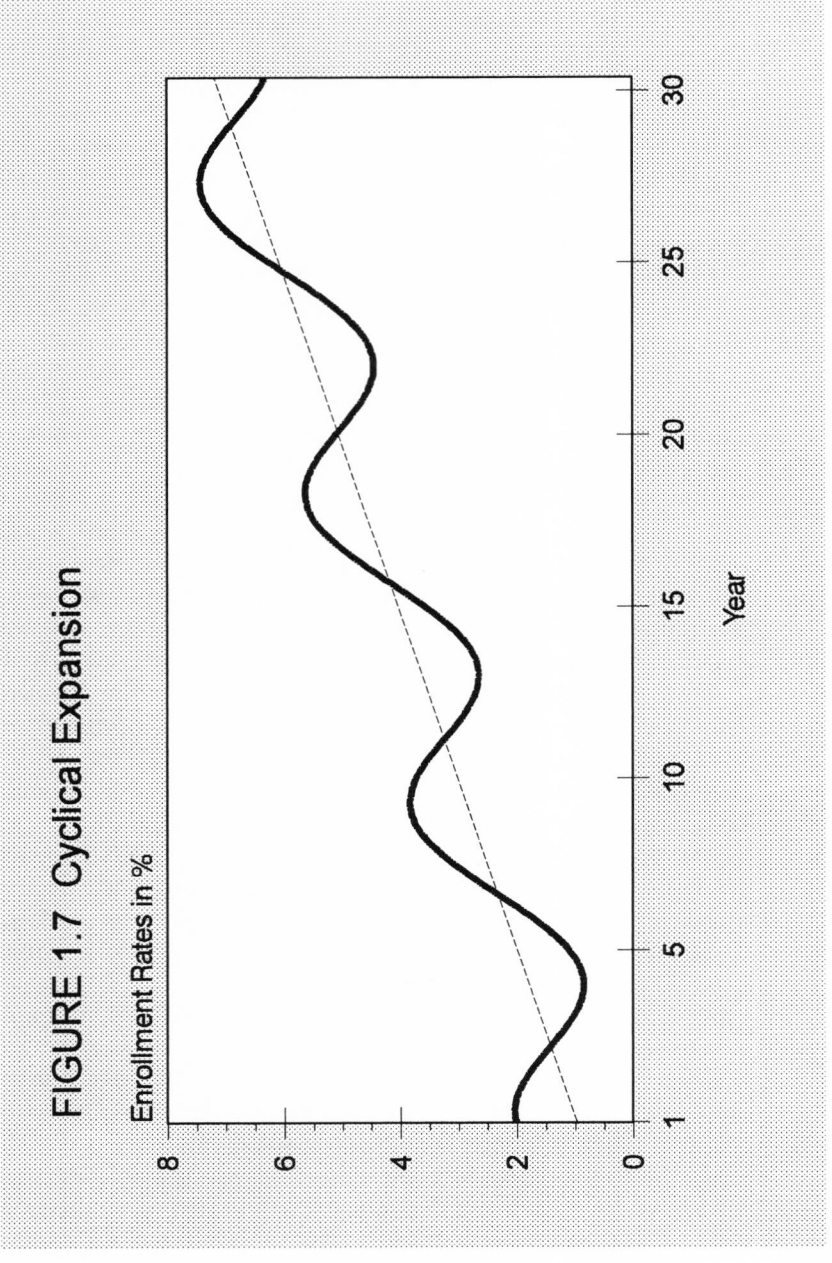

FIGURE 1.7 Cyclical Expansion

war experience.[22] Within a few years this "backlog" had been accommodated, and by 1925 the number of students was only slightly higher than that before the war. The steep decline during the years 1923-1925, however, cannot be explained simply by a large percentage of drop-outs among the war veterans; rather, the drop in university attendance was due largely to the hyperinflation which had wiped out the savings of many in the middle class, who were then no longer financially able to support university study.

This effect of economic conditions on university enrollment was thus not a response on the part of potential or actual students to the current relationship between supply and demand in the labor market but due to the parents' lack of resources to finance higher education for their children. The impact of this hyperinflation is documented in the financial records kept by some families throughout this period. For example, it has been estimated that the family of a higher civil servant spent 27% of its income on food in 1913, but 66% by the first quarter of 1923. Earlier savings from capital investments were decimated, and current saving was impossible under these circumstances. The proportion of national income stemming from capital investment was 14.5% in 1913; by 1925 this had sunk to 2.9%. During the same period the proportion from wages and salaries rose from 45.3% to 56.3%.[23]

This period of falling university attendance, however, was then followed by one in which student numbers rose at a rate that German universities had never previously witnessed. Within six years university enrollment rose from 90,000 to almost 140,000. At individual universities this swelling of student numbers led to extensive changes. The previously elite universities were now becoming mass universities, with the accompanying potential for explosive social discontent. In 1900 there were about 6500 students at the University of Berlin and about 5700 at the University of Munich. With the exception of Bonn and Leipzig, other universities in Germany at that time were attended by fewer than 2000 students. However, by 1930 enrollment had risen to 15,000 in Berlin and 8200 in Munich. It was then predicted that there would be over 100,000 unemployed university graduates by 1935.

These figures attest to the social discontent that was rife in the early 1930's, and that found expression in virulent polemics particularly from conservative and radical right-wing educationalists. Beginning in 1932 stasis in the growth of student numbers set in, and in 1933 the new Nazi regime imposed strict admissions ceilings, expelled non-"Aryan" students, and screened applicants' political affiliations. By the outbreak of the Second World War the number of students in Germany stood at approximately the same level as before the First World War.

·For France there exist comparable data only since 1890. Here, as in Germany, the curve of educational expansion was fairly continuous until the First World War; only in 1896/1897 was there a slight decline in student numbers. The War then interrupted this rise.[24] As in Germany, enrollment rates increased immediately after the war due to the "backlogged" demand; but by 1927 university enrollment had fallen back to the prewar level. In the years following the War France did not experience such severe economic and political turbulence as Germany, and its educational expansion therefore did not undergo such disruption: there was neither the steep decline due to hyperinflation, the repeated rise with students escaping economic hardship around 1930, nor totalitarian restrictions thereafter. Only in 1935-1937 did enrollment begin to decline. This decline in absolute numbers, however, is largely the effect of demographic factors and does not reflect a lower rate of enrollment for the individual age cohorts, for the cohorts then completing secondary education were born during the First World War, when birthrates had been depressed.[25]

University expansion is the result of two overlapping effects. One is the simple growth in the size of the population, and the other is the diffusion of the demand for higher education through the middle class. These two effects are differentiated in the data presented in Table 1.1. The gross growth rate refers to the average annual rise in the number of students in the respective periods and reflects the combined effect of the two factors. The net growth rate, on the other hand, reports the expansion as controlled for demographic influence, i.e., assuming a constant cohort size, or stationary population size. This therefore shows only the social diffusion process. (The difference between gross and net rates measures the proportion of the educational expansion that would be expected solely on the basis of population growth.)[26]

One can also see the cyclical process of educational expansion in the data of Table 1.1. Phases of rapid growth (e.g., 1890-1900 in the United States; 1890-1895 in France) are followed by phases of relatively low growth or even decline (e.g., 1900-1910 in the United States; 1921-1925 in France). Universities in all the countries examined here went through a phase of relatively high growth in the second half of the 1920's; the annual net increase (among men) was 11.2% in the United States (1920-1930), 6.7% in Germany (1925-1931), and 4.6% in France (1926-1930). This period of expansion was followed in the mid-1930's by one of stasis. Only in Germany was the effort made by the Nazis to break the "ratchet" effect of educational expansion. However, when one considers the net growth rate in Germany, it appears that a part of the decline in the size of its student population in the late 1930's can be explained by the demographic effect discussed above: among men the annual gross decline averaged 10.2%, but the annual net decline was only 4.2%.

The growth rates for enrollment among women were almost always greater than those for men. The proportion of women at universities in the United States was high even before the First World War, but their real influx at European universities began only during the 1920's. Whereas 20% of all university graduates at American universities were female at the turn of the century, only 3.3% at French universities were. Records of student numbers in Germany were differentiated by sex only beginning in 1911, at which time women made up 3.6% of the total enrollment. By the 1930's the relative balance had shifted. In 1931 (at the peak of student enrollment in Germany) the proportion of women among all university students was 16% in Germany, 25% in the United Kingdom, 27% in France, and 40% in the United States.

Thus from the beginning of the period under discussion here, American enrollment rates were higher than was politically possible in European countries – both for men and, particularly, for women, as can be seen from the following table (enrollment rates in percent for 1931):

	Men (%)	Women (%)
United States	6.9	4.2
Germany	4.1	1.1
France	3.4	1.2

While enrollment in the United States and France continued to rise throughout the 1930's, that in Germany fell annually by an average of 4.2% among men and 6.7% among women.

The American head start in educational expansion is also evident at the level of secondary education. In 1935 approximately 45% of adolescents attended school until at least the 11th grade; in Japan the corresponding figure was 25% (Cummings and Naoi 1974). In Germany, less than 4% of a cohort graduated from *Gymnasium* (male).[27] Universities in the United States could therefore resume expansion more or less at the level at which they had left off before the War. The educational systems of European countries, on the other hand, had to first expand at the secondary level before there could be an effective demand for university seats.

These figures indicate not only the level of educational expansion before the Second World War but also the relative development potentials

Table 1.1: Growth Rates in Higher Education, 1870 - 1940: United States, Germany, France

	United States							
	1870-80	1880-90	1890-00	1900-10	1910-20	1920-30	1930-40	
Men								
gross	3.0	2.4	7.3	3.0	1.1	13.0	4.9	
net	-0.9	0.2	5.6	0.3	1.2	11.2	4.2	
Women								
gross	8.0	0.8	9.5	6.1	9.7	19.4	5.8	
net	4.8	-1.4	7.5	4.0	9.1	17.7	5.1	
	Germany							
	1871-90		1891-1914		1925-31		1933-37	
Men								
gross	3.9		5.5		6.9		-10.2	
net	2.9		3.3		6.7		- 4.2	
Women								
gross	+		+		33.5		-12.8	
net	+		+		33.4		- 6.7	
	France							
	1890-95	1896-99	1900-05	1906-10	1911-20	1921-25	1926-30	1931-36
Men								
gross	10.4	2.3	2.9	2.3	1.5	1.7	5.3	-1.7
net	10.1	3.4	3.0	2.6	2.3	-1.9	4.6	1.0
Women								
gross	+	+	22.4	14.9	8.5	13.5	13.0	0.1
net	+	+	22.6	15.3	8.0	12.8	13.5	2.4

Percentages give annual average growth rates of students enrolled in Universities and Technical Universities (polytechnics). For the United States the percentages give annual average growth rates of students receiving the bachelor's degree or first professional degree. Periods refer to periods of population census in the respective countries. + Data not available.   Source: See Appendix I

in different countries after the War. The social, cultural, and economic consequences of educational expansion become evident only with a considerable time lag. The expansion of university enrollment between 1925 and 1932, for example, manifested itself outside of the university only some 10-20 years later, when these graduates were integrated in the work force and were themselves carrying economic and political responsibility. The polemics directed against university expansion at time reacted only to the immediate effect of increasing the numbers of highly educated among the unemployed and disregarded the effects that restrictions on university admissions would have in the future.

There is the danger in times of overfilled universities that government education policy will orient itself too strongly along the lines of the theory of human capital. With rising unemployment and falling income among university graduates the effective value of a university degree and of educational institutions may appear – both for the individual and for society – to be rather diminished. Such a short-sighted policy, however, entails potentially serious disadvantages in terms of long-term development prospects.[28]

1.4 Time-Series Analysis

As we have seen, the process of educational expansion over the past century has been a cyclical one, with periods of accelerated growth following, and being followed by, those of less rapid growth. In this section these cycles are subjected to a time-series analysis, seeking to determine, first, the length of such variations, that is, the cyclical duration (period) and, second, the relationship between the cycles in educational expansion and those in economic development. Did the phases of university expansion correspond to those that the economy was going through at the same time, or did the educational system expand in phases unrelated to those of the economy?

(a) This analysis is carried out on the data on five countries which during this period underwent industrialization and modernization, and which also experienced a substantial educational expansion; these five are Germany, France, Italy, Japan, and the United States. A further criterion for this selection was of course the availability of complete data sets for educational expansion. The cycles of educational expansion over two periods for three of these countries are presented in Figs. 1.8-1.10 (Germany, Japan, United States).

To examine specifically the cycle, as opposed to the trend, these two components were isolated out and analyzed separately. To describe the trend an exponential rather than a linear function was used, as this allows a better estimation of the trend.[29] The data presented in Figs. 1.8-1.10 are the residuals, i.e., the variation along the trend (depicted here as a vertical line with a value of zero), and thus present the cycles of university growth above and below the overall expansion during the entire period. In calculating the cyclical variations, demographic effects have also been controlled for; this means that the curves present solely the (residual) rate of enrollment defined as the proportion of those of a given age who attend university (in the United States, those receiving the bachelor's degree). A complete cycle is defined as the period from one peak to the next.

Points to the right of the zero line indicate enrollment higher than the trend, i.e., above-average growth, and those to the left enrollment lower than the trend, i.e., below-average growth. Thus, even when the curve

runs to the left of zero, universities may still have expanded, but at a rate
that was less than average for the overall period. A turn of the curve to
the left means that the rate of expansion declined, and, conversely, a turn
to the right means an acceleration in the rate of expansion. One must
determine for each period – particularly those of economic downturn –
whether the rate of university expansion was above or below average, and
whether the expansion was accelerating or slowing down.

The figures above each curve indicate the average annual growth rate
over the period, which is particularly high for Japan in 1878-1940 (4.3%)
and particularly low for men in the United States in 1950-1991 (0.7%).
The duration of cycles before the First World War was 25-35 years,
between the World Wars 10-22 years, and after the Second World War
(1950-1991) again 25-30 years.[30] The alteration between expansion and
stasis in Germany during the interwar period was rapid and volatile. Here
the short cyclical variation reflects the political crises which the country
experienced during these years.

In Germany and Japan the cycles reached a turning point in 1975 (in
the United States already in 1972), and the enrollment rates thereafter
rose only slowly or, in Japan and in the United States for men, fell for a
time (Fig. 1.10). One can assume that another turning point was reached
in the late 1980's/early 1990's, and that the expansion of higher education
accelerated since then again (new take-off), after a period of
approximately 13-15 years during which the speed of expansion
continually declined. This was thereby the longest phase of decelerating
expansion speed since 1870.

The cycles for gross national product are also calculated, using the
same procedure as that for cycles in educational expansion, determining
the variations along the trend and the mean cyclical variation (cycles not
shown). Here the cycles are less pronounced, more regular, and shorter in
duration than those for educational expansion. This is an early indication
that in some countries the two systems did not developed in pace with one
another but followed independent courses, and such independence rules
out a statistically significant relationship between them.

(b) These data allow us to test Eulenberg's thesis (1904, p. 256) that
university expansion is greater in times of economic recession and high
unemployment than during years of increased economic activity. The
period covered by the present data saw three severe international
depressions, during which living standards declined and unemployment
rose sharply in most industrialized countries – those of 1876-1893, 1928-
1935, and from the mid-1970's to the mid-1980's.[31] Data from these
periods provide the basis to test whether economic recession discourages

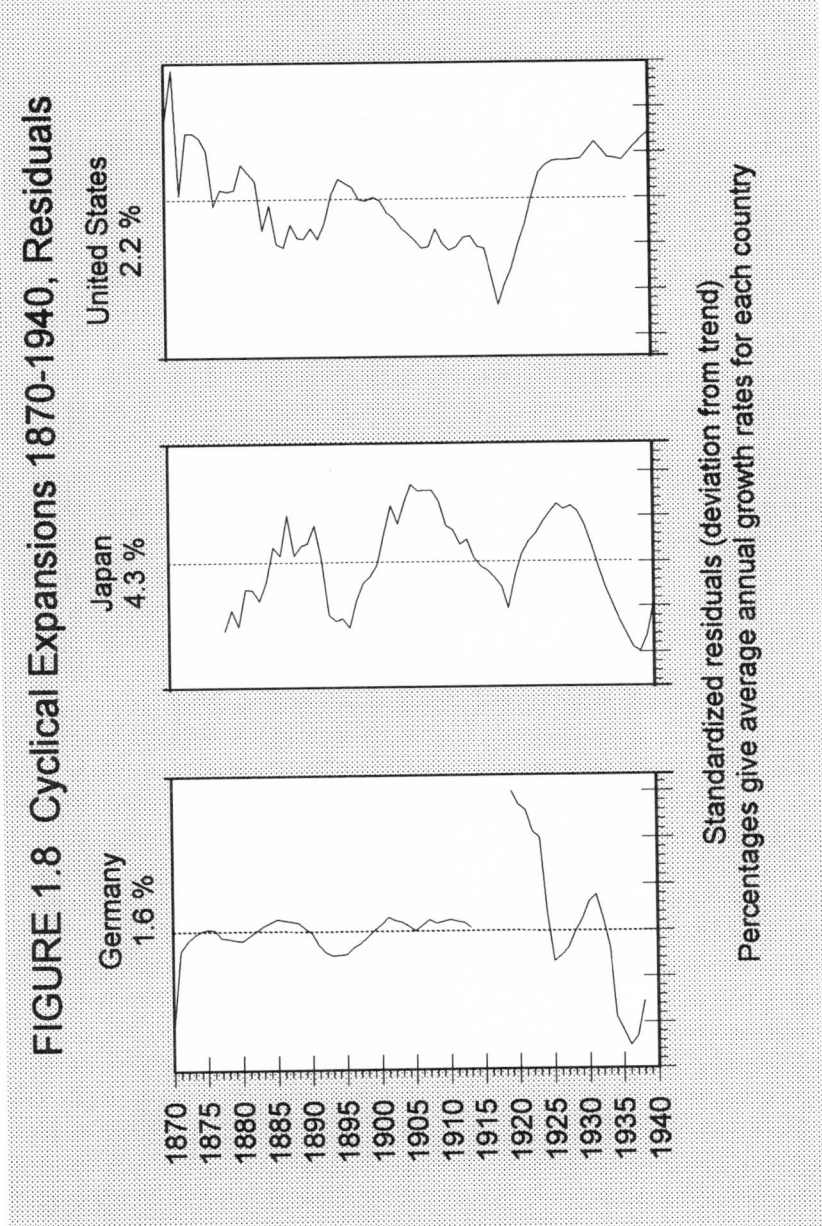

FIGURE 1.8 Cyclical Expansions 1870-1940, Residuals

Germany 1.6 %

Japan 4.3 %

United States 2.2 %

Standardized residuals (deviation from trend)
Percentages give average annual growth rates for each country

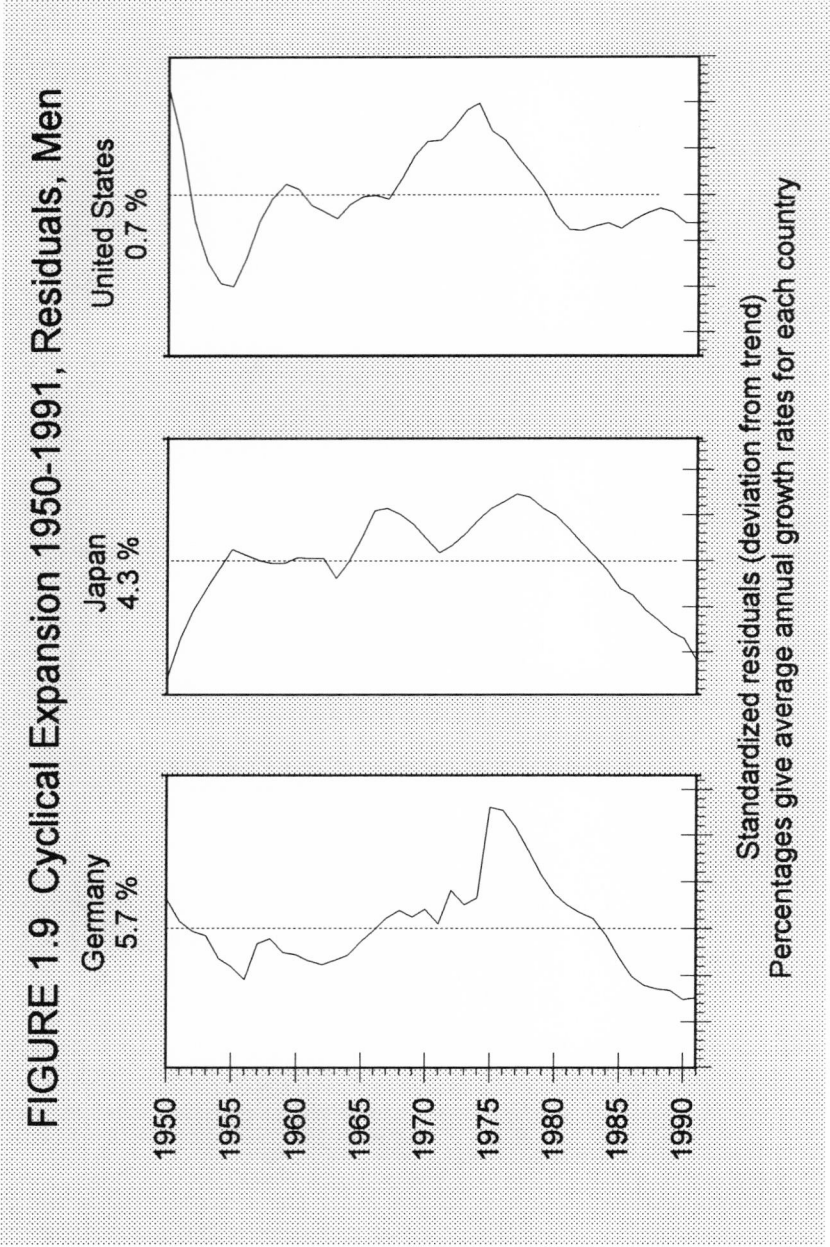

FIGURE 1.9 Cyclical Expansion 1950-1991, Residuals, Men

Germany
5.7 %

Japan
4.3 %

United States
0.7 %

Standardized residuals (deviation from trend)
Percentages give average annual growth rates for each country

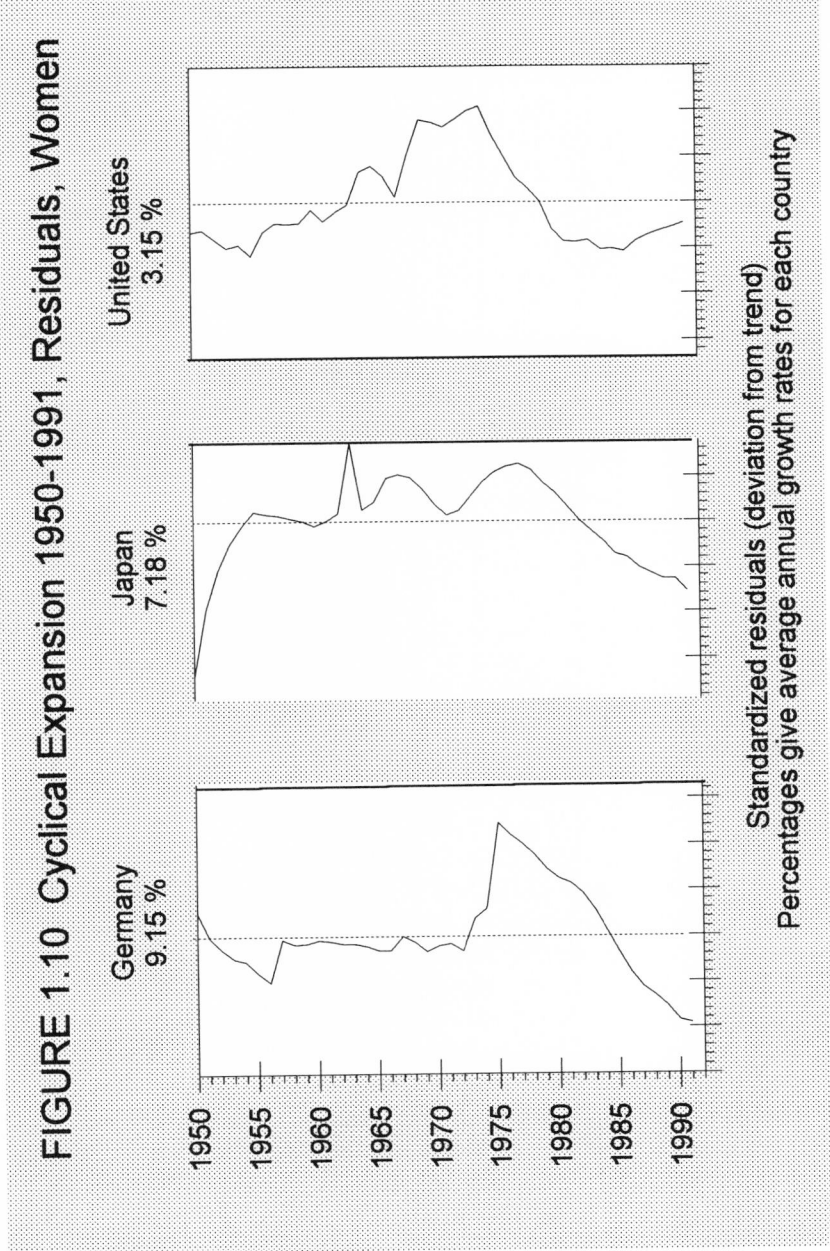

FIGURE 1.10 Cyclical Expansion 1950-1991, Residuals, Women

Germany
9.15 %

Japan
7.18 %

United States
3.15 %

Standardized residuals (deviation from trend)
Percentages give average annual growth rates for each country

or – as the theory of status competition maintains – encourages university expansion.

Data are available for the period under discussion on net national product, unemployment, and size of the civil service. According to Eulenberg, we should expect a positive correlation between unemployment and university enrollment and a negative correlation between economic growth and university enrollment. These hypotheses have been tested by means of a multivariate regression analysis; the results are presented below in Tables 1.2 and 1.3.

An important premise of normal (ordinary least squares) regression analysis is generally violated in the case of time-series data by the existence of autocorrelation, that is, the value of a variable at a given observation point (t) is usually highly correlated with its value at the previous point (t-1). Under these conditions neither the regression coefficient nor the standard deviation provides genuinely meaningful information about the data. This problem can be corrected for by the use of specialized estimation procedures (generalized least squares).[32] A further problem is that presented by an underlying trend which, as in the case here, shows a continual rise in values for the independent variables of civil servants and net national product. In statistical terms this is the problem of multicollinearity, i.e., the correlation among the independent variables themselves. The problems due to the trend are more difficult to eliminate (see Gunst and Mason 1980, p. 300).

The following analysis considers the relationship between educational and economic expansion from two different perspectives. First, a regression analysis was carried out with the help of an autoregressive procedure. The results are summarized in Table 1.2.

The dependent variable is the enrollment rate in higher education, and the independent variables used in this analysis are: per capita net national product (NNP), unemployment rate (UR), and number of civil servants (CS). In the case of some variables data are not available for every year in the period under discussion (gaps have been filled by interpolation). The last column in the table (N) presents the number of years to which the analysis applies. The NNP is measured in constant prices (adjusted for inflation) and therefore represents an indicator of real national wealth.

The regression equation in Table 1.2 shows a number of statistically significant coefficients that support the hypothesis of the status competition school. For Germany and the United States there is a significant positive correlation in the years 1880-1939 between unemployment and educational expansion. Thus in times of high unemployment the expansion of university enrollment was high, and, conversely, falling unemployment was associated with stasis in the expansion of universities. This correlation serves to support Eulenberg's observation. The same relationship is also found in France, however, only among women and only since the Second World War.

Between economic growth (NNP) and educational expansion there is a positive correlation for the United States in the period 1880-1939. Again, this is the case of France only for women and only after the War. This relationship, on the other hand, indicates that the economic and educational systems expanded together, which contradicts Eulenberg's position. Although the relationship between NNP and number of students is often negative here (e.g., in West Germany and in Japan after the Second World War), the correlation never achieves statistical significance.

Remarkable is the significant positive correlation between the size of the civil service and educational expansion. Significant coefficients appear for Germany, France, and Italy in the first period (1880-1939) and for West Germany, Italy, and the United States in the second period (1950-1985). Thus, universities and the government bureaucracy grew in

Table 1.2: Auto-Regression (trend included)

	a) 1880 - 1839 Men and Women					
	NNP	CS	UR	R^2	D.W.	N
Germany	.07	.65**	.08*	.74	2.14	41
France	.01	.43**	-.01	.66	1.86	37
Italy	.15	.71*	+	.62	2.04	20
Japan	-.03	+	+	.01	2.02	62
US	.13*	-.11**	.06*	.25	1.65	52
	b) 1950 - 1985 Men					
	NNP	CS	UR	R^2	D.W.	N
Germany (West)	-.31	1.50**	-.11	.80	1.99	28
France	1.08	-.18	.13	.87	2.02	38
Italy	-.03	.72	-.11	.20	1.99	34
Japan	-.79	1.51**	-.14	.84	1.29	26
US	-.10	.93	-.06	.43	1.87	38
	c) 1950 - 1985 Women					
	NNP	CS	UR	R^2	D.W.	N
Germany (West)	-.13	1.23**	.06	.93	2.20	28
France	.87**	.06	.09*	.98	1.91	38
Italy	.48	.41	-.04	.51	1.93	34
Japan	-.15	.90**	.12	.91	1.89	26
US	.09	.90**	.00	.95	1.75	38

Non-standardized regression coefficients (Generalized Least Squares).

Independent Variables: NNP=Net National product per capita; CS=Number of civil servants;

UR=Unemployment rate. Dependent variable: Enrollment rates; BA + First professional degree in the US. D.W.= Durbin-Watson Test; N=Number of years. + = Data not available.

Level of significance: *: $\alpha \leq .05$; **: $\alpha \leq .01$. Sources: See Appendix I.

the same cycles. At least for European countries and for Japan (before the Second World War) this finding is hardly surprising, for the civil service there is the principal employer of university graduates.

In case of the United States, however, there is a *negative* correlation for the period between 1880 and 1939 between educational expansion and the explosive growth in the size of the civil service (-0.11). This indicates a qualitatively different relationship in the United States between the bureaucracy and the educational system. In contrast to the situation in European countries, university graduates thus appear to have prepared themselves from the outset of their studies at the university for employment in the private sector – positions in the civil service being awarded largely on the basis of political patronage (spoils system). Particularly in times of economic recession political parties in the United States sought to distribute civil service positions not on the basis of merit (university degree) but to those who had supported the winning party. It was only after the Second World War that political patronage was largely eliminated in the awarding of civil service positions (see Chap. 5).

In the regression analysis presented in Table 1.2 the factor of autocorrelation was controlled for, but not that of the trend. When there is a similar trend in any two variables, for example, university enrollment and economic growth, it is not surprising to find a significant relationship between them. Once the trend has been eliminated, however, the question is: do the cycles representing growth and stasis in the two systems overlap or not. In the second regression analysis the trend was therefore subtracted, and only the variations along it were examined. In contrast to the case in the first analysis, it is the residuals that are used, thus eliminating – with the trend – the trend-induced multicollinearity. (As in the first analysis, an autoregressive procedure was used here as well, thus eliminating also the problem of autocorrelation.) In this second analysis, then, only particularly pronounced relationships can attain statistical significance. Table 1.3 presents the results of this analysis.

In this case, no significant correlations appear for the first period (1880-1939) between NNP/unemployment rate and the dependent variable (enrollment rate). This indicates that the significant coefficients that emerged in the first analysis, using the raw data, were due to the underlying trend.

In the second period (1950-1985) four coefficients are significant: in France among men for NNP (+0.63) and for unemployment (-0.50), in France among women for NNP (+0.82), and in Italy among women for NNP (+0.54). These findings contradict Eulenberg's hypothesis. None of the correlations which would support the theory of status competition (negative for NNP, positive for unemployment) are statistically significant. The conclusion that one can draw, therefore, is that the cycles of educational expansion have been more closely related to economic cycles since the Second World War than they were previously. In some cases the coefficients for the relationship between educational expansion and the size of the civil service are also significant, thus offering further support to relationship between the academic labor market and the state bureaucracy.

There is the possibility, however, that significant correlations were not found among the variables because the respective cycles do not correspond to one another in time.[33] Such correlations can be uncovered by building into the analysis a time lag or time lead between the systems. It may, on the one hand, for example, be the case that students base their decisions about whether to attend university on their perceptions of *past* economic conditions; to determine this a time lag vis-à-vis NNP would reveal significant relationships. On the other, however, and somewhat more plausibly, students may orient themselves in terms of their expectations about the *future* course of the economy; this would require incorporating a time lead in the analysis. While the introduction of both time lags and leads can thus be justified from a theoretical perspective, another consideration casts doubt upon the validity of such an analysis. This is the simple fact that the data about the economy which we possess are those of objective economic conditions; the *perceptions* of the individual actors concerning economic conditions – which is what actually would have influenced their decisions – must remain shrouded in mystery to us, however. For this reason I have chosen not to carry out such an analysis.

In summary, then, does this analysis permit us to regard either the theory of human capital or that of status competition as verified? Unfortunately, it is rather a tie game. Both theories can muster a few coefficients for its side, so that each can find some comfort in the ambiguous score. It is noteworthy, nonetheless, that the coefficients from the first period (1880-1939) favor to some extend the theory of status competition whereas those in the second (1950-1985) tend to support the human capital theory.

Those who are inclined to find the major influence upon educational expansion in political rather than in economic conditions can marshall a number of statistically nonsignificant coefficients from this analysis. These suggest that there is in fact no relationship between the level of economic activity and educational expansion. The results of the second analysis (Table 1.3), which imposes the more stringent verification

Table 1.3: Auto-Regression (residuals)

| | a) 1880 - 1939 Men and Women | | | | | |
	NNP	CS	UR	R^2	D.W.	N
Germany	.01	.28	.00	.03	2.35	41
France	.07	.23*	-.05	.21	2.22	37
Italy	.02	-.05	+	.01	1.98	20
Japan	-.05	+	+	.02	2.12	62
US	.07	-.17*	.06	.18	1.87	52
	b) 1950 - 1985 Men					
	NNP	CS	UR	R^2	D.W.	N
Germany (West)	.98	.45	-.38	.32	2.13	28
France	.63*	-.36	-.50**	.72	1.94	38
Italy	.33	.18	-.12	.16	1.93	34
Japan	-.19	.90**	-.27	.67	1.95	26
US	.26	.49**	.21	.42	2.13	38
	c) 1950 - 1985 Women					
	NNP	CS	UR	R^2	D.W.	N
Germany (West)	.37	.68*	-.01	.54	2.22	28
France	.82**	-.12	.03	.33	2.02	38
Italy	.54*	.16	.00	.23	1.89	34
Japan	-.63	.84**	.14	.45	1.99	26
US	-.13	.83**	-.11	.66	1.78	38

D.W.= Durbin-Watson Test; N=Number of years. + = Data not available.

Level of significance: *: $\alpha \leq .05$; **: $\alpha \leq .01$.   Sources: See Appendix I.

conditions, can be seen as providing some support, albeit rather weak, for the view that the motor behind educational expansion lies in the collective struggle of social groups for political and cultural emancipation. However, an interpretation that finds its support principally in nonsignificant correlations is ultimately unsatisfying, and I shall return to this problem at the end of the next section (1.5).

1.5 Educational Expansion and Choice of Academic Discipline

In terms of the number of students enrolled in them, the various academic disciplines[34] reach their respective zeniths and nadirs at different times. Some enjoy overfilled classrooms while others lack students to instruct – only for the relative popularity to be reversed at another time. Titze (1984, p. 96) has observed that, "the preferences of students among the various subjects is not constant over time but is always changing. The periodic oversupply of those in certain occupational fields is generally accompanied by prospects that are 'still bright' or even expanding in others."

If Titze's view is correct, the cycles of popularity of individual university subjects should not correspond to those in the overall number of students enrolled in universities. Total university enrollment may expand at a time while enrollment in specific subjects are contracting due to changing conditions in the labor market. Such changing economic conditions may thus find a response not in prospective university students' decision concerning *whether* to study, but *what* to study. The ability of the university to absorb these changing student preferences for the individual subjects can be seen as necessary for its continuing expansion at times of altered conditions in the economy and therefore in the labor market.

Such changed conditions *within* the university as regards subject preferences of students could perhaps explain the absence of a clear relationship in Tables 1.2 and 1.3 between economic and educational expansion. Evidence that certain subjects are expanding along with cycles in the economy while others are not would help to explain the overall lack of a relationship between economic cycles and cycles of university expansion.

To posit such a differing response among subjects to labor market conditions presumes a differentiated educational decision. At a first stage the prospective student (or his/her family) makes the decision as to whether to attend university, and at a second stage he or she confronts the choice of subject. The first decision may have little to do with perceptions of economic conditions, particularly in Germany with a differentiated school system, where the important decisions about future occupational possibilities may be made while the person is still in childhood; this decision may also depend upon family background and for this reason be made far in advance of the actual enrollment at a university. It is at the second stage that economic considerations may influence the person's educational decisions, and this decision may be made only relatively late before beginning university study. The results of the following analysis shows this in fact to be the case.

Data are available for the numbers of those enrolled at German universities in the various subjects for the period 1867-1914.[35] Figure 1.11 presents the variation of certain subjects from the overall trend curve. The same procedure is used for this analysis as for that discussed above (sect. 1.4): the vertical line represents the overall trend and the individual curves (residuals) the variation from it.

Ignoring certain irregularities in the cyclical duration of the various curves, the subjects can be divided into two groups. In one are the subjects with cycles that correspond to those of the economic cycle, such as law and technical subjects; the other comprises those with cycles that run precisely contrary to the economic cycle, including medicine, the humanities, mathematics, natural science, and theology. These data show the enrollment in law and technical subjects to be at a low ebb during the economic depression of 1878-1890 while that in medicine to be particularly high. The curves for law and for medicine are seen to be offset by approximately one-half of the cyclical duration: when the former is to the right of zero (high enrollment) the other is to the left (low enrollment). Thus these subjects have a substitutive relationship to one another: full classrooms in law mean few students in medicine, and vice versa.

Similar substitutive relationships exist between enrollment at universities and that at polytechnics. Between 1875 and 1883, for example, enrollment at polytechnics fell by some 43%, at a time when the overall system of higher education was expanding by 23%. Some subjects and institutions suffered falling attendance despite the fact that educational expansion was continuing in the overall system. Barbagli (1974, p. 135) has presented similar data on Italian universities. During the economic depression there between 1888 and 1896 universities were expanding at an above-average rate (see Fig. 1.6), while the number of students studying engineering subjects was declining; however, when the economy was expanding again, the total number of students declined, but enrollment in engineering increased substantially.

In Germany the depression beginning in the mid-1870's put an end to the economic boom of the early unification era. Graduates from polytechnics, whose job prospects lay principally in the private sphere, faced a diminished labor market. Students starting their higher education at this time were discouraged from enrolling in technical subjects and chose instead to pursue other subjects; during this time the number of those enrolled in medicine rose by 87% (from 3370 to 6303), in the humanities by 23%, and in mathematics and science by 47%. Thus when the prospects for employment in industry were not bright, students decided to become physicians or teachers, but not to give up a university education.

Table 1.4 presents the cyclical variations in enrollment in specific subjects; these support our interpretation of Fig. 1.11. The correlations here are those between the residuals for the respective subjects. A value of +1 indicates that enrollment cycles in the two subjects correspond in time to one another perfectly, and a value of -1 that the cycles are exactly opposite in time (decline in one means rise in the other). As a rule of thumb, the higher the coefficient the more synchronous are the two cycles; if the coefficients reach 0 the two subjects are temporally offset.[36] For example, the correlation coefficients for medicine and law ($r = -0.45$) and

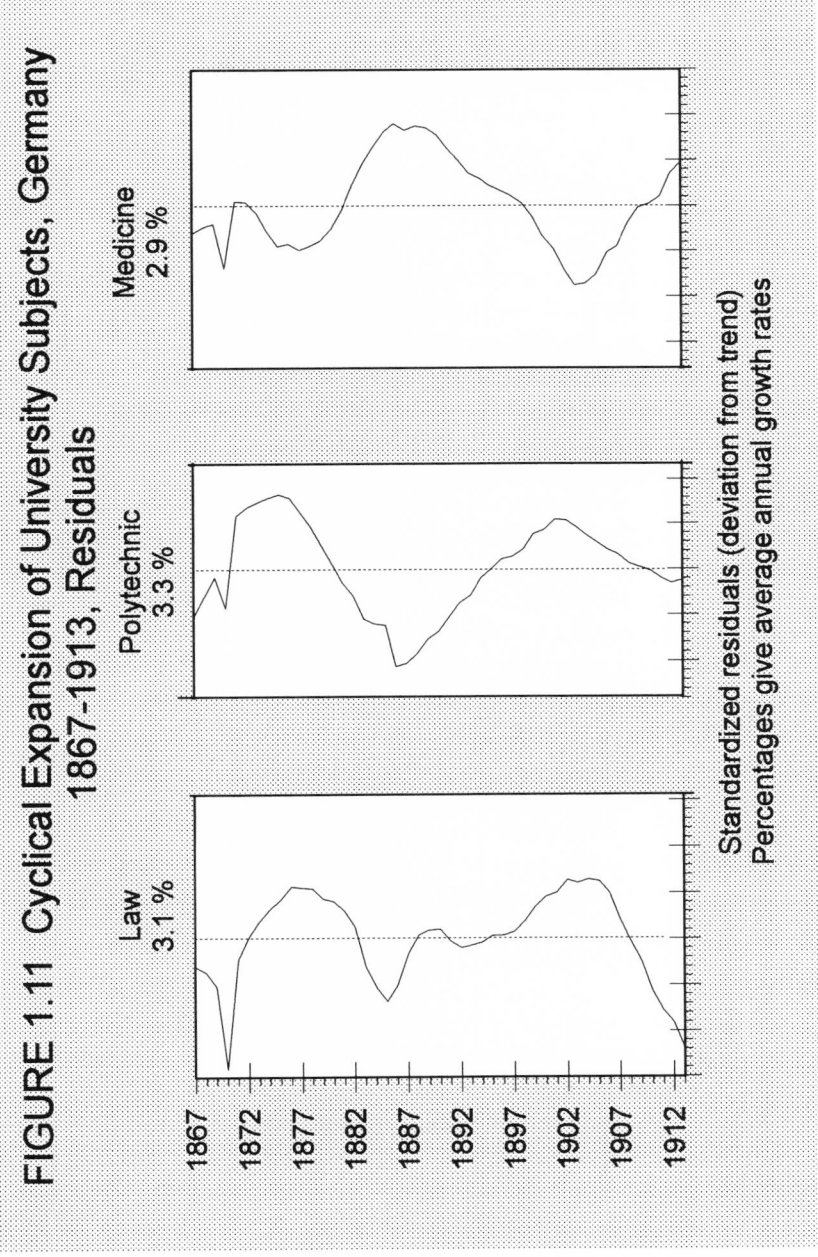

FIGURE 1.11 Cyclical Expansion of University Subjects, Germany 1867-1913, Residuals

Standardized residuals (deviation from trend)
Percentages give average annual growth rates

those for technical subjects and Lutheran theology ($r = -0.69$) show that the cyclical variations in enrollment in these pairs of subjects tend to be "anti-cyclical"; on the other hand, that for medicine and Lutheran theology ($r = +0.91$) shows very similar, synchronous cycles between these subjects.

To determine the relationship between the various subject-specific enrollment cycles and the cyclical variations in the economy, Table 1.4 also presents the correlation coefficients between enrollment in the individual subjects and NNP (also residuals). Here we see that the enrollment in law and technical subjects expanded along with the economy, but that enrollment in medicine and Lutheran theology tend to be "anticyclical" in comparison with the economic cycle.

On the basis of these results we are now in a position to answer the question posed at the beginning of this chapter. Eulenberg's thesis – that university enrollment is negatively related to the business cycle – is true only for certain subjects. As the figures in Table 1.4 show, particularly strong expansion of enrollment is seen during times of economic recession in medicine, Lutheran theology, and education-related subjects. In contrast to these, however, enrollment levels in law and technical subjects react positively to economic conditions and tend in times of economic downturn to decline or to expand less rapidly than at other times. Because the cyclical variations in enrollment in the various subjects are offset in relation to one another, the overall enrollment level in higher education presents no clear relationship in its cyclical variations to cycles in economic conditions, or does so only for certain specific periods.

We can summarize these results as follows. The economy does have an influence on educational expansion, and students are not immune to economic signals related to their future employment prospects. However, this form of economic rationality is seen not in their decision as to whether to attend university but rather in their choice of subject once they get there. University education opens the way to upward mobility and provides graduates with the freedom of self-determination and political participation, and prospective students are not willing to forego these social privileges unless forced to do so. Unfavorable conditions in the labor market seldom represent such a compelling reason and incline prospective students not to seek another occupation as a substitute for university education but to choose an economically "rational" subject of study at university.

However, accommodation of the university to the economy has had only limited success. Setting aside the subject of theology, enrollment in all subjects has expanded over the past century, and the student's change

Table 1.4: Correlation-Matrix, University Subjects (residuals)
1866-1914

	LT 1	CT 2	Law 3	Med 4	Hum 5	MNS 6	Eco 7	PO 8	NNP 9
1 Luth.Theol.	1.00	.19	-.42*	.91*	-.40*	-.06	.18	-.69*	-.58*
2 Cath. Theol.	.19	1.00	-.33	.10	-.39*	-.80*	.41*	-.26	.04
3 Law	-.42*	-.33	1.00	-.45*	.00	.39*	-.10	.66*	.33
4 Medicine	.91*	.10	-.45*	1.00	-.42*	-.03	.01	-.50*	-.37
5 Humanities	-.40*	-.39*	.00	-.42*	1.00	.47*	.08	-.05	.01
6 Mathem./Nat.	-.06	-.80*	.39*	-.03	.47*	1.00	-.09	.23	-.05
7 Economics	.18	.41*	-.10	.01	.08	-.09	1.00	-.27	-.27
8 Polytechnics	-.69*	-.26	.66*	-.50*	-.05	.23	-.27	1.00	.64*
9 NNP	-.58*	.04	.33	-.37*	.01	-.05	-.27	.64*	1.00

NNP=Net National Product; N=46 (number of years); Level of significance: *: $\alpha \leq .001$
Source: See Appendix I.

of university subject can only marginally improve his or her employment prospects in the labor market. Oversupply in one area of the labor market generally means a similar oversupply in others. The students' attempt to evade particularly difficult labor market areas by means of changing the subject that they study at university can therefore bring rewards for only a small number of students, and for the overall labor market this accommodation of the university to economic conditions can promise success only in the short term. It is precisely the reaction to predictions of future labor market prospects that leads to these predictions eventually not being fulfilled.

2

Educational Expansion
and Social Background

2.1 Processes of Social Closure 1870-1934

Even if status competition is the driving force behind educational expansion, not all social groups will necessarily be able to take part in the competition. In Germany and other European countries, access to the university and to the range of employment possibilities available to university graduates remained the province of a small number of privileged groups until the First World War. Between the two World Wars the middle class gained access to the university, and after the Second World War the working class was granted a limited right to university admission. Behind the history of educational expansion lies the struggle for university access, with times of social openness being followed by periods of social closure and of attempts – generally unsuccessful – to control the self-defeating consequences of the earlier expansion.

The various arguments that have been put forward regarding measures to open the universities socially tend to belong to one of two camps.[1] On the one hand have been the liberal reformers who have maintained that university openness will ensure equality of opportunity and social justice. Particularly those from the lowest socioeconomic groups are presumed to benefit from the possibility of upward mobility that this would provide (Dahrendorf 1965).

Very early, however, there were skeptics who warned of the unintended consequences of educational expansion.[2] These observers believed that the expansion would not in fact eliminate social inequality but rather would only further solidify the existing structures of power and authority, for it is the children from the upper classes who would attend university and would therefore be able to add the symbolic power of a university degree to their already privileged social and economic position. In fact, the term that was introduced in Prussia for the university degree was that of "entitlement." As the basis of social position began to shift from ascribed status to meritocratic achievement, the traditional elites added the symbolic power of academic degrees to their traditional economic and social privileges.[3]

This section examines which social classes took part in the educational expansion between 1870 and 1934 and the effect that economic depressions had on middle class attendance of universities. Was it the case, for example, that a form of "seniority" principle existed in effect, such that the most recent social groups to arrive at the university were the first to be driven from it in times of economic hardship?

The following statistics on student enrollment illustrate the structural change that German universities underwent during the decades before the First World War: The proportion of students from aristocratic families at the University of Bonn (Germany) declined between 1840 and 1910 from 13% to 2%. Whereas over half of all students in 1840 were children of university graduates, only 22% of them were so by 1912. During this time the proportion of students from the capitalist-industrial sector rose from 4% (1840) to 15% (1911). Thus it was largely the sons of factory owners, managers, commercial tycoons, and of higher level qualified white collar workers who, after economic success, sought academic success. Enrollment at German polytechnics rose between 1860 and 1901 from 2,000 to 13,000, at which time they comprised one-fourth of all seats in higher education. Those enrolled in theology (Catholic plus Lutheran) comprised 38% of all students at German universities in the winter semester of 1830/1831, but only 6% in the winter semester of 1911/1912.[4]

At the beginning of the 19th century the universities stood at the periphery of social life, and their principal function was the training of ministers, physicians, and attorneys. By the turn of the century they had come to occupy a central role in society, governing the reproduction of political and cultural elites. One can regard the time of German unification (1871) as something of a caesura in the history of universities' expanding role: before that time they were attended by a small educational elite in a small number of professions, whereas in the period thereafter and down to the First World War they were opened to the commercial-industrial classes (still excluding the working class).

The universities assumed an important role in the political emancipation of the bourgeois classes, as specialist training and professional experience helped to legitimate the demand of these classes to participate in political power. The university degree often competed against traditional privilege in the filling of high-status positions, and the late 19th century saw the balance tip gradually in favor of meritocratic ability and against feudal privilege.

Introduction of the entitlement system, however, did not lead to the creation of an open society. Open access to education and the filling of positions on the basis of ability and performance were by no means guaranteed, even on paper. The university created a new set of "rights" and a new class of "entitled" citizens, and while the university degree did help to legitimate their demands for status, it did not guarantee social equality. In the Weimar Republic the entitlement system became even more important due to the high unemployment (Bäumer 1930, p.58). Those possessing university degrees claimed a permanent right to high public positions and a life-long entitlement. The university degree therefore intensified the conflicts between those possessing it and those not, as well as between the educated middle class and the uneducated working class.

The meritocracy developed a dynamic of its own. The university degree was the key to gaining access to positions in the bureaucracy and the professions but also closed the door to those without it. Once the middle class gained the key, they sought to prevent it being passed to further groups. The more important the university degree became in achieving political and cultural participation in bourgeois society, the more educational institutions moved to center stage in the arena of class conflict. These ceased to be institutions merely for the imparting of "humanistic" education, as in the past, and took on the role of distributing important positions in the state, the established church, and the economy – they came, in short, to be the distributor of "opportunities for life" (Schelsky 1959, p. 18).

Max Weber (1956, p. 202) referred to this process as "social closure": a social group seeks to protect its economic power by excluding other groups from gaining the resources and means by which to challenge it. This monopolization of economic opportunity eliminates otherwise potential competitors by branding them with a characteristic, either positive or negative, which effectively excludes them from competition and maintains them in a permanent position of outsiders as regards social and economic opportunity. Parkin (1974, p. 4), in elaborating this concept further, pointed out that it is not only those already in possession of power who develop such strategies, for those excluded from power develop their own counterstrategies to combat them. The class conflict during the

German Empire and the Weimar Republic was characterized by the exclusion of the working class not only from possession of the means of production but also from attaining educational degrees.

The history of the Polytechnique in Paris provides an example of this. This technical elite school was founded by the moderate Jacobins following the fall of Robespierre in 1794. The students were to be admitted to this school without consideration of their social background, birth, or wealth but only on the basis of their ability and performance. A contemporary wrote that most of the students at the Polytechnique did in fact come from humble backgrounds. Of the 274 students graduating in the class of 1799, 160 were described as being from "poor" families, 75 from the middle class, and 39 from "rich" families.[5] Within 50 years, however, the social composition of those enrolled at the school had altered substantially. The reforms of 1830 redefined the admission criteria, requiring applicants to have attended an academic secondary school for two to three years; the subjects to be tested for admission were again to include classical languages and literature – although the principal subjects of instruction at the school were mathematics, physics, and engineering. A tuition fee of 1600 francs was also charged (the average annual working class income in 1850 was about 1400 francs). But even if the prospective student were able to meet these conditions for admission, he still faced the requirement that the mayor of the city attest to the political responsibility and social standing of his family. In the years between 1850 and 1880 some 60% of the institution's students therefore came from the upper class and fewer than 1% from the so-called *classes populaires* (Shinn 1980, p. 185). The social openness which had come in the wake of the Revolution had thus been reversed by the subsequent opposition of bourgeois society. Introduction of the educational degree led to neither equality of opportunity nor to an open society but provided in the end a further instrument for social closure.

The example of the French Polytechnique illustrates that over the past century universities have had to walk a fine line between openness and closure to maintain their central role in society. As the doors are opened to new social groups, we see repeatedly that these new groups attempt to close the door behind them. Upward mobility is possible through a university education only so long as the university degree remains a scarce commodity. While it is undeniable that the expansion has enabled those from previously excluded social strata to participate politically, the university has been forced at times to restrict the expansion to prevent an inflation of those holding the university-guaranteed "entitlement."

We examine below the effect that historical events had on the social composition of the student body at German universities between 1887 and 1934. This analysis shows how economic depression and stasis in university enrollment rates, on the one hand, and accelerated educational expansion, on the other, altered the social profile of the students. The analysis concentrates on four periods in particular: 1890-1893, as enrollment rates remained constant after the depression of the 1880's; 1923-1925, at the time of hyperinflation; 1929-1932, at the beginning of the world depression and before the Nazi seizure of power; and the period of the Nazi regime.

Table 2.1 presents the backgrounds of students between 1887 and 1934. Unfortunately, data are not available or not comparable for the entire period. Comparability is made difficult here in particular by the use of varying categories, as Bavaria, Prussia, and the German Empire used different classification schema for their respective populations (noted where appropriate in the table). These differences affect the profiles that emerge from the data. The cutoff between small and large firms is set differently, for example, in Bavaria and in Prussia, and in the latter no distinction was made at all before 1908. Also lacking is the division in Prussia between middle and lower civil service, and that in Bavaria between large and middle or small farms.

The first column in Table 2.1 shows the social background of Prussian students at the end of the first phase of rapid growth (1887) and the second column the subsequent "cooling-out" phase in expansion; in the third column are the data for the period immediately before the outbreak of the First World War. Although the overall number of university students almost doubled during this period, when one examines the social profile of the students, one finds, with few exceptions, an astonishing similarity.

Only few trends can be ascertained with certainty here. One is the decline in the proportion of students whose fathers were *higher* civil servants or ministers; a compensating rise was among those from *middle-level* civil service backgrounds, from 20.6% to 27.3%, indicating the class that was able to best exploit the expanding educational opportunities. Thus, the proportion coming from any level of civil service family rose from 37.2% to 41.4% (see Table 2.1, bottom).

A number of case studies have confirmed the continual decline during the 19th century in the proportion of students whose fathers were university graduates. At the University of Leipzig (Germany), for example, this decline was from about 50% to 30% between 1860 and 1885 (Eulenberg 1904, "Appendix"). As is shown in Table 2.1 (bottom), however, this proportion rose in Prussia between 1887 and 1891 from

25.7% to 27.5%. These data suggest that during this period of stasis in university enrollment it was principally the students from the middle class who were the first to be driven from their studies by the economic hard times. While the difference is minimal and should therefore not necessarily be taken as an indication of social closure, they do point in the expected direction. With the rapid expansion that took place after 1896 the proportion of students from families with university education decreased again, falling to 22% at the beginning of the First World War.

Table 2.1: Social Background of German Students 1887-1934

Occupational categories (father)	PRUSSIA			BAVARIA			GERMANY		
	1887-1891 %	1891-1896 %	1911-1912 %	ST 1920 %	ST 1923 %	WT 1924 %	ST 1928 %	ST 1931 %	WT 1933/34 %
Higher civil service	7.0	6.6	5.9	7.8	10.3	11.3			
				12.5	15.1	15.4			
Teachers with univers. degree	3.3	4.1	4.0	4.2	5.1	5.0	Σ 13.5	Σ 12.7	Σ 14.1
				9.1	11.8	9.8	Σ 22.0	Σ 20.6	Σ 21.7
Ministers (Lutheran)	7.0	7.2	4.6	2.9	2.5	2.6			
				2.4	1.6	2.6			
Professionals	5.1	5.3	4.4	10.4	9.1	9.7	6.2	5.6	5.6
				14.0	11.3	13.8	9.1	8.5	8.8
Higher military officers	1.0	1.1	1.1	2.5	2.4	2.4	1.3	1.3	1.4
				3.1	2.3	2.6	1.7	2.0	3.3
Large farmers, 'Junker'	1.9	1.9	1.4	*	*	*	1.4	1.2	1.4
							1.2	1.0	1.9
Entrepreneurs	**	**	**	22.9	20.0	17.9	5.7	7.3	6.2
				29.7	22.4	18.6	6.3	8.9	7.7
Managers	1.8	1.7	2.5	4.2	4.3	4.2	5.3	6.5	7.1
				6.1	6.5	5.1	4.7	6.1	7.4
Middle civil service	20.9	20.8	27.3	18.7	20.4	18.7	28.1	28.5	29.5
				11.7	13.6	13.8	27.2	28.5	26.4
Small farmers	12.5	11.6	9.4	8.2	7.4	7.2	4.3	5.0	4.6
				2.7	3.4	4.3	1.7	2.0	1.9
Artisans/ merchants	35.4	35.6	36.1	8.6	8.8	9.1	21.0	17.8	15.9
				2.7	4.3	5.1	17.7	13.7	11.7
White-collar employees	0.2	0.6	1.5	2.3	4.2	4.8	7.3	6.7	8.4
				2.0	4.6	5.4	5.4	5.1	6.1
Lower civil service	***	***	***	2.9	1.4	2.1	1.7	3.0	2.1
				1.1	0.6	0.8	0.6	1.3	0.7
Manual workers	0.2	0.2	0.2	2.0	2.5	3.0	2.0	3.5	3.0
				0.2	1.5	0.8	0.6	1.5	0.7
Other	3.7	3.3	1.6	2.4	1.6	2.0	2.2	0.9	0.8
				2.7	1.0	1.9	1.8	0.8	1.9
All Students N=100%	12565	11752	24218	9937	11421	8247	82391	109813	6035
				881	1078	869	11705	21073	702

Columns add to 100%.   Upper row: men; lower row: women (shaded).

Table 2.1: Social Background of German Students 1887–1934

Social back-ground indicators	PRUSSIA			BAVARIA			GERMANY		
	1887-1891	1891-1896	1911-1912	ST 1920	ST 1923	WT 1924	ST 1928	ST 1931	WT 1933/34
	%	%	%	%	%	%	%	%	%
University graduate	25.7	27.5	22.0	+	+	+	21.0	19.5	22.5
							32.9	30.3	33.9
Civil service	37.2	38.2	41.4	39.0	42.1	42.1	45.3	45.6	47.1
				39.9	45.0	45.0	52.7	52.5	52.1
Women	-	-	3.7	8.1	8.6	9.5	11.6	16.0	10.4
Upper class	+	+	35.6(e)	+	+	+	33.4	34.6	35.8
							45.0	47.1	50.8

Upper row: men;   lower row: women (shaded)

University graduate = proportion of students whose father is university graduate.

Civil service = proportion of students whose father is tenured civil service employee.

Women = proportion of female students

Upper class = Sum of the first eight occupational categories in Table 2.1, part 1, above.

For Prussia no data on social background of women is available.

Key to symbols used:

Σ GERMANY 1928 - 1934: The first three occupational categories collapsed.

* BAVARIA 1920 - 1924: The statistical sources do not distinguish between large and small farmers.

** PRUSSIA 1887 - 1912: The statistical sources do not distinguish between (large) entrepreneurs and (small) artisans and merchants.

*** PRUSSIA 1887 - 1912: The statistical sources do not distinguish between middle and lower civil servants.

+ Data not available.   (e) Estimated from 'Preußische Statistik', Vol. 236 (1911/1912), pp. 54-170.

ST = Summer term;   WT = winter term.   Sources: See Appendix I.

Thus, even if the sons of middle class families were temporarily forced from the university, this effect was only short lived.

The dynamic of university expansion was in fact supported by this decline in the representation of university graduates' children at universities. Those from previously excluded social strata who do obtain a university degree will, themselves, tend to send their own children to university. This behavior follows an "iron law" that social analysts have observed in the case of various social groups (Bofinger 1977; Halsey et al. 1980), as the upwardly mobile attempt to guarantee their children the privileges which they themselves have managed to attain, including linguistic facility, an understanding of educational institutions, and the desire for upward mobility. Therefore the declining proportion of students from university families signals a dynamic in the educational expansion in which the demand for university admission grows from generation to generation (see Chap. 1, note 6).

Table 2.1 demonstrates that the major beneficiaries of the educational expansion were those from middle-level civil service and employee backgrounds. Their rise came with a corresponding decline in the proportions from farming families (from 12.5% to 9.4%) and families of ministers and higher civil services. The working class was not represented at the universities at this time; their proportion remained throughout this period (1887-1912) fairly constant at 0.2%.

The data for Bavaria present a good example of the developments at universities during the crisis years following the First World War and the relative stabilization achieved with the Stresemann government in 1925. In 1923 the value of the Reichsmark, the German currency, was set at 20,000 to the United States dollar, and the preceding period of hyperinflation had wiped out the savings of the middle class. In his address in Oslo upon being awarded the Nobel Peace Prize, Stresemann described the consequences of this hyperinflation: "The greatest loss, in my opinion, was the support of a pillar upon which the state traditionally rests, the industrious commercial middle class, for after showing their complete dedication to the state during the War it cost them their wealth and proletarianized them."[6]

Two tendencies can be identified in the data on the social backgrounds of students during this period. One is the decline, from 22.9% to 17.9%, in the proportion from the (self-employed) commercial middle class, the second strongest group at the university after civil servants, as the loss of their savings had rendered them less able to support university education for their children.[7] The other is the rise (among men) from 39.0% to 42.1% in the proportion of those from civil service families; least of all affected by the general decline in enrollment were those from the higher levels of the civil service, whose proportion increased from 7.8% to 11.3%.

The effects which the inflation had on the lower social strata cannot be interpreted clearly in terms of social closure. Total enrollment at German universities fell between 1923 and 1925 from 125,700 to 90,000, and it was particularly sons from lower level civil servants and from farming families who suffered most; however, the proportion from working class backgrounds attending Bavarian universities during this time rose from 2% to 3%. Social analyses have shown that those with fixed incomes (including the unemployed) were hardest hit by the inflation, while the position of the working class was improved relatively. "Those drawing regular wages and salaries can be seen as the group deriving the greatest lasting advantage from the redistribution associated with the inflation, while entrepreneurs were able to just maintain their position, and those receiving unemployment benefits were the greatest losers in the process" (Holtfrerich 1980, p. 268). These relative responses help to explain the changes in student profiles shown in Table 2.1 for this period.

The data for the German Empire cover the period from 1928 to 1934; the university expansion of the Weimar era reached its peak in 1931. The data for the winter semester 1933/1934 apply only to those beginning the university (entering students) and thus already show the restrictions imposed by the Nazis. Between 1928 and 1931 the proportion of students from working class backgrounds rose from 2.0% to 3.5% and that from lower civil service families from 1.7% to 3%. Thus, although the lowest socioeconomic groups did participate in the expansion, the working class representation at German universities remained so low that one can hardly speak of a social opening to them in terms of university admissions. The middle class was not able to take great advantage of the expansion in the second half of the 1920's, and their proportion fell from 19.3% to 15.8%; this may be explained by the continuing effects of inflation and the high rate of bankruptcies during the early years of the depression.

With the Nazis' coming to power, only small changes took place in the social background of university students. The selection mechanisms were too established in the social institutions for the political revolution to have an immediate effect, and thereafter selection criteria were instituted that were directed at political attitudes of the students that were not reflected clearly in the statistics on social background (see Chap. 3). The winners in the political revolution were the civil servant families, whose proportion among the students increased from 45.3% in 1928 to 47.1% in 1934. It is remarkable how little the political events during this time interfered with the intergenerational careers within civil service families. While the proportions of entrepreneurs, commercial middle class, and farmers were undergoing considerable reductions, that of the civil service did not, and the university appeared to be becoming even more of a "civil service institution" than it had been before.

Within just a year of the Nazis' seizure of power they had achieved their first goals in the *antimodernization* of the universities: the absolute number of students and the proportion of women had been returned almost to their levels before the First World War, the proportion from university families was higher than in 1912 (22.5%), and the proportion from working class families was declining (already from 3.5% to 3.0%).

Nevertheless, in spite of the changes that we have identified here in the social profile of German students between 1880 and 1934, one is still struck by an amazing constancy. Of all students 35.6% were from the upper classes in 1911, 34.6%; in 1931, and 35.8% in 1934. Thus, the upper classes did not allow the educational expansion to escape them and to profit only the middle classes, but maintained their position. In the middle of the 1920's 45% of the labor force was employed in blue-collar jobs, but the proportion of students from the working class was only 2%-3%. In contrast, only 4.6% of the labor force were civil servants, but 40% of all those enrolled at German universities were from civil service families.[8] In other words, the relative proportions of social classes in the population were roughly the reverse of those at the university.

The social background of *female* students underwent the same changes as have already been described for their male counterparts, but at a higher social level. The proportion of women increased from 8.1% to 16% during the Weimar Republic, only to fall to 10.4% in 1933. Due to the stricter social selection among women their social profile was higher than that among men; for example, whereas 34.6% of male students were from the upper class in 1931, the figure among women was 47.1%. Of the few women who, under the Nazi restrictions, were able to attend university one-half (50.8%) were from the upper class. Enrollment rate differences between men and women were greatest among the working class and farming population; the chance that a son from such a family would be able to attend the university was, as we have seen, very slim – that of a daughter doing so was twice as slim.[9] As far as women's emancipation can be documented in figures on university enrollment, this emancipation clearly began in the upper classes. The notion of a woman from the working class obtaining a university education was accepted only 40 years later.

2.2 Social Selection in the Secondary School System

The changes in social profile of students that we see in Table 2.1 cannot be explained at the level of university education itself. The universities themselves have only a minimal role in determining the social profile of students, for this profile can but reflect that of pupils leaving secondary school with the qualifications needed to attend university. Until 1933 possession of the school-leaving certificate (*Abitur*) from an "academic" secondary school was sufficient to obtain admission to university; the university could turn no one away, and only in exceptional cases could it admit an applicant without this qualification.

In the first half of the 19th century the *Gymnasium* had not yet assumed the role that it was later to have in selecting students for university study but still had a largely "comprehensive" character. In today's context it is somewhat misleading to describe it as "comprehensive," for even then it was not open to all children but principally to those of the middle and upper classes; no such "comprehensive" school existed for the lower socioeconomic groups. It was largely families of the commercial middle class who sent their children to *Gymnasium*, not as later would be the case to secure for them the credentials of access to university but to provide them with a middle-level education that would open the doors of bourgeois society to them, as well as certain privileges regarding military service. "The 'humanistic,' elite *Gymnasium* of the late 19th century had remained an integrated comprehensive school until well after the middle of the century. The majority of its pupils learned the trade of artisan or businessman, and only a small number stayed on until the upper grades, and of these only some obtained *Abitur*" (Müller 1977, p. 41).

The social tensions that came to be unleashed by the educational expansion and the overflooded labor market for university graduates were focused only in part upon the universities themselves. Many saw it as the responsibility of the secondary schools to award the school-leaving certificate to only that number of pupils that the labor market for university graduates could accommodate. During the time of the German Empire as well as that of the Weimar Republic conservative educationalists were agreed that the educational expansion and the perceived slackening of standards accompanying it could be halted only in the secondary schools. It was therefore seen as the role not of the university but of the secondary schools both to select the individuals to obtain university degrees and to determine their overall numbers – thus guaranteeing the scarcity of the commodity.

The struggle in the second half of the 19th century over the monopolization by the *Gymnasium* of the right to award *Abitur* must be seen in the context of this debate concerning the overfilled educational facilities (Kraul 1984), for extending the right to include the more practically or professionally oriented secondary schools would have further accelerated the educational expansion.

In the middle of the century the university became a central institution in the recruiting of political and economic elites. University education came to be regarded as an indispensable aspect of one's inheritance, along with social status and privilege. At the same time a new market opened for those with academic qualifications. Under these conditions it was impossible for the *Gymnasium* to become an open, nonselective school for the middle class. This would have been possible only if the universities had themselves taken the responsibility for selecting students and instituted entrance examinations. A number of such suggestions were made during the Weimar Republic (Schairer 1932); however, these were not incorporated into government education policy because they did not accord with the highly centralized structure of university administration. Such a change would have meant increased autonomy on the part of the individual universities and thus diminished the government supervision of higher education. Such proposals ran too counter to the Prussian tradition for them to be accepted. The development of education policy in Prussia and the German Empire did not diverge from its course; *Gymnasien* became elite institutions, and the age of student selection was pushed back effectively into childhood.[10]

At about the turn of the century it became evident, however, that the only way in which the classical *Gymnasium* would be able to maintain its elitist, humanistic educational goal would be by sacrificing its monopoly of the right to grant *Abitur*. The economic power of the middle class had grown so substantially that its demands for alternative avenues to the university could no longer be resisted.[11] In 1901 the decision was made to include the more professionally orientated secondary schools among the schools that could award the school-leaving certificate, but initially only a conditional form which entitled its holder to study only certain university subjects (excluding, for example, medicine, law, and theology).

Until the end of the 19th century it was the emphasis in the *Gymnasien* that pupils master classical languages which had acted as a selection barrier deterring the lower classes from this type of school – and thereby from acquiring the academic credentials to attend university. This diversification in university-preparatory secondary education was now needed to absorb the increasing demand for educational expansion. In addition to the *Gymnasium*, there were now several forms of secondary schools from which the school-leaving certificate entitled its holder to university study.[12] Similarly as for middle class men, women were able to attend university only after the corresponding school type for them (the *Oberlyzeum*) was granted the right to award *Abitur*. These newly "upgraded" schools replaced the emphasis on classical languages with one on modern languages and science and were therefore able to attract the previously excluded social groups.

The figures in Table 2.2 attest to the considerable change that occurred between 1886 and 1931 in the type of school that students had attended before reaching university. The proportion of students who had attended the classical *Gymnasium* fell during this time from 84.9% to 35.9%, while that from the more professionally orientated secondary schools rose from

Table 2.2: Type of Secondary School Attended by University Students, Germany 1886-1931

Type of secondary school attended	PRUSSIA 1886-91 %	PRUSSIA 1911-12 %	GERMANY 1931 Men %	Women %
Gymnasium	84.9	68.9	35.9	6.3
Professional secondary school	6.9	24.6	55.2	48.9
Professional sec. school for women	-	-	6.9	41.8
No school-leaving certificate(Abitur)	8.2	6.5	2.0	3.0

Columns add to 100%.   Sources: See Appendix I.

6.9% to 55.2%. These data also demonstrate the substantial extent to which the *Gymnasium* monopoly of the *Abitur* privilege served as a brake on the educational expansion in the late 19th century.

On the other hand, however, this diversification relieved the pressure on the *Gymnasium* to absorb the expanding numbers of middle class children wishing to participate in higher education and thereby enabled it to maintain its social exclusivity. The diversification in university-preparatory school types entailed a corresponding social differentiation among pupils preparing for university: those from the upper class attended *Gymnasien* and those from the middle class the professional secondary schools. This hierarchicalization is evident in the data presented in Table 2.3 on the social backgrounds of Prussian pupils in the various types of schools in 1921. Among higher civil servants' children who attended secondary school 70.1% were enrolled in *Gymnasien* and only 29.9% in the professional secondary schools; among working class children the corresponding figures were 26.9% and 73.1%.

The issues faced by the German educational system in confronting the problems of expansions, diversification, and maintaining standards can perhaps be illustrated by comparison to the educational system of the United States at that time. The German universities were noted for their uniformly high level in both research and teaching, a feature that was widely emulated abroad. While elite universities in the United States were able to vie with or even surpass them, mass universities there were generally unable to keep up with their rigorous standards. As early as the 1930's 45% of American school children completed high school, and these large numbers of high-school graduates represented a vast reservoir of

Table 2.3: Social Background of Students in the Secondary School System – Prussia 1921

Occupational categories	Gymnasium %	Other* %	All (N)
Higher civil service	70.1	29.9	12,264
Professionals	67.2	32.8	5,840
Large farmers	61.4	38.6	3,260
Higher military officers	58.8	41.2	2,267
Farmers	52.9	47.1	7,421
Middle civil service	43.4	56.6	44,486
Entrepreneurs	39.4	60.6	9,040
Artisans/merchants	36.8	63.2	47,486
Lower civil service	34.6	65.4	7,278
Managers	33.6	66.4	7,947
White-collar employees	28.0	72.0	21,416
Manual workers	26.9	73.1	8,001
All Students (N)	73,509	103,197	176,706
%	41.6%	58.4%	100.0%

* Professional secondary schools (Realgymnasium, Oberrealschule)
Rows add to 100%.   Source: Keller (1926).

potential students for selection by the various universities in terms of their own requirements and specialization. Postsecondary education in the United States became very diversified, with both peaks of excellence and numerous technical and specialized colleges below the university level. The training of physicians at that time offers an example of the structural weakness in this highly diversified system, with myriad forms of dubious methods being taught (Flexner 1930). This weakness of the decentralized American system of higher education has often been noted. Brubacher and Rudy (1968, p. 402), for example, have observed that, "precisely the autonomy of the American university, its differentiation and the fact that no uniformity was forced upon it, has been criticized as a sign of its lack of coherence. These conditions made possible an invasion of quackery of all kinds; expansion was wild and uncontrolled. Critics were dismayed by the naive faith in size and progress, by the excessive materialism, and the lack of qualitative standards." This uncontrolled growth and diversity was the price which the system of higher education in the United States paid for its democratic openness.

The homogeneity and high academic standards of the German university depended upon the homogeneity and preselection of the secondary school system (Gymnasium), as well as the diversity and "openness" of the American university was a result of the diversity and relative openness of the high school system in the United States. The institutional structures of secondary and of higher education influence each other and cannot be analyzed separately.

Hartnacke (1931, p. 119), a renowned pedagogue in the Weimar Republic who became Minster of Education in Saxony after the Nazi Party seized power formulated a clear alternative in the 1930's: "Either liberally protect the individual's right to university admission and, as a consequence, the eroding of university standards to the level of inferior mass institutions, or return to elite standards and impose the most stringent selection on students. The question is not, how can we best avoid doing anyone an injustice in preventing him from obtaining higher education, but rather, how can we support those who will best repay the public investment in his education. The answer lies in beginning the selection as early as possible." Selection as early as possible meant at the age of 12 or younger at which the children were selected for *Gymnasium*.

The reforms enacted during the era of German Empire were directed not at the working class but at the middle class. This was clear in the decision in 1901 to extend the right to award the *Abitur* to the professional secondary schools, which ended a decades-long *Kulturkampf* over the monopolization of the *Abitur*. Defenders of the *Gymnasium* had recognized that the only way to maintain the ideal of classical education which the humanistic *Gymnasium* represented was to allow a differentiation in the educational system. Enabling other types of schools to meet the demand for modern languages and science as an avenue to the university left the *Gymnasium* free to pursue its traditional emphasis on classical languages. However, this controversy was one that affected only the bourgeoisie of German society, for over 90% of working class children still attended the *Volksschule*, the lowest tier in the school system and one from which advancement to the university was ruled out due to the nonacademic nature of the education that it imparted. It hardly touched their interests whether professional secondary schools were able to award the *Abitur* or not.

It was only later that the lower socioeconomic groups joined the conflicts over public education policy. The struggle on the part of working class organizations at this time was over political participation; with the lifting of the ban on socialist organizations and the electoral victories of the Social-Democratic Party this goal was largely achieved. The continuation of their class struggle into the area of education policy required first a period in which the working class organizations consolidated their newly won power. Modest gains in the proportion of working class students attending universities were made during the Weimar Republic, but their actual breakthrough had to await the substantial educational expansion following the Second World War.

The next section analyzes the social backgrounds of students enrolled in the various subjects and concentrates in particular upon (a) the social strata of students who were later to assume leading positions in the government bureaucracy and (b) changes in the choice of subject studied between 1887 and 1934 by those from different strata.

2.3 The Social Profile of University Subjects

In Germany, law departments prepare students for positions as attorneys, as judges, and for higher levels of the state administration. Humanities departments train future teachers for state-operated *Gymnasien* – an occupation for which the opening of the university played a key role. Those studying theology take positions in one of the two established, state-financed churches in the country. While analyses of the social backgrounds of those enrolled in these subjects do not provide certain information about those filling such state positions, they do give some insight into the social groups that have tended to pursue certain occupations. After the system of entitlement became entrenched in all areas of the state bureaucracy, no one without the appropriate degree would generally have been considered for such positions, and social groups that were denied access to these subjects at the university were therefore absent from the occupations.[13]

In modern mass democracies the bureaucracy has become an efficient administrative organization that fulfills a range of important political and economic functions. Weber (1956, p. 716) observed that the operation of a fully developed bureaucratic mechanism operates in comparison to traditional forms of administration as a machine does in comparison to nonmechanized forms of production. Nevertheless, the bureaucracy is not a neutral instrument for the objective administration and implementation of the laws. It also represents an autonomous center of power, whose interests in survival and maintaining its privileges must be respected by any political elite. A once fully established bureaucracy is one of the hardest social organizations to destroy, to quote Weber again (1956, p. 726).

The more indispensable the bureaucracy becomes, the more important is the control over avenues of recruitment to it and over the personnel who staff its higher positions. Upon winning office in the new Weimar Republic the Social-Democratic Party (SPD) was soon confronted by the fact that it lacked a very important basis of support in the state bureaucracy, for the civil servants who still ran it had not surrendered their loyalty to the Kaiser and remained hostile to the new political leaders (see Chap. 5). Even in the interwar years the clientele of the SPD – the blue-collar and many of the lower white-collar workers in Germany – was effectively excluded from positions in the bureaucracy by virtue of the barriers to university study that would qualify them for these positions. Despite their electoral victory with the SPD these social strata therefore still lacked representation in the key positions of the civil service. The selection procedures for the university-preparatory schools had indeed had the intended effect: these positions were almost exclusively in the hands of the traditional higher strata of German society. The political party of the lower strata lacked not the electoral but the bureaucratic basis that would have been necessary to consolidate its power. The SPD was thus something of a general without any troops to command.

The simultaneous opening of the universities to the middle class (particularly its upper strata) and closure of them to the working class was not merely an educational issue but one related centrally to the basis of the bourgeoisie's reigns on power in the capitalist society of the day. By excluding certain social groups from the university they were able also to exclude them from the higher positions of power in the state bureaucracy. The central importance which the selection procedures for the humanistic *Gymnasium* held in the *Kulturkampf* of the Imperial era is seen in the struggle to maintain its monopoly of the *Abitur* privilege.

Although this effort to hold on to power was characteristic of a still half-feudalistic state administration, it could not be maintained indefinitely in the face of the growing welfare state. Equality of opportunity represents not merely an educational ideal of democratic society but a functional precondition for the state bureaucracy. The modern welfare state has taken over many functions from the family, business firm, and other societal bodies and replaced them with government regulation. The varied experiences, preferences, and value systems of all social classes must be represented in the bureaucracy and judiciary, and the state cannot perform these functions if it is administered by a class-based civil service. Even bureaucratic power is dependent upon popular legitimation, and the bureaucracy cannot enjoy legitimation unless it is open to all the social groups whose interests it is expected to protect.

In the United Kingdom, for example, the social closure and homogeneity of the judiciary generated an attitude on the part of the trade unions toward the state administration which has had wide ramifications. Judges were drawn almost exclusively from the traditional elites, and for the unions any decisions of a court of law could amounted to nothing but "class justice." British trade unions have taken the position of "voluntarism," which admonishes reliance upon their own organizational strength and the avoidance of state adjudication of their disputes with management. This stance still finds expression in unions' ideological statements and political strategies today (Flanders 1975, pp. 277-278), in particular, in their rejection of state involvement in collective wage negotiations. What were the reasons for this position of British unions?

Winston Churchill – an impartial witness, given his anti-union attitudes – commented on a draft of a trade unions bill before the House of Commons in 1911 as follows: "The courts hold justly a high, and I think, unequalled pre-eminence in the respect of the world in criminal cases, and in civil cases between man and man, no doubt, they deserve and command the respect and admiration of all classes of the community, but where class issues are involved, it is impossible to pretend that the courts command the same degree of general confidence." In a speech delivered to judges gathered at the University of Cambridge in 1920 Lord Justice Scrutton explained to his colleagues on the bench the source of this prejudice: "The habits you are trained in, the people with whom you mix, lead to your having a certain class of ideas of such a nature that, when you have to deal with other ideas, you do not give as sound and accurate judgments as you could wish. This is one of the great difficulties at present with Labour. Labour says 'Where are your impartial Judges? They all move in the same circle as the employers, and they are all educated and nursed in the same ideas as the employers. How can a labour man or a trade unionist get impartial justice?'"[14]

To generalize the argument of Lord Justice Scrutton, one could maintain that the state may assume a regulatory role in industrial relations only when the personnel who comprise it include members of the social groups who are the objects, and perhaps the victims, of its intervention. However, this argument can be further generalized beyond industrial relations to include also the personnel of the state bureaucracy.

When access to the civil service or to leading positions in large organizations is obtained exclusively by means of the system of university entitlement, the social selection at universities automatically carries over to the state bureaucracy. Denying certain social groups admission to the university also denies them entry into the bureaucracy. Just as their experiences and values are sacrificed at the university, their input is lost in the decision-making processes of the state.

Examining the social backgrounds of students furnishes information about tomorrow's civil servants – about their social networks, the spheres in which they are active, and the influences which have shaped them. Their behavior once in positions of public trust will likely stem at least in part from the backgrounds out of which they have come. Thus the selection of students for the university has consequences not only for the degree to which equality of opportunity is ensured in society, or inequality is legitimated, but also for the social openness of public bodies, the administration of justice, and the possibility of carrying out programs of social change. Education studies have documented, for example, that teachers who themselves are from the middle class tend to give better grades for the same work to pupils from the middle class than to pupils from the working class (Ingenkamp 1974). A relationship has also been shown between the social backgrounds of judges and the nature of the decisions that they reach.[15]

The data presented in Table 2.4 on the social profile of university subjects are to be interpreted in this light. The first (upper) figure for each item is that for Prussian universities in 1908 and the second (lower) for German universities in 1931. The columns add vertically to 100% and represent the social background rates in the respective subjects. The last row shows the proportion of students in that subject who were from civil service families.

Similar changes are seen in almost all subjects between 1908 and 1931: the proportion of self-employed (in commerce, industry) decreased and that of civil servants increased. In the humanities the proportion of those from civil service families rose from 42% in 1887 (data not shown) to 50% in 1908 and then to 54.4% in 1931; between 1908 and 1931 their proportion among law students increased from 40% to 47.3%. Thus the civil service families were able to augment their already dominant position during the interwar era.

It must also be noted in this context that structural changes were taking place in the population. The processes of economic concentration were accelerated during periods of depression, and many self-employed were forced to seek employment with others. The proportion of the labor force classified as self-employed declined from 28% to 16.5% between 1882 and 1925, and that classified as civil servant or white-collar employee rose from 6.1% to 17.3%.[16]

At the same time as the structural shift in the labor force from *self-employed* to *employed* there was occurring a shift among university students from *self-employed* to *civil servants*. Toward the end of the Weimar Republic 43% of all students came from civil service families, although their proportion in the labor force amounted to only 4.6% (Achner 1931, p. 486). As the lower socioeconomic groups were striving through the SPD and the labor unions to wrest political power from the hands of the traditional bureaucracy, their offspring were either barely

Table 2.4: Social Background of Students by University Subject

Occupational categories (father)	Law %	Medicine %	Humanities %	Natural sciences %	Lutheran theology %	Catholic theology %	Polytechnics %
High civil service	19.2	13.0	12.5	11.5	36.5	1.7	+
	18.5	17.2	12.8	12.2	21.9	2.4	12.9
Professionals	4.7	12.6	1.7	3.4	1.1	1.5	+
	7.5	14.1	3.6	4.1	1.8	0.9	4.3
Higher military officers	2.6	0.8	0.5	1.7	0.6	-	+
	2.2	1.5	2.1	1.2	1.0	0.2	1.7
Entrepreneurs	17.3	12.6	8.2	14.8	4.5	4.6	+
	10.4	8.6	4.8	7.2	2.3	1.8	9.8
Large farmers/'Junker'	6.1	4.9	2.7	3.2	2.1	4.3	+
	1.6	1.2	0.6	0.7	0.7	0.5	0.9
Managers	1.7	1.9	3.4	3.5	2.2	4.9	+
	6.6	5.8	5.8	7.0	4.4	2.9	9.7
Middle civil service	18.2	18.3	37.0	26.8	33.6	21.7	+
	24.9	23.6	36.6	32.6	32.3	21.8	25.5
Small farmers	3.4	4.8	6.7	5.5	5.0	22.5	+
	3.2	3.2	3.7	4.3	5.0	22.4	2.7
Artisans/merchants	24.8	28.3	24.0	27.1	12.6	27.6	+
	16.5	17.3	15.8	15.7	13.2	20.1	18.3
White-collar employees	0.4	0.3	1.7	1.3	0.4	5.9	+
	4.5	4.0	7.0	8.0	7.7	6.3	7.5
Lower civil service	**	**	**	**	**	**	+
	1.7	1.6	2.9	2.9	4.7	7.2	2.8
Manual workers	-	0.1	0.4	0.1	-	1.4	+
	1.8	1.2	3.6	3.5	4.1	12.1	2.8
Other	1.6	2.4	1.2	1.1	1.4	3.9	+
	0.6	0.7	0.7	0.6	0.9	1.4	1.1
All 1908	5694	2704	5376	2417	1019	877	+
N = 100% 1931	20839	21541	26703	16314	6511	4229	16951
Father: Civil	40.0	32.1	50.0	40.0	70.7	23.4	+
Service %	47.3	43.9	54.4	48.9	56.1	25.8	42.9

Upper row: Prussia 1908; lower row: Germany 1931 (shaded)

Columns add to 100% (inflow).   + Data not available.   ** The Prussian statistics do not distinguish between "middle" and "lower" civil service.   Sources: See Appendix I.

(white-collar employees) or virtually not at all (blue-collar employees) in the student body of German universities; in 1931 only 6.3% of all students came from families classified as manual workers or white-collar employees in the private sector.

Although the basis of the state's self-image had changed from that of a centralized, authoritarian to that of a liberal social welfare state, the target groups of its welfare were denied participation in the bureaucratic administration of the state. Despite the participation rights of the lower socioeconomic groups in the new democracy, the reproduction of personnel in the courts, schools, Lutheran Church, and in the state bureaucracy remained closed. The self-recruitment of bureaucratic personnel occurred less from among the ranks of upper-level civil servants than those at the middle levels. It was the latter who appeared most aware of the consequences and advantages of the entitlement system, and they were determined not to let the careers of their children be limited by the barriers that had limited their own careers.

These conditions were described in 1930 by an observer in the *Sozialwissenschaftliche Rundschau* in the following way (Keiser 1930, p. 1029): "No less than half of all university students are the children of civil servants. It can be presumed that one of the major reasons for their increase among the student body is the substantial growth in the size of the civil service since the war.... The German bureaucrats have managed to guarantee themselves both with life-long jobs and with salaries that rise with age, and it cannot be seen as a socially healthy circumstance that this should lead to the present boom in student numbers and to a kind of incest within the bureaucracy."

Bureaucrats constituted a dominant social group not only among university students. In the German Empire and the Weimar Republic they also made up a sizable proportion of delegates to the Reichstag. Among representatives to the National Assembly in 1848 59% had been civil servants. In the Reichstag of 1871 they still accounted for 43% of delegates. Although their numbers fell to 25% during the Weimar Republic, the figure had risen again to 42% by 1976.[17] Between the bureaucracy and the Parliament there developed a personal union which impaired the latter's check on the former.

Thus, intergenerationally the bureaucracy recruited from within itself, and its strong representation not only in the state administration but also in the university student body and Parliament protected its position as a closed caste. It would be incorrect to speak of occupational "inheritance," as most students came from families of the lower or middle levels of the civil service and looked forward to a career promising upward mobility. What was inherited from one generation of the civil service to the next, however, was a value system and a code of behavior that had its roots in a predemocratic society. This highly effective reproduction strategy welded the bureaucracy and the university into a single social interest for stabilization of the status quo and social closure of the university (Ringer 1969, p. 34).

A final comment should be made regarding the recruitment of Catholic priests. A remarkable proportion of Catholic theology students were drawn from the families of farmers and small shopkeepers – 54% in 1908 and 43% still in 1931. While the proportion of those from the working class rose during this period from 1.4% to 12.1%, the increase came principally during the Weimar era, so that the social profile of Catholic priests in the 1930's closely resembled that of the student body (Catholic theology) at the beginning of the century. That which we observed above concerning the judicial system also applies to the Catholic clergy: it was incapable of integrating within its organization the new social strata of the industrial age, the white- and blue-collar employees. The Catholic Church thus remained culturally an institution of the agrarian sector, with all of the consequences which this entailed for its ideology, organizational structure, and membership recruitment. The social origin of the Catholic clergy may explain, at least to some extent, the support the Nazi regime found among the establishment of the Catholic Church.

In contrast to the only 17% of Catholic theology students who were from the higher socioeconomic groups or from the families of university graduates at the turn of the century , 47% of those enrolled in Lutheran theology showed this background.[18] If one views the economic and administrative elites as the principal force behind modernization processes, the social strata from which the Catholic Church recruited its personnel can be regarded as one of the obstacles to its participating in this modernization. At the turn of the century it was still recruiting its priests principally from social groups that were dwindling in size and importance – farmers and shopkeepers. In this sense the Catholic Church was therefore allied neither with the elites of the traditional society nor with the working class of the new industrial society.

2.4 Choice of University Subject and Social Background

The preceding section examined the social strata of students enrolled in the various subjects. The present section turns the perspective around and asks what subjects were studied by those from the various social strata.[19] This analysis will demonstrate the role which the choice of subject played in the establishment (and inheritance) of the individuals' status within the higher socioeconomic groups. The changes over time also reflect the secularization and rationalization of a society which, at the turn of the century, was still largely influenced by feudal institutions.

The changing social backgrounds of those choosing the various subjects, from the late 19th to the early 20th century, are presented in Table 2.5 (Prussia, 1887 versus 1911) and Table 2.6 (peak of university enrollment in 1931 versus the beginning of the Nazi regime's admissions restrictions). The two tables cannot be compared directly with one another; whereas Table 2.6 refers to all students in higher education, the data for students at polytechnics are not available for Table 2.5.

The "secularization" of subject choice is striking in the first of these two periods. In 1887 Lutheran theology was still the subject chosen by 16.4% of the sons of university and *Gymnasium* teachers, but by 1911 the figure had fallen to 4.7%. Among those whose fathers were teachers without educational training the proportion dropped from 41.7% to 8.9%. Even the sons of Lutheran ministers tended at the later date more strongly to secular professions (58.2% in 1887 versus 34.7% in 1911). Their preferences shifted from theology to teaching subjects (humanities) or those of mathematics and science. Minister's sons became teachers, and primary school teachers tried to make *Gymnasium*.

By the middle of the 19th century the sons of higher civil servants, physicians, aristocrats, and military officers no longer felt called to the ministry. Between 1887 and 1911 this occupational preference on their

Table 2.5: Choice of University Subject by Social Background of Students, Prussia 1887-1912

Occupational categories (father)	Lutheran theology %	Catholic theology %	Law %	Medicine %	Humanities %	Natural sciences %	Economics %
Higher civil service	8.0	0.9	49.8	23.7	9.0	6.5	2.1
	2.0	0.5	53.4	16.7	12.0	8.0	7.4
Teachers with university degree	16.4	1.0	23.6	26.3	21.3	10.7	0.7
	4.7	0.6	23.4	19.6	28.2	16.6	6.9
Ministers (Lutheran)	58.2	-	9.3	19.9	8.3	3.4	0.9
	34.7	0.1	14.8	13.7	24.2	8.6	3.9
Professionals	5.3	0.8	16.6	62.3	6.1	7.0	1.9
	1.4	0.9	22.9	49.5	9.5	9.2	6.6
Higher military officers	8.8	0.8	52.0	12.0	11.2	9.6	5.6
	3.0	0.8	57.4	11.3	8.3	8.3	10.9
Large farmers/ 'Junkers'	4.1	0.4	55.7	14.3	3.7	6.2	15.6
	1.5	3.3	42.2	12.2	9.0	6.4	25.4
Small farmers	22.7	10.4	14.8	30.3	9.6	5.9	6.3
	3.3	11.3	16.6	17.7	23.9	10.8	16.4
Enterpreneurs/ artisans	17.7	7.0	14.9	31.7	14.1	11.9	2.7
	2.8	6.9	20.9	17.2	26.1	17.3	8.8
Merchants	9.4	2.6	20.6	43.0	12.2	10.2	2.0
	2.4	1.9	28.0	23.3	23.0	12.9	8.5
Teacher without univers. degree	41.7	6.9	6.8	23.1	15.5	4.7	1.3
	8.9	3.7	10.8	12.7	42.0	17.0	4.9
Lower civil service	22.8	3.9	17.1	30.2	16.0	7.7	2.3
	5.4	3.1	16.8	14.8	37.1	15.8	7.0
Manual workers	36.9	15.8	-	10.5	31.6	5.2	-
	6.8	11.4	6.8	6.8	40.9	18.2	9.1
All students 1887	20.3	4.6	19.2	32.5	12.5	8.1	2.8
% 1912	5.4	3.9	22.5	19.0	26.8	13.9	8.5

Upper row: 1887; lower row: 1912 (shaded). Rows add to 100% (outflow). N = 11,385 students; 1912: N = 24,218 students.   Sources: See Appendix I.

part declined even further, falling to under 5% in almost all groups of the higher strata. Instead they tended to choose law or the humanities. For some the teaching profession offered an acceptable alternative; for example, the proportion of sons of higher civil servants studying humanities increased from 9% to 12%. A comparable increase is also seen among the sons of physicians and teachers themselves. The declining percentage of medical students from all social strata is due to the below-average expansion in the medical profession during this period (Table 2.5, last row).

Other preferences, however, remained fairly stable. About 50% of the sons of higher civil servants, military officers, and aristocrats continued to

Table 2.6: Choice of University Subject by Social Background of Students, Germany 1931-1934

	Law %	Medi- cine %	Econo- mics %	Humani- ties %	Natur. scien. %	Far- ming %	PO %	Theo- logy %	Diff. 31-34 %
Higher civil	20.1	24.6	3.8	19.5	10.4	1.2	12.5	7.9	-22.8
service	16.9	34.5	3.4	14.1	9.6	1.9	10.8	8.8	
Higher military	21.2	18.9	5.7	22.1	9.1	3.1	16.5	3.4	-29.0
officers	19.3	26.1	7.2	15.1	9.8	3.3	15.5	3.7	
Professions	18.4	45.2	4.1	11.9	7.8	0.8	10.0	1.8	-26.0
	13.8	57.6	3.6	7.4	6.3	0.9	8.2	2.2	
Entrepreneurs	20.3	21.3	12.9	13.1	10.8	0.9	18.6	2.1	-42.4
	15.5	28.6	14.2	8.6	9.8	1.6	19.1	2.6	
Managers	15.2	19.6	7.5	18.4	12.7	0.8	21.2	4.6	-31.5
	13.9	29.7	8.5	12.8	11.2	1.9	17.2	4.8	
Large Farmers/	20.1	24.4	6.3	10.4	6.8	20.1	7.8	4.1	-41.1
'Junkers'	20.5	28.8	5.5	8.5	6.8	19.2	7.0	3.7	
Middle civil	13.3	20.5	4.1	30.1	13.6	0.7	9.9	7.8	-24.9
service	12.9	31.3	4.0	18.8	11.1	1.1	10.7	10.1	
Small farmers	10.7	20.2	3.8	20.6	11.3	6.2	6.8	20.4	-12.8
	8.8	29.9	3.3	13.7	7.6	5.7	5.0	26.0	
Artisan/	14.8	23.7	7.7	23.2	11.1	0.6	11.5	7.5	-29.6
merchant	11.8	32.8	7.1	14.3	9.6	1.0	12.4	11.0	
Professions with-	13.3	27.1	6.2	15.3	8.6	0.6	23.1	5.8	-30.9
out univers.educ.	9.8	36.9	6.1	12.2	9.0	0.9	20.5	4.6	
White-collar	10.7	15.6	6.7	29.2	14.8	0.9	13.4	8.7	-11.0
workers	9.8	22.9	6.2	17.5	12.9	1.4	16.4	12.9	
Lower	9.8	15.0	4.7	29.5	13.2	0.8	10.1	16.9	-28.1
civil service	10.0	20.5	6.2	24.2	10.2	0.7	7.8	20.4	
Manual workers	8.8	8.3	5.5	39.7	13.4	0.2	5.8	18.3	-21.0
	7.5	13.0	5.4	29.9	10.2	0.6	6.2	27.2	
All students 1931	15.1	22.5	5.9	23.3	11.8	1.3	12.3	7.8	-26.1
1934	12.9	31.6	5.2	16.2	10.1	1.7	11.7	10.6	

Upper row: 1931; lower row: 1934 (shaded)　　Rows add to 100% (outflow).

Last column: Decrease in number of students by fathers' occupation between 1931 and 1934 (percentages). PO=Polytechnics; Theology=Lutheran plus Catholic theology.

1931: N=136,863 students;　1934: N=101,116 students.　　Sources: See Appendix I.

study law; many sons of Prussian *Gymnasium* teachers followed in the occupational footsteps of their fathers. In 1887 about 62% of sons whose father was classified as "professional" chose medicine as university subject, in 1934 this proportion was about 57% (Tables 2.5 and 2.6).

It appears that students from middle class backgrounds reacted more strongly to market signals than did those from the upper class – not in the sense that an excess supply of university graduates discouraged them from pursuing a university education, but that they chose their subject of study on the basis of perceived conditions in the labor market.[20] Higher strata children were more bound by family tradition; in fact it is principally among these that one can even speak of a family tradition that could be "inherited." The relative concentration in the higher strata on a small number of professions means a lack of diversity in the choice of university subject. Almost three-fourths of the students from this background in 1887 were enrolled in only two subjects (law and medicine). On the other hand, only 52% of the sons of civil servants without academic education were enrolled in the two most frequently chosen subjects among this group (Lutheran theology and medicine). When one calculates this concentration in the two most frequent subjects for all upper class as opposed to all middle class students, the figure for the former is 72.2% and that for the latter 55.7%. Although by the end of the Weimar Republic this difference had decreased, it is still evident in the data for 1934: 52.1% versus 42.9%.

The "inheritance" of the father's profession is particularly strong in certain occupations. The following figures are the proportions of matriculating sons in 1887 who chose their father's profession in the three occupations in which this "inheritance" was most common. The corresponding figures for 1934 show an even greater concentration:

Professional inheritance

	1887	1934
Physicians	63.2%	70.3%
Pharmacists	59.7%	83.0%
Attorneys/judges	63.0%	76.6%

Table 2.5 also shows the strong preference by the sons of aristocrats and military officers for the law profession. A dominant influence in this choice of subject on the part of those from the Prussian *Junker* class was presumably family tradition combined with the desire to maintain their sociopolitical hegemony. By the turn of the century at the latest it was considered an advantage for a magistrate[21] to be not only *Junker* but a

lawyer as well.

These groups with "inherited" professions are an exception, however, and the further the educational expansion proceeded the more marginalized they became within the overall student body enrolled in the subjects. In general, the "inheritance" of professions declined over time. Ever more middle class families were sending their children to university without a family tradition in a particular occupation. Moreover, around the turn of the century and again during the interwar period university study became newly mandatory for many occupations, and this further diversified the range of subjects available and increased the number of alternative career paths from which to choose.

With the increasing importance of one's occupation for shaping the type of life that one leads, the individuals' demand for freedom in making their choice of occupation is strengthened. The role of family tradition in the choice of university subject declined in parallel with the similar decline of considerations of wealth and inheritance prospects in the choice of spouse. For the individual this meant greater personal freedom of choice; for the universities, however, it meant greater uncertainty, as they became subject to more extreme and less predictable cyclical variations in student preferences. Overall student enrollment may have been increasing year after year, but that in the individual subjects varied over time and relative to one another. Once students' choice of subject came to be governed more by their individual wishes and talents and less by stable family traditions, long-range university planning became more fraught with miscalculations.

Until the middle of the 19th century a number of features were fairly stable at German universities: The number of departments was restricted, generally to the classical four,[22] each with a rather clearly identifiable clientele. Civil servants' sons studied law or medicine, ministers' sons studied Lutheran theology, and Prussian teachers' sons studied languages. A function of the university was to reproduce the occupational and family traditions of the upper class. Toward the end of the Weimar Republic the university became an arena of competition, where individual and class-specific interests overlapped and conflicted. Family traditions had ceased to play such a dominant role in students' choice of subject. The doors had been opened to increasing numbers of students from the middle class. In addition, the working class was beginning to see university access as the next step in its economic and cultural emancipation. The experience of the SPD during the Weimar Republic had shown that the working class could play a genuine role in the life of the country only when it could count on those from its own ranks occupying positions of power in the state bureaucracy. And its path into that bureaucracy led through the university.

As the interwar expansion in university enrollment reached its peak in 1931, students from certain social strata were still choosing predominantly their respective subjects; however, the differences between strata had narrowed. Whereas half of the children of higher civil servants attending university still studied law in 1887, only 20.1% did so in 1931. At the same time, 10.7% of working class men and 8.8% of working class women at university were enrolled in law. In view of the polytechnics' origin as a vocational school one might have expected their technical subjects to attract most of the children from the working class. However, of the 4268 students from working class families attending German universities in 1931 only 5.8% were enrolled at a polytechnics while almost 40% studied subjects leading to the teaching profession. The polytechnics were preferred, rather, by children of entrepreneurs and higher level white-collar employees.

The cooperation that developed between the professional secondary schools and the polytechnics, on the one hand, and the *Gymnasium* and universities, on the other, sheds light on the differing career paths typically taken by the two types of higher socioeconomic groups. The wealthy commercial/industrial class, for example, tended more strongly than the traditional upper class to attend the polytechnics. There were also differences between university students versus polytechnic students in terms of their secondary education: 33.5% of university students had received their *Abitur* from the *Gymnasium*, but only 24% from the professional secondary school, while the corresponding proportions among polytechnic students were almost the reverse (22.1% and 39.1%). The differences between the two higher social strata are thus seen in the differing ways in which they passed their social status on to their offspring. Children from the more traditional upper-middle class continued to attend the *Gymnasium* and university, after which they sought positions in the civil service (or the free professions). The educational and career alternative offered by the professional secondary schools and the polytechnics was one that appealed principally to the sons of entrepreneurs, who after their studies either returned to the family firm or sought high-level positions in other large companies.

Evidence for this differentiation between the educational institutions is also seen in the social backgrounds of students from the respective higher strata attending universities versus polytechnics. At the former the sons of entrepreneurs comprised only 14% of the student body but at the latter 20.6%. While this difference is not very great, it does indicate that the process of social reproduction took different forms, with the *economic* elite tending to one set of educational institutions and the *bureaucratic* elite to the other.

A final feature of the data in Table 2.6 is the social profile of the German student body in 1934, one year after the Nazi imposition of restrictions on the total number of university admissions (the second, lower, figure for each item in the table). These restrictions led to a 26.1% decrease in the overall number of students between 1931 and 1934. The decrease was most marked among the children from families with large industrial or commercial enterprises (-42.4%; presumably including many Jewish students) or large farming interests (-41.1%); the least decline was among children of white-collar employees (-11%) and smaller farmers (-12.8%).

While the size of the student body in almost all other subjects was sharply reduced, however, that in medicine increased between 1931 and 1934, by 4%. Although their goal was to radically turn back the process of university expansion, the Nazis were evidently content to allow the size of medical departments to continue expanding. One reason for this have may been the massive expulsion of Jewish physicians from the profession. In the six years down to 1931 the number of medical students in Germany had increased from 11,000 to 31,000, and the professional interest organization of physicians had begun to do all that it could to discourage a continued influx. The expulsion of Jewish physicians was evidently taken by non-Jewish students as a signal of suddenly improved labor market conditions. Throughout the period of totalitarian rule, however, medicine remained a propitious choice of career for another reason as well: those going into the law profession or the state bureaucracy would either have to suffer political conflicts or collaborate with the Nazis – a fate that could more easily be avoided in medical practice. One may also speculate that a further reason for the Nazis' allowing medicine to continue expanding was their anticipation of war.

Not only medicine expanded at German universities under the Nazis, however, but also theology. The reasons for the increased popularity of this subject can also only be speculated upon. One may have been the desire to escape to the nonpolitical refuge of otherworldly contemplation and spirituality. Many who might otherwise have chosen the teaching profession may therefore have preferred this career to avoid the militantly Nazi educational policies which teachers were required to propagate. On the other hand, for some the choice of a career as minister may have been politically motivated, for the churches were seen as belonging to the few large organizations in which a degree of political opposition was permitted (notwithstanding that this expectation was later disappointed).

3

The Opposition to Educational Expansion

For the class society of late 19th century the German university had two relatively clearly defined functions: it awarded "entitlement" to higher positions in the government bureaucracy and legitimated the inheritance of social privileges. For the university to fulfill these functions of social stabilization it had to be open exclusively to the upper class and thus exclude the middle and lower classes. However, a process of social opening was initiated in educational institutions; though cautious at first, this process was to snowball out of control over the coming decades. As soon as access to the university becomes a universal right to all in society, the university degree can longer be a basis for legitimating traditional social inequalities. As the university opened its doors to those further and further down in the social hierarchy, it increasingly became itself an arena and a subject of the class conflict which it had earlier served to control. Thus, rather than helping to stabilize the social order, the university gradually came to compound the threat to it.

The more the universities expanded, the more vociferous became the criticism of conservative politicians who opposed their social openness. At every opportunity they lamented the growing "anarchy" in the labor market and in the universities, which in their view could be traced clearly to the ever more accessible doorstep of the university. Even many liberal politicians and educationalists, however, also felt they could no longer close their eyes to the paradoxical consequences of educational expansion and were eventually willing to accept countermeasures which they had earlier rejected. This chapter describes the restrictive – and sometimes totalitarian – measures undertaken by the German and other European governments between the World Wars to put a brake on the accelerating educational expansion. The dilemma that continually faced education policy in these years was the need to limit educational expansion but without violating the democratic principal of equality of opportunity.

3.1 Unemployed University Graduates During the Depression

Attempts to open higher education socially had succeeded over the years by expanding the universities so as to provide a place in them for the middle class. The eventual undoing of this liberal education policy lay in the particularly rapid growth in the student population and to the overfilled university classrooms that it engendered between 1925 and 1931 – just the as deepening Depression was causing ever longer lines of unemployed job seekers. Rather than training the young to take positions in the economy after completing their degree studies, the universities – by ensuring all students a subsidized life-style during their studies at government expense – offered them a refuge from the unemployment that would otherwise await them outside the university. The flooding of the universities by social parvenus deprived the upper class of its former monopolization of the university precisely at the time that such monopoly of access could have been of most benefit. The high unemployment among university graduates served as a welcome opportunity for the critics of educational expansion to demonstrate the injudiciousness of socially nondeferential university admissions policies and to demand a tightening of the standards for university access.

Expanding unemployment and expanding universities, both out of control, would have posed a serious challenge to the state and to the labor market even if they had been faced in isolation, but their coincidence in time only further aggravated the already intensified class conflict and deepened the crisis of the Weimar Republic. It also increased the appeal of "radical" solutions being offered to overcome these problems. Below, the conditions are portrayed that characterized the labor market for university graduates in the later years of the Weimar Republic. At the end of this chapter we then consider the attempts of the subsequent Nazi regime to counteract the liberal educational policies of the Weimar years and return to the enrollment rates of the prewar years.

(a) The six years between 1925 and 1931 saw university enrollment in Germany explode from a level of 90,000 to one of approx.140,000, an expansion that entailed consequences for the labor market that could not be postponed for long. Germany's new democracy demanded a respect for each citizen's equal opportunity to obtain educational advancement; however, it was the observance of this democratic principle that prevented it from restricting the increasing numbers of young persons attending the

Gymnasium and later the universities. When a similar situation, albeit in less extreme proportions, occurred in 1890, Bismarck could still call for examinations to be made more difficult and for university fees to be increased – with the express aim of hindering the influx of the masses to the universities (Titze 1984, p. 116). This option, however, was no longer a politically viable alternative to policy makers in the Weimar years.

(b) On the other hand, an institution which the Weimar Republic did inherit from the bureaucratic-authoritarian German Empire was the system of "entitlement." Competition in the labor market – for positions both in the state administration and, increasingly, in the private economy – led to rising demands being placed on applicants for academic qualifications. The caricature here is that of the craftsman required to prove not only specialized vocational training but academic credentials as well (M. Müller 1931, p. 11). The negative consequences of the entitlement system were accentuated by the Depression and entailed an "arms' race" in educational credentials: The more, the better. Rather than deterring potential students from the university, high unemployment only encouraged them further to seek additional qualifications. Compared to being unemployed, enrollment as a university student – however minimal the stipend – seemed the lesser of two evils; at least the status of student was less degrading than that of the unemployed. "The university is the waiting room for those leaving school..." (Hadrich 1931, p. 484).

(c) War reparations, inflation, and economic recession had wreaked fiscal havoc on the German state. The civil service was nevertheless still able to expand between 1925 and 1930/1931; the number of those on the public payroll grew during these years from 870,000 to 1,100,000 (Flora 1983, p. 214), and this provided jobs for at least some of those leaving the university. In fact, the growth in the educational system was one cause of this expansion. In the ten years between 1921 and 1931 the number of pupils receiving *Abitur* at German schools rose from 17,000 to 40,000 per year, and this expansion required the hiring of more teachers. In Prussia the number of fully employed teachers at higher schools for boys grew during this period from 9,000 to 12,000 (Titze 1985, p. 108). Women also benefited from this expansion in the civil service, albeit principally at the lower levels; the proportion of female civil servants rose from 16.6% in 1907 to 28% in 1925 and to 32.4% at the beginning of the 1930's (Preller 1949, p. 125). However, beginning in 1930 no new civil servants were hired, including teachers, and some positions began to be terminated. Since the government had been the principal employer of new university graduates, this meant even more of them now joining the unemployment lines.

(d) A declining birth rate also increased the hardship facing teachers. In Germany between 1913 and 1929 the annual number of births per 100,000 population fell from 27.5 to 17.9. Germany was not the only country in which this was the case, however; in the United Kingdom during the same period the birth rate declined from 23.9 to 16.8, and in the United States in 1921-1933 the drop was from 22.5 to 16.4 (J. Müller, p. 622; Kotschnig 1937, p. 33). The smaller size of families increased resentment toward the modernization and industrialization of society – and in particular against the increasingly apparent emancipation of women.

(e) Women, who in Germany had been prohibited from attending university before the turn of the century, began to flood to universities after the First World War. In this regard the development in Germany can be seen as a catching-up with other Western democracies, where women had gained access to the university by the turn of the century. Conservatives' nostalgia for the old days was encapsulated in the title of a book which Hartnacke published in 1931: "The Education Fad and the Demise of the *Volk*." Women not only swelled the student population and added to the inflation of the university degree; they also used their education in the search for jobs and further increased the ranks of the unemployed. For Hartnacke there was no doubt but that the falling birth rate was a direct and deleterious consequence of the expansion of educational institutions and economic emancipation of women.

(f) As the effects of inflation and Depression were crippling the government's ability to act, increasing demands were being put on it for regulative and welfare outputs (see Borchardt 1982). The individual and collective efforts to deal with certain aspects of the crises only made other conditions even more critical. The attempt by ever greater numbers of young persons to evade the plight of the uneducated unemployed by obtaining a university degree led them to the benches of the educated unemployed. The discouragement of women, many of whose husbands were unemployed, from the labor market impoverished their families even further. It is against the background of these economic and political conditions that one must view the unemployment among university graduates, which is examined below.

No exact statistics exist on the number of unemployed university graduates during the Weimar Republic, but later estimates have put the figure at about 40,000-50,000. If one takes the number of employed university graduates as having been some 350,000, the unemployment rate among graduates would come to 11%-14%. It has also been estimated that natural turnover would have provided around 12,000 jobs each year. By contrast, however, there were 25,000 annually completing university degrees. Rainhold Schairer in 1932 predicted that the oversupply of degrees would surpass 100,000 within three years.[1] Schairer also had a clear notion of what had led to the overfilling of the universities (p. 8): "These conditions are not in fact due principally to a recession-induced contraction in the labor market for graduates. The real reason does not lie with the market for university degrees, and a sudden, surprise improvement in economic conditions likewise cannot overcome the problem in any satisfactory way. Rather, it is the entitlement system which has to be seen as the ultimate cause." The entitlement system, that carry-over from the German Imperial days that made career and upward mobility dependent upon a university degree, had set in motion a competition for academic qualifications which, given the means available to the liberal-democratic state, could not be controlled.

The oversupply of graduates was seen in virtually all fields; the yearly excess of physicians was estimated at 1,000, for example, and in 1931 the number of unemployed engineers had grown to 19,000.[2] The hardest hit were the teachers. In May 1930, 23,147 unemployed teachers were registered alone with the Prussian school authorities; against a total of 109,631 teaching positions this amounted to a jobless rate of 21.1%. Of those without jobs more than half had taken temporary employment of some sort in the school system, some 3,000 were working as assistant teachers, and another 4,000 were serving as replacement teachers for others who were taken ill, but almost 9,000 were without employment of any kind (*Deutsches Philologen-Blatt* 1930, p. 606). Statistics show, however, that in the same year almost 30% of all students at German universities – a total of 15,932 – were planning to become teachers. In view of the country's declining birth rate German school authorities at that time were planning on filling only some 500 turnover-related vacancies per year – a demand that the already unemployed teachers could meet for the next 45 years. Notwithstanding the already depressingly large surplus of teachers, 12,000-14,000 new university graduates were being expected to apply for teaching positions by the end of the 1930's. The *Deutsches Philologen-Blatt*, a professional publication for teachers, announced in a banner headline in December 1931 (p. 693): "15,000 Male Job Seekers and 13,600 Employed Male Teachers; 7,500 Female Job Seekers and 1,900 Employed Female Teachers."

The unemployment among teachers had reached such an extreme that it could no longer be compared to the temporary oversupply at the end of the 19th century (Herrlitz and Titze 1977). The educational system and the employment system had become detached from one another and had entered a "meritocratic vicious circle" (Bäumer 1930, p. 74). The response of the labor market was an ever higher demand for educational qualifications.

In the *Sozialwissenschaftliche Rundschau* of 1930 Müller gives an example for this vicious circle from the region of Baden (p. 407): "According to the still applicable law of 30 February 1926, to be accepted at an education college in Baden one must have either *Abitur* or, if there is a dearth of applicants with *Abitur*, a lower level certificate. However, what is the situation in practice? No one with only a lower level certificate would ever apply because there is such an oversupply of applicants who do have *Abitur*. In fact, even *Abitur* alone is not enough to gain admission; one must even have the highest grades in the *Abitur* examination. Others simply do not stand a chance.... Everyone tries to protect himself against the oversupply, and thereby drives the requirements ever higher."

Even when university graduates did manage to find a job, it was often one for which they were overqualified, or that did not match their expectations. Such underemployment was common in all areas of the economy at the end of the 1920's. As Müller (1931, p. 67) noted: "In 1930 among 3,000 higher level postal employees 1,300 occupied positions for which they were overqualified, and among 47,000 middle level employees there were 16,000 who were overqualified. As early as 1927 a professional organization for those in the book trade estimated that for only 20% of the jobs held in that branch by university graduates was a university degree required, and that 80% of employed graduates were thus overqualified. A similar organization for those with a university degree in commerce reported in summer 1929 that of its 1732 members 898, in other words, one-half, were not in positions commensurate with their education."

The forces of supply and demand thus led to a vicious circle in regard to educational qualifications: the more these were required to find employment, the greater the number who attended educational institutions in order to obtain them; the greater the number finishing their education with them, the higher the standards were set. It seemed to many that only the intervention of a deus ex machina could put a stop to this spiral. The system of *Numerus clausus*, discipline-specific admissions ceilings, which the Nazis introduced upon coming to power in 1933 did in fact stop the spiral – by government fiat. Although this repressive measure was rejected by many educationalists, the way had been prepared for its introduction by the debates that had gone on over education policy in the Weimar Republic. A general consensus had emerged that the government would have to take action of some sort to stop the uncontrolled university expansion and to reduce the size of the student population. The ever growing numbers of unemployed university graduates served as a strong argument for the failure of the "liberal" education policy of the Weimar Republic.

The uncertain job opportunities during the Weimar years led to shifts in student preferences for the various university subjects, and the substantial increase in the number of students was distributed unevenly across the individual disciplines. No overall consistent pattern emerges from the statistics, but they seem to reflect, rather, the momentary prognoses of oversupply in the different occupational branches. The proportion of students attending polytechnics, for example, at first rose but then fell again at the end of the 1920's. Just the opposite curve is seen in medical colleges.[3] Instead of "rational" decisions on the basis of real opportunities in the labor market the changing student preferences for the individual subjects seem to reflect resignation and uncertainty. One such reaction was the shift to the self-employed professions at the end of the 1920's. For example, the number of medical students in Germany rose between 1927 and 1931 from 11,900 to 24,100; there was a comparable rise in France during these years, from 7,336 to 10,242 (Kotschnig 1937, p. 116).

However, competition also rose in these professions, as there was an increasing backlog of university graduates from earlier years who had not found adequate positions. In addition, these were competing for a dwindling number of jobs. Compared to the 10,817 attorneys in Germany in 1911 there were 19,208 in 1933, while 2,290 received accreditation in 1930 alone. Within a few years there would have been one new attorney seeking entry to the profession for each one already practicing. Many attorneys were barely making ends meet. In 1933, 41.9% of attorneys in Germany were earning less than 3,000 marks per year, whereas the average yearly wage of a blue-collar worker in the commercial/industrial sector was 1,650 marks (*Studium und Beruf* 1935, p. 103).

Studies have also attested to the difficult conditions on the labor market for university graduates in France and the United States. A system of unemployment benefits was introduced in the United States only during the New Deal. A survey was conducted among the employment offices in 1935-1936 on all those registered as unemployed, at a time when the overall unemployment rate stood at 25%. This survey showed that the professions were less affected by unemployment than blue- and white-collar employees, but that among those most affected were such occupations as teachers, engineers, and tax consultants. Some 80,000 teachers were registered as unemployed (unemployment rate 7.4%), and 13,000 tax consultants and accountants (unemployment rate 5%-6%). The authors of the report stressed that those least affected seemed to be skilled workers, although largely because they had not registered for unemployment benefits. Thus, these figures represent conservative estimates, and the real levels of unemployment were likely substantially higher.[4]

The labor market in France also saw a backlog of university graduates at the beginning of the 1930's who had little prospect of employment. However, the Depression had rather less dramatic consequences there than in Germany and the United States. The official unemployment figures for 1934 showed "only" 340,000 jobless. Nevertheless, conditions were depressed in many highly qualified occupations, and political pressure was mounting for the government to do something about them. For example, of the 1,775 students who received their degree in 1934 for teaching humanities at higher level schools, fewer than half (approximately 700) found jobs. Conditions among law students were not better: while about 800 vacancies were announced in the government bureaucracy for attorneys in the year 1933, some 2,000 law students were finishing their degrees (Kotschnig 1937, p. 115; Rosier 1936, pp. 305-309).

3.2 Countermeasures I: Prologue

In the middle of the 19th century physicians, teachers, pharmacists, engineers, and others began to form professional associations. As pressure groups these associations enjoyed substantial influence with political parties and were thus able to do much toward promoting the group interests of their members (Carr-Saunders and Wilson 1933; Starr 1982). Examples include the influence of the interest organization of teachers on education policy (*Deutscher Philologenverband*) and that of the physicians' on health policy (*Hartmannbund*). The most important distinction between these interest groups, on the one hand, and labor unions, on the other, was the university degree held by the members of the former, and a principal goal of theirs was protecting the privileges associated with this degree. The considerable interest that professional associations expressed in the government's policy toward universities also grew out of their concern to protect their class privileges, and the social opening of the universities was regarded as a direct challenge to the exclusivity of their status.

By the beginning of the 1930's the *Sozialwissenschaftliche Rundschau* had become a major forum for the debate over the overfilling at German universities. A frequent commentator was Wilhelm Hartnacke, quoted a number of times above. He often presented his writings here on "Liberal Education and Its Natural Limits" and "The Education Fad and the Demise of the *Volk*." (When the Nazis came to power Hartnacke was made Minister of Education in Saxony.) Another opponent of social openness at the universities was Prof. Müller, who often quoted the race biologist Lenz. In criticizing the oversupply of medical students and physicians,[5] Müller maintained (1930, p. 731) that, "No one can really claim that we need 45,000 physicians in Germany today. It is an open secret that less than half of physicians' professional duties are devoted to the genuinely ill. The oversupplied health insurance benefits are exploited by the oversupplied physicians to fill out their time with essentially nonmedical busywork. If there were only 25,000 physicians in Germany instead of 45,000, we would be no less healthy than we are today. Moreover, hundreds of billions of marks would be saved every year."

A subject discussed at every convention of the physicians' association were the "disastrously overfilled conditions" in the medical profession. Demands were made time and again for measures to limit access to the profession, for example, making examinations more difficult and introducing *Numerus clausus*. Similar demands were being made by the attorneys' association, which in May 1930 called for a drastic limitation in the number of those receiving government accreditation – only as many as were needed to fill the need in public service and in private practice.

Such demands for halting the university expansion and for protectionism toward the professions were heard not only in Germany at this time but also in many other Western nations, and these were often taken up by political parties. The responses of different governments were many and varied, ranging from moral persuasion aimed at discouraging young persons from attending university to the institution of strict systems of *Numerus clausus*. A number of these are detailed below. Most, however, were emergency measures or unsystematic, ad hoc responses, ant they were too weak to have a real effect upon the expansion.

In France, for example, the Bureau Universitaire de Statistique was established to collect data on the country's student population. In a study commissioned by this office, Rosier in 1936 examined the labor market for university graduates, and expressed the view (p. 276) that, "Public opinion in France supports the prohibition or at least the restriction of foreigners' access to certain professions; however, it also does not want any damage to be done to the incomparable intellectual prestige of our country."

There was a relatively large proportion of students at French universities in the 1920's and 1930's from the colonies or from countries in southern and eastern Europe. Of the 79,000 students there in 1930/1931, 17,300 – 22% – were foreigners. (The corresponding figure in Germany was 5%.) In 1933 the *Loi Armbruster* was enacted, prohibiting foreigners from practicing medicine in France who had not received their *baccalauréat* in France. In spring 1935 French medical students went on strike for a *stricter selection* (sic!) after the first year of medical study, although ever more students were already failing the examination for admission to the second year of study – in 1932 only 61% had passed and in 1933 only 49% (Rosier 1936, p. 315). As a result the law restricting foreigners' right to practice in France was changed in July 1935, prohibiting them from medical practice altogether, and naturalized immigrants were allowed to practice only 10 years after obtaining French citizenship (Kotschnig 1937, p. 225).

In France, as in many other countries, the principal barrier to university admission – and therefore the strongest instrument for limiting university expansion – was the *baccalauréat*. Only 36% of pupils taking this test passed it in 1934, and the French government was planning to make it even more difficult. In the United Kingdom, the Universities of Glasgow and Edinburgh imposed *Numerus clausus* for medical study in 1933. In the Netherlands, the "Limburg Report" proposed the increasing of university tuition to reduce student numbers, and similar plans were being made in France and Germany (Kotschnig 1937, pp. 185-195). The Social-Democratic government of Prussia doubled school tuition between 1928 and 1932, from 120 marks to 240 marks; the highest rates were imposed in Lübeck with 360 marks and Hamburg with 288 marks (*Deutsches Philologen-Blatt* 1932, p. 62).

Professional associations also sought the imposition of restrictions to protect their members from competition, discriminating particularly against women and foreigners. In September 1933 the Dutch Minister of Education was given the authority to deny foreigners the right to attend university in the country; this was followed in May of the next year by a law preventing foreigners from taking academic examinations. One could go on seemingly forever with the list of such protectionist policies. The measures were an aspect of the wave of pathological nationalism that was sweeping through Europe at the time; in the area of international trade protectionism had already led to disastrous consequences. In his pamphlet entitled *La trahison des clercs*, Benda (1927) accused European intellectuals of selling out to the nation-state and thereby betraying the idea of "Europe;" the nation-state was becoming the fulcrum of political decision making, and the mistakes being made in foreign policy in one country after another were being repeated in education policy.

In Germany, Schairer in 1932 called for wide-reaching structural changes that would stop the influx to the universities. His proposal of giving the individual universities the right to set their own admissions standards was a departure from the traditional German policy of restricting university access not at the university level but in the *Gymnasium*, which still held the *Abitur* as a sacrosanct institution. Schairer (p. 124) maintained that, "Especially in such times of overfilling such as the present, the ultimate responsibility should lie not with the schools but with the universities. Only this is in keeping with the essence of academic education. Any measure must begin with the fundamental autonomy of the university in the selection of its students and in establishing a plan for its own development.... A function of this selection must be the imposition of restrictions so that the numbers admitted to a discipline correspond to those actually needed in that discipline."

One of Schairer's proposals involved a mandatory "work year," according to which no German school-leaver would gain admission to university before previously spending a year engaged in some sort of practical work. To first introduce this work year, the matriculation of the beginning class for 1933 was to be postponed until 1934, and courses for these beginning students canceled in the 1933/1934 academic year. The idea of students performing a year of practical service to society was presented as a first step toward the intellectual service to society that would be expected of them later.

Another proposal of Schairer's (1932, p. 112) was that of a "free year" for professionals, who through such a sabbatical would provide a new graduate the opportunity to enter the profession. The person taking the sabbatical would receive from the government an additional 20% of the average professional's income; this would be financed by their paying 3% of their income each month into a special fund. This proposal Schairer presented as an emergency measure to last ten years, which would both protect the professions themselves and spare those seeking entry into them the probability of unemployment and despair.

Of Schairer's ideas for dealing with the oversupply and unemployment among university graduates, only of the "work year" was to gain official ratification: the idea was taken up by the Nazi regime and implemented one year later than Schairer had called for. His suggestion for giving the universities autonomy in setting admissions criteria ran completely counter to the centralizing principles of the new totalitarian state. The proposal of a "free year" was to find supporters only 50 years later.

Women's participation in the new educational opportunities had contributed to a significant part of the expansion that was taking place. This became a subject of controversy in almost every country, and numerous measures came to be instituted to actively discriminate against women. Cecelia Goetz, for example, a judge for bankruptcy proceedings in New York, was interviewed in 1969 about her experiences as a novice examining attorney in the 1920's: "The Anti-Trust Office of the Justice Department, which was headed then by a liberal, made no secret of the fact that women would not be hired. Even where women were not automatically ruled out, they were still not welcome....

I was reproached for trying to steal the bread from a married man by competing against him for a vacant position" (Epstein 1983, p. 84).

In France women were excluded from the higher levels in the civil service. The inner circle of power there was comprised of those with top positions in the judiciary, internal revenue, and treasury (*grand corps*). These positions were awarded to applicants with the highest grades on an special examination (*grands concours*), and this examination was structured in a way that generally only those who had attended the *grandes écoles* would stand a chance of passing it.[6] Although women were admitted to the *grandes écoles* (but not to the Polytechnique), they were not allowed to take this examination.

In Germany the discrimination against women was part of explicit public policy. An official statement of the Justice Department (quoted in *Studium und Beruf* 1934, p. 138) on the recent Judicial Training Law of 22 July 1934 read: "Although the Judicial Training Law contains no special regulations in reference to women, it nevertheless regards the performance of juridical duties to be the responsibility of men. Inasmuch as the law of 11 July 1922 permitting the hiring of women as judges and state attorneys has not been rescinded, women cannot be denied admission to courses or examinations for these juridical positions. It must be pointed out, on the other hand, that women cannot count on being hired for such positions. They are in effect barred from public positions in the judiciary. As regards the private practice of law, experience shows that as a rule there is also here no chance for a woman to earn a living. Women are therefore strongly discouraged from pursuing the study of law."[7]

This policy finally closed a labor market to women to which their access had already been very restricted. Of the 10,359 judges and state attorneys in Germany in 1934 only 26 (0.3%) were women, and among the 17,668 private attorneys there were only 167 (0.9%) women.

Such measures, enacted into government policy by the Nazis, grew out of a tradition which had enjoyed the support of a number of political parties. For example, in the Berlin City Council the Deutsche Volkspartei (a conservative middle class party) on 9 December 1930 had taken the following position: "All married women employed in the public or private spheres whose husbands earn an income which, in terms of the present economic conditions, is commensurate with the family's social standing should be awarded the appropriate severance pay and dismissed from their jobs." A coalition of parties representing economic interests in the Reichstag called on "All national, state, and local authorities to limit the hiring of female employees to the absolutely minimum. Those women who are already employed by national, state, and local governments to be dismissed, especially if they are holding men's jobs, and provided they are not responsible for the support of their parents. The wives of public and private employees and of those on pensions to be forbidden from practicing an occupation that is economically detrimental to employment conditions."[8]

Women had begun in the 1920's and 1930's to use their university education to gain access to the professions and to positions requiring high qualifications. Coming at the time of the economic crisis, this further increased competition for the jobs that were still available. By the beginning of the 1930's it was evident that their full integration into the labor market would soon be a matter of fact. This confronted upper class males with an even greater threat to their monopolization of power than that of the university-educated middle classes. However, their discrimination against women was not based solely on the attempt to limit competition for positions of power. It also represented an opposition to the general trend in industrial society toward modernization and democratization.

3.3 Countermeasures II: The Hour of the Radicals

Since the middle of the 18th century anyone receiving *Abitur* in Germany was automatically granted admission to university, but in the 1920's the rapidly growing student population led many to demand that admission be made conditional upon passing a university entrance examination.[9] Nevertheless, until 1933 the *Abitur* remained the necessary and sufficient accreditation for admission.

In March 1933 the Nazis came to power, and in April they imposed a system of *Numerus clausus* on German universities as part of a law intended to deal with the overfilling of schools and universities. Rather than the additional examination which many had called for, this system instituted a selection procedure that vetted applicants, among other things, on the basis of their political views. This law set a ceiling of 15,000 school leavers per year to be admitted to German universities. Of the 39,500 pupils receiving *Abitur* in 1934 only 15,979 were in fact granted admission, thus barring the door to 60% of potential new students. The law also limited the proportion of women to 10%. In the course of the 1920's the number of women at German universities had increased by 600%, but there were thus now permitted only 1500 new matriculations per year – the same level as that before the First World War. Moreover, a quota system was instituted for the individual states, based on the relative size of their respective populations. For example, 8984 were admitted from Prussia, 1670 from Bavaria, and 1339 from Saxony.[10]

The proportion of non-"Aryan" students was limited to 1.5%. At first, exceptions were made in the case of children of Jewish First World War veterans, but these were eliminated by new regulations enacted in January 1934, which extended the anti-Semitic discrimination even to those enrolled only on a nondegree basis. Kotschnig (1937) estimated that approximately 7000 Jewish students were directly excluded from study as a result of the new law.

The new authoritarian regime thus put an abrupt end to the liberal education policy of the Weimar Republic. Rather than providing the universities more autonomy in selecting their students, as many had proposed, the *Numerus clausus* system of the Nazis continued the policy of centralized selection, substituting one based solely on the *Abitur* with one including nonacademic characteristics of the applicant. A protocol accompanying the law in the state of Prussia described these criteria in the following way: "As important as academic ability may be in granting permission to study, this alone does not suffice. Other qualities must also be taken into consideration, such as integrity of character, truth of convictions, strength of will, and devotion to the aims of National Socialism. No less important is bodily constitution [and] participation in national organizations (SA, Hitlerjugend, Bund der deutschen Mädchen)."

The procedure was mandated as follows: "University admission requires application for permission to study. This application along with the assent of the applicant's legal guardian is submitted to the director of the applicant's school. The applicant may provide witnesses to attest to his participation in the SA or Hitlerjugend. The director forwards the application along with accompanying documents to the Admissions Commission. Notwithstanding the full jurisdiction of this Commission, the school director informs the District Party Leader of the applications that he has received, with the request to submit possible objections regarding the applicants to the Commission within a reasonable period of time."[11] This procedure thus took the decision on the application out of the hands of the school, for the school director did nothing but receive the application and pass it on to those who did make the decision – political and party-political authorities. In instituting this procedure the Nazis extended to the universities their policy of subordinating social institutions to political control. It led to the rejection of over half of all applicants, and those who were accepted presumably included enough Nazi sympathizers that political activities could be counted on to be carried out by them once they got to university.[12]

Political reliability was also encouraged by the work service system for youth and students that had been in operation since 1928 in Germany, particularly in localities with high unemployment. Beginning in 1931 government support was granted to the camps for those in the project. In the second half of 1932 there were some 260,000 young persons in the project, carrying out such work as road building, farmland clearance, and public gardening. This system served as a model for the CCC introduced in the United States as part of the New Deal.

The idea of work service camps grew out of the radical-democratic tradition, and they were seen as a social melting pot in which class distinctions and prejudices could be overcome. Most of those participating in the project were of privileged backgrounds and had had little previous contact with the working class, and it was thought that the new fund of social experiences provided by involvement in this scheme would foster solidarity across class lines. Politicians were quick to recognize the potential that these camps offered for political indoctrination, and members of the Nazi student organization often managed to become leaders of the camps.

Participation in these camps was to become the second hurdle that university applicants were required to pass in order to obtain admission to their studies. As early as February/March 1933 Prussia took the lead in mandating work service for university applicants. At first a 6-month stint in the service was described as voluntary, but in the course of 1934 this was made a formal requirement for admission to university in addition to *Abitur*. While the *Numerus clausus* system had reduced the number of new students to 15,000, the work service camps in the summer of 1934 meant the loss of an entire beginning class in one semester. As a result of the two measures together, the number of male students declined between 1933 and 1934 from 98,000 to 77,000 and the number of female students from 19,000 to 12,000.

Thus, immediately after taking power the Nazis gained effective control over the selection of university students. The *Numerus clausus* ceilings, the vetting criteria, the mandatory work service participation – these new political institutions guaranteed the Nazis not only a certain type and number of students at the university but also a source of political pressure on politically questionable university staff. Moreover, it assured them a supply of reliable recruits to serve as future leaders of the regime (Hartshorne 1937; Giles 1985). The expulsion of Jewish professors and those opposing the Nazi regime was supported by an incoming student body that was following the party-line and devoted to the new regime and its ideology.[13]

The Nazi education policy managed to put an end to a vicious circle that had arisen during the Depression, and which the liberal education policy of the Weimar Republic, with the limited means available to it, had not been able to cope with. The size of the student population had risen dramatically in almost all Western countries during the interwar period, and this despite of (or precisely because of) the high unemployment among university graduates. Only Germany departed from this pattern in the 1930's, ending the rapid educational expansion and imposing a political definition of the "need" for university graduates. It was evident also in the other Western countries that the extent of university education was greater than the social "need" would have dictated; however, in these countries the numbers of students continued to climb throughout the 1930's and was halted temporarily only with the outbreak of the Second World War.

The Nazis envisaged the *Numerus clausus* ceilings as only a temporary measure, with the selection of university students being shifted in the future to earlier stages in the pupils' education. The appended protocol stated that, "In subsequent years the numbers admitted are to be gradually decreased. In addition, this intervention between *Abitur* and university admission is to be made unnecessary by shifting the responsibility for selection to the university-preparatory schools" (*Studium und Beruf* 1933, p. 4).

Indeed, the new selection system proved such an immediate success that there was in effect an "overkill," and the limitation on the overall number of students was lifted in February 1935. The restrictions had reduced the number of students to below the level that was statutorily permitted: of the 16,000 students granted the right to enroll at university in 1934/1935 only 14,000 had in fact done so. The *Numerus clausus* system was therefore modified to university-specific ceilings. The maximum number of students allowed at the University of Berlin, for example, was set at 6900 students, that at the University of Munich at 5400, and that at the University of Frankfurt at 1700. Limitations specifically on the large universities that had been centers of student activity were intended to divert the student influx to smaller, provincial universities. In the event that the number of students registering at a university exceeded the statutory limit, the following criteria were established for the selection of those actually permitted to enroll: (a) Nazi Party members with membership numbers below 1,000,000; (b) soldiers under orders to attend university; and (c) students who had been enrolled for at least two semesters at the University of Königsberg (today, Kaliningrad), the University of Breslau (Wroclaw), the Polytechnic of Breslau, or the Polytechnic of Danzig (Gdansk). The ostensible purpose of the latter priority was to encourage the integration of those from eastern Prussia; however, the real reason was the increased control that this provided the political authorities over the student body.

Summarizing the Nazis' set of restrictions, Kotschnig (1937, p. 208), the General Secretary of the International Student Service in Geneva observed that, "The *Numerus clausus* system of Germany and the way in which it is applied can no longer be considered an emergency measure. It means nothing less than the end of the university as we understand it, and as it was understood in Germany until the National Socialist seizure of power."

What Kotschnig was criticizing, however, had grown out of measures that had, in part, been called for during the Weimar Republic by many educationalists and politicians, and that had originally been seen as "liberal" (see Sect. 3.2 above). It was the extremism of the *Numerus clausus* and the party-political criteria of student selection which made the measures so reprehensible. R Schairer, a conservative among the liberal educationalists, had supported the introduction of a ceiling on the number of students and a mandatory work service for prospective students. However, even W. Hartnacke, a strong supporter of the Nazis and opponent of higher education for women spoke out against the selection criteria in a newspaper article in April 1936.[14]

At a conference of university educationalists in Davos, Switzerland, in 1931, Adolf Löwe presented an address on "The Contemporary Education Problem of the German University" in which he analyzed clearly the situation immediately before the Nazi seizure of power. He traced the crisis of overfilled universities in Germany to two factors. One was the financial collapse of the middle class as a result of war, inflation, Depression, and economic concentration. The flight to "academic" occupations, especially the civil service, appeared as the only safeguard against downward social mobility (1932, p. 5): "Tens of thousands are flooding to the university to escape the dwindling and downwardly mobile middle-level, nonacademic occupations."

The second cause of the overfilling Löwe identified as the economic and political decline of the "Old World." He maintained that it would be an illusion to see the overfilling of universities and academic occupations as nothing but a temporary problem due to the current economic conditions (p. 5): "The actual roots of the occupational crisis lie, on the one hand, in the rationalization and monopolization of the world economy and, on the other, in the loss of the European lead in world economic terms." The economic ascent of the United States after the First World War had put an end to Europe's leading role. The innovative production methods pioneered by Taylor and Ford had unleashed a productive capacity with which the guild-based productive institutions of the Old World were unable to compete (see also Maier 1985). Löwe concluded that, "Inasmuch as the heart of the problem lies in the nonacademic occupations, the only really effective solution requires the integration of the German economy within a larger context. In the current situation this means within the context of a European economic and foreign policy."

Löwe also saw that the educational expansion had a political dimension, one that grew out of the class conflict of the Weimar Republic. The lower strata were aspiring to political, economic, and cultural participation in the new state. It was not merely a matter of equality of opportunity but of participation in the cultural institutions of democracy. Löwe was aware that cultural power also meant political power, and that to be excluded from the cultural and educational institutions of society rules out true political equality. The cultural integration of the lower strata is not merely the result of increased political power of the working class but is a necessary condition for its political integration.

This insight into the ultimate roots of the current problem did not stop him from offering practical steps for dealing with the overfilling of universities which involved introducing more restrictive selection criteria (p. 1): "By far the politically and socially most urgent need is the introduction of selection procedures that will avoid the proletarianization of intellectual work." He continued: "The overfilling of especially nonacademic women's occupations is driving women now to the university, who *both in their own interests and in those of university policy should be denied access through a more rigorous selection procedure.*" Thus, although Löwe was able clearly to analyze the problems of educational expansion in the 1920's, his thinking remained in the conservative mode of traditional German society. He did not recognize that there was a political dimension also to the influx of women into the universities, that women also constituted a group struggling for political, economic, and cultural equality, and that women's emancipation was also a part of the overall process of societal emancipation. If he had considered the case of the United States (with which he was well acquainted), he would have seen that women's attendance at universities and the "overfilling" which this entailed were an inevitable trend as well for European universities, and that this could not be held back simply by instituting more rigorous selection procedures.

It was precisely such a policy, however, which the Nazis instituted. They turned back the clock to the prewar situation and within their first year of power had, in terms of their objectives, reached a thoroughly satisfactory result. An editorial in *Studium und Beruf* commented in August 1935 (p.96) that, "The overfilling of the university has been overcome – this is shown by the statistics on German student enrollment in the summer semester of 1934."

Löwe's analysis highlighted the dilemma of education policy in the Weimar Republic: the demands by the middle and lower social strata were in opposition to the traditional quality standards of the university. The conditions at the University of Berlin must have been a nightmare for professors whose educational ideals were still based on those of the Humboldtian university. Dibelius (1930, p. 265) remarked: "Before the War the largest classroom, with its 1000 seats, was only rarely used for lectures, but today it is packed from morning to evening. Today the largest classroom seats 1500, and even it is in constant use. Some professors cannot even find seats enough for all their students in one classroom and have to use two: they hold their lectures in one and broadcast them in the second by loudspeaker." Löwe (1932, p. 6) saw only one possible solution: "Basically the strata that dominate the university today, with their mediocre level of abilities, must be reduced in numbers." Löwe's practical suggestions for dealing with the problem were in effect a denial of reality.

The area of education policy was one in which the Nazis encountered the least resistance. They took up all the ways in which Löwe in his address in Davos had denied reality. From an essentially clear-sighted analysis of the problem, conclusions for education policy were drawn which tried to restore the "golden days" of the German Empire. Not only the proletariat but also women were treated as a menace, and one whose social self-assertion had to be opposed by the traditional upper class.

In an article[15] entitled "The flood of University Graduates 50 Years Ago" Karl Fromme commented in 1983: "The measures taken by the National Socialist state were certainly drastic. However, a close look reveals that many of them bear a great similarity to proposals which today's democratic state is being forced to consider in order to deal with the flood of school leavers." The problems facing today's democratic state do indeed bear a certain similarity to those at the end of the 1920's. Since the beginning of the 1980's the universities have witnessed a continual expansion, accompanied by rapidly rising unemployment among university graduates. Many see this paradox of rising university enrollment together with rising unemployment among those leaving the university as grounds to question educational expansion and to propose appropriate changes in government education policy.

However, the measures being proposed today for dealing with university overfilling are more subtle than those of 50 years ago. The imposition of *Numerus clausus* ceilings was seen as an exception and is continued today only with certain pangs of academic conscience. No one speaks today of outright restrictions on university access. Rather, differentiation and selection within the university have become an important instrument of control. The next chapter examines the way in which this differentiation within the university answers the problem of overproduction of university graduates today. On the basis of internal differentiation and hierarchicalization the university manages to maintain social openness but at the same time to accommodate the needs of the labor market. Differentiation is the "democratic" response to growing enrollment rates and "overeducation" in many European countries since the early 1970's.

4

Institutional and Social Differentiation
in Higher Education

4.1 Elite and Mass Education

The idea of giving special support to the intellectually gifted and to the education of an elite has enjoyed substantial attention in Germany since the beginning of the 1980's.[1] With the schools and universities having expanded rapidly in recent years, interest has turned to universities' internal structural problems and to the quality of education which they provide. This chapter compares the internal organization and hierarchicalization of universities in several countries. In meritocratic societies with democratic political systems it is easier to respond to overfilled universities with internal selection procedures and hierarchical differentiation than with bureaucratic limitations on access. The following four points are dealt with here:

(a) Differentiation among institutions of higher education into mass and elite sectors is frequently a political reaction following a phase of rapid educational expansion. After a period of social openness and democratization there often comes one of social closure and internal selection. The simultaneous economic recession and rapid educational expansion of the 1980's meant a leap in the numbers of unemployed university graduates, which, as at the end of the Weimar Republic, deflated the value of a university degree. Internal differentiation enables universities to maintain a policy of social openness while controlling this deflationary effect. While a degree from the "mass" sector still demonstrates qualifications, it does not automatically entail "entitlement." The process of differentiation resembles that of a currency reform: old "paper money" (credentials of the mass sector) is devalued and replaced by a new currency (elite sector).

91

(b) The structures of the secondary and tertiary educational systems are interrelated. When selection at the secondary level is inadequate, selection procedures at the tertiary level must become more rigorous. The long-range effects of introducing comprehensive schools may have the paradoxical effect of increasing the pressure for differentiation and hierarchical organization at the universities. Whereas a school system with different structural tiers can exist alongside an undifferentiated system of higher education, a secondary system consisting exclusively of comprehensive schools virtually requires differentiation at the university level.

(c) The comprehensive school is not a stable institution, and it can serve only temporarily to "free" young persons from their social backgrounds. Once comprehensive schools have been instituted, elite universities exert strong pressure on the secondary school system for a redifferentiation. Students wishing to apply for admission to an elite university improve their chances considerably by attending an elite secondary school. Parallel to the public comprehensive school system private elite schools have developed in many countries which serve as feeder schools to the elite universities. The nonselective school leads to tendencies in the higher education system in the direction of closure and selection, and the selective institutions here have a feedback effect on the secondary system toward redifferentiation. Although the overall level of education in society is higher than it was in the past, the result is a system that was characteristic of the 19th century: elite education for 5% of the population and mass education for the rest.

(d) Along with the institutional differentiation into elite versus mass universities and elite versus mass schools comes a social differentiation among students and pupils. The elite institutions are attended exclusively or at least predominantly by those from the upper socioeconomic groups. While those from the middle and lower socioeconomic groups are not barred from attending university, as was the case before the Second World War, the elite universities do not accept them. Selection at the elite institutions is not based directly upon social background; their students are those with the highest qualifications. However, these students do in fact come from the upper strata, for it is only here that the conditions exist that allow pupils to attain these qualifications. Selection based on (school) performance and selection based on social background are not alternatives but rather are highly intercorrelated, which increases the exclusivity of these institutions.

The following sections illustrate these four points, taking the example of private schools and universities in the United States. These institutions have remained outside the movement to educational expansion, and many of them have not increased the number of their students. Following this examination, the social profile of students at elite universities is analyzed in different countries.

4.2 Expansion and Differentiation in the School and the University

(a) As early as the 18th century private schools were founded on the east coast of the United States along the lines of the English "public" school. At the time these were the only institutions in the country that offered academic education, and they were open only to children from the upper strata. Among the oldest and most exclusive of these were Andover (founded in 1778), Exeter, St. Paul's, and Groton. Such schools imparted not only the education that prepared pupils for study at university but also the training which they needed to take over the family firm thereafter.[2]

Strong competition arose to these private schools at the end of the 19th century with the founding of public high schools, which were free of charge and frequently offered a better and broader education. Due to lack of pupils many private schools were forced to either close their doors at this time or to transform themselves into public schools. The number enrolled at Exeter, for example, sank from 355 to 123 between 1880 and 1890. Others were able to survive as private schools only as the result of generous donations from wealthy alumni (Levine 1980, p. 65).

It was the enormous success of the public schools, however, that allowed the private schools to become competitive again. Whereas 3.5% of pupils in public schools completed all 12 years of schooling in 1890, by 1925 this figure had risen to 25%.[3] Public schools in the United States were becoming comprehensive, providing education to the mass of the population. At the same time, they lost the social intimacy of institutions in which the upper strata gathered among themselves, and suffered the anonymity and bureaucratization of large institutions. Teachers became self-consciously "expert" and rejected the "lay" influence of "uneducated" parents. With the growing flood of immigrants to the country in the early 20th century the public schools also began to face seemingly insurmountable problems of social integration (Tyack 1974, p. 229; Katz 1971).

The response of private schools was a form of "product differentiation," becoming institutions expressly for the elite. They eliminated their vocational courses and concentrated solely on a university-preparatory curriculum. The elite selection became more exacting; at St. Paul's 1600 applications were received in 1920 for something over 100 places (Levine 1980, p. 74). Many private schools invested heavily to transform themselves into boarding schools in order to accommodate elite pupils from greater distances. As boarding schools these institutions were then able to exert greater influence upon their pupils, thus increasing the social exclusivity of the education which they provided (Bourdieu 1981, p. 9).

In a country the size of the United States such private boarding schools played an important role in the social and cultural integration of the upper strata (Domhoff 1983, p. 25), bringing together those who otherwise would never have met and furnishing them with a common educational background. More importantly at that time, however, these schools isolated the "white Anglo-Saxon Protestants" from the flood of southern and eastern European immigrant children, who were neither culturally nor linguistically integrated into the American mainstream. These schools left the task of Americanizing the immigrant children to the high schools, while they socialized the children of the elite into an exclusive life-style based upon the cultural homogeneity of the American upper class. This goal, in fact, took priority over that of imparting academic knowledge to their pupils.

Private schools thus offered an enclave away from the socially comprehensive schools and largely outside the control of public authorities. They were generally small institutions, and their dependence on tuition and donations guaranteed the parents a strong say in their operation and curriculum. In contrast to the comparative "laissez-faire" stance of the high schools, the private institutions based their scholastic socialization squarely on the Protestant ethic (Labaree 1984).

Since the Second World War private schools have enjoyed a virtually undisturbed independence, as the public school system has expanded continually. Government education policy has aimed at ensuring enrollment and literacy figures that are as high as possible in international comparison, and private schools have played no role in this policy. Since the early 1980's the subject of private schools has drawn much greater public attention in the United States as a result of the debate over the quality of education in American schools. The controversy stemmed in large part from a study which confirmed the superiority of private (especially Catholic) schools over public schools in terms of pupil performance and discipline, scholastic environment, and the percentages going on to university.[4] The differences also remained significant after controlling for social background.[5]

This study came at the same time as the report of a government commission investigating the quality of the public education system in the United States. This report began with the following observation: "Our Nation is at risk. Our once unchallenged preeminence in commerce, industry, science, and technological innovation is being overtaken by competitors throughout the world.... We report to the American people that while we can take justifiable pride in what our schools and colleges have historically accomplished and contributed to the United States and the well-being of its people, the educational foundations of our society are presently being eroded by a rising tide of mediocrity that threatens our very future as a Nation and a people."[6] The focus of this quotation are the poor conditions at the average public high school in the United States which the upper classes have long since left to send their children to the private sector. Taking the message of the research of Coleman et al. (1981, 1982) and of "The Nation at Risk" together, it seems, that high educational standards are met only outside the (public) mass sector, i.e., in the (private) elite sector.

The social openness of the American school system had been lauded since the early 1960's as guaranteeing everyone irrespective of class and racial background the opportunity to obtain an education and even a university degree. Many European countries began at this time to introduce their own comprehensive schools based on the American model. Coleman (1982) had pointed out, however, that in addition to the public schools there existed institutions in the private sector that served only 10% of the country's children, and which were far more efficient and successful than the public schools. These studies gave added weight to voices that had been heard since the beginning of the educational expansion claiming that the price of this expansion is a lowering of the educational standards of schools.

Along with the development of comprehensive school systems, private schools in other countries have also enjoyed increased popularity. In Japan and France private schools and selective public schools play a major role in channeling students to elite universities (Rohlen 1983). The growing importance of these schools is not necessarily reflected in an increasing number of pupils attending them; in fact, elite schools and universities hardly expanded throughout the 1960's (Bourdieu 1981, p. 61). *The exclusive institutions did not expand – they selected.* For this reason, changes in this sector are difficult to document in terms of empirical data (see sect. 4.5).

(b) This process of differentiation, as a concomitant of expansion, has also taken place among institutions of higher education in the United States. Harvard, Princeton, and Yale were not always elite universities in the sense in which we apply the term to them today. Harvard, for example, was effectively accessible to almost every applicant to it in 1880; there were entrance examinations that had to be passed, but these were based on internal university standards (Schudson 1972). These standards were somewhat lowered for sons of alumni and those from families making contributions to the university (Levine 1980). What was important at such exclusive universities was less the knowledge needed to assume a technical function in society after graduation than the class-specific socialization and integration which the university offered.

Even in the 1950's the dearth of applicants had made it difficult for Yale Law School to fill all the seats available to students (Sacks 1978, p. 225). It was only with the expansion in the public sector of higher education that the private universities came to form a closed sector of their own, with precisely defined selection criteria and performance standards which became subject to court control. It was then that they became "exclusive" in the sense of universities for the "elite." Their area of recruitment ceased to be the immediate vicinity and spread out over state lines to the entire country. Universalistic criteria were established for admission to them. Such a selection policy presumes a large number of applicants, and the admissions criteria have sometimes been raised expressly to make acceptance even more attractive and thereby to draw even more applicants. The difficulty of gaining entrance became a measure of the institution's prestige and reputation. Moreover, there developed a form of corporatist relationship between the elite sector and the labor market, with alumni controlling access to leading positions in government and economy, and these recruited their staff and thus successors from the new graduates of these institutions.[7]

Herrnstein and Murray (1994, p 30) argue that "Harvard was not so hard to get into in the fall of 1952." And they continue: "... suddenly, but for no obvious reason, Harvard had become a different kind of place. ... Instead of rejecting a third of its applicants, Harvard was rejecting more than two-thirds." There is an "obvious reason" why it became "suddenly" so hard to get into Harvard: The pressure of the expansion made the university more selective and the pressure of the civil rights movement made selection criteria more universalistic.

It is often the case that the founding of new mass institutions serves to protect the institutions in the elite sector. Community colleges, for example, function as a cordon sanitaire around elite universities, protecting them from an invasion of the lower classes. Selection for the differentiated tertiary level is thus shifted from the secondary level to the tertiary level itself; the responsibility for distributing students to mass or elite universities lies not with the schools but with the elite universities. This allows the overall system of higher education to present the appearance of social openness, with virtually everyone being theoretically able to attend university. At the same time, however, it maintains differentiated selection on the basis of performance, class, sex, and race.[8]

(c) The changes in the American educational system that are reviewed briefly above cannot be summarized adequately simply as those of educational expansion. Such a model was proposed by Trow (1974), oriented strongly to experiences in the United States particularly since the Second World War. This rather mechanistic model was one purely of educational expansion for both secondary and tertiary levels and described the stages of elite education (10% of a cohort), mass education (20%-50%), and truly universal education. This model purported to be applicable to European countries and to predict the future development of their educational systems. Trow's predictions, however, as almost all such predictions in the field of educational research, have proven incorrect. Even in the United States the stage of mass education has not been completed. The major shortcoming of the model was its isolation of events in the educational system from those in society and the economy upon which the former depend. Expansion was taken to be a given, as a fundamental world-view, and to constitute the normal and universal course of development.

A more complex model is necessary to accommodate the development of educational institutions: when the expansion attains the stage of mass education, counterforces are mobilized that either put a brake upon continued expansion or lead to a differentiation in the educational institutions. With the latter, an "exclusive" sector develops alongside the mass sector which in most cases is one that caters to an "elite." For the education system *institutional differentiation represents a reaction to, and in some ways against, educational expansion.* The evidence shows that university expansion is not a process which continues automatically; rather, a necessary (although not sufficient) precondition for continued expansion has proven to be the differentiation of an elite sector.

Thus a "three-stage model" is proposed here which suggests that the development of education systems progressed from institutions which served only a small proportion of a cohort (stage 1) to a process of expansion up to the point of "mass" education (stage 2), and finally to the differentiation of the education system into a mass and an elite sector (stage 3).[9] In some countries exclusive institutions existed already in the early 19th century and have gradually been transformed in "elite" institutions as they are defined here (e.g., United States, United Kingdom).

In other countries higher education expanded strongly during the past four decades without internal differentiation, for instance, in Italy. However, in this case we find very high drop-out rates which increased with increasing enrollment rates (see Fig. 4.1 below).

The "critical" threshold seems to be the attendance of one-third to one-half of pupils in comprehensive institutions, for at this level the middle and upper strata react to the compulsory integration of culturally heterogeneous groups by founding their own, socially segregated educational institutions. (Levin 1979, p. 599). While there may still exist a single government authority to oversee all educational institutions in the country, the actual freedom of these institutions is usually considerable. Educational institutions play an important role in maintaining the stability of social classes and in the inheritance of social status. School reforms threaten the traditional balance of power among social classes and may trigger strong opposition (see sects. 4.7-4.9).

If such democratic reforms are introduced from above by an "enlightened" government (for instance, the comprehensive schools in Germany) the newly introduced institutions fail because they are left to wither – after enough parents "vote with their feet" and seek alternatives. A good example of a reform institution falling victim to this form of protest is the comprehensive school in West Germany, which despite the great hope originally placed in it when it was introduced in the 1970's is attended today by no more than 3% of the country's pupils (Voit 1989, p. 171).[10]

4.3 Differentiation by Sector, Subject, and Geographical Segregation

The differentiation can take any of a wide range of forms. Hierarchicalization of the educational system into *mass and elite sectors* is only one of these. Another is *geographical segregation*, such as one finds among American high schools since the Second World War, with those in affluent suburbs resembling the German Gymnasium or the French lycée while those in the inner-city ethnic ghettos are nearer to the lowest tier in the vertically differentiated German school system. The latter form of segmentalizing the educational system assumes the residential segregation of social strata, and the more segregated they are, the more effective is the resulting de facto differentiation among the educational institutions. The impermeability of this form of differentiation can in fact be greater than that in a system based on de jure vertical differentiation, for working class children would be able to attend a middle class high school only if their parents were to move to a middle class residential area, which seldom occurs (Litt and Parkinson 1979, p. 107).

A third form which the differentiation may take is that based upon subject of study. This means of segregating the classes at university has characterized German universities since the middle of the 19th century (Titze 1981): law and medicine have been the domains principally of the upper socioeconomic groups while subjects leading to occupations as teachers or engineers have been preferred by the middle and lower socioeconomic groups. However, if the elite subjects are not "protected" by a *Numerus clausus* system, such an informal system of differentiation tends to break down as a result of educational inflation. A contemporary example of this is the study of law at German universities, where expansion has been substantial despite the declining employment prospects of law students after obtaining their degree.[11]

Differentiation in terms of hierarchicalization (elite sector), subject, and geographical segregation are functional equivalents, and nationally specific traditions play a crucial role in determining the form which the differentiation in any given setting takes.

A range of possibilities are at the disposal of the authorities setting education policy for controlling or counteracting the inflationary consequences of educational expansion. In decentralized market systems the differentiation may either take place, as it were, "naturally" (e.g., with the "ivy league" institutions in the United States) or be officially mandated (e.g., with the *grandes écoles* in France). In some European countries the vertically differentiated secondary educational systems still fulfill an important role in the preselection of university students (Germany), while in the undifferentiated systems of the United States and Japan the inflation in the number of those qualifying for university admission is counterbalanced by the encapsulation of an elite sector of higher education.

Selection for the labor market can take place either in the school or in the university. In this respect, the two levels cannot be regarded in isolation, for if the selection is lacking in the former, it becomes a responsibility of the latter. This connection between the two levels is evident in the discussion of education policy in Germany, where a movement to establish comprehensive schools led to calls for the introduction of elite universities. (In some urban areas the proportion of pupils advancing from elementary school to the university-preparatory Gymnasium is 60%-70%, which effectively transforms the traditional Gymnasium into a comprehensive school.) Conversely, one could expect a nondifferentiated system of higher education, i.e., one unable to ensure social selection, to increase the political opposition to comprehensive schools. Proponents of comprehensive schools where these are not already the rule may therefore be faced with the paradoxical conclusion, that one way in which to strengthen their political hand would be to support the establishment of elite universities, as the lesser of two evils.

However, there is a fallacy in this line of thinking, for the acceptance of elite universities as a short-term tactical move to gain a comprehensive school system would defeat itself in the long term as a result of the feedback effect which this differentiated tertiary sector would have for a redifferentiation of secondary education. Competition for admission to elite universities would merely lead to pressure to establish elite preparatory schools appropriate to them. Even in Japan and the United States the formally comprehensive school system today comprises institutions of widely varying standards.

Thus, the selection function of the educational system may be located at different levels within it. Relative lack of differentiation at one level can be compensated by heightened differentiation at another. Such a functional analysis makes it easier to put into a wider perspective the conflicts that characterize debates over the introduction of educational reforms.

4.4 Economic Recession and Institutional Differentiation

With the dramatic increase in the numbers of those holding educational certificates, the educational expansion has meant a relative devaluation of such degrees. The paradoxical effects of this in the labor market were not long in manifesting themselves: to the same extent to which individuals from the lower socioeconomic groups make *personal* use of the expanded educational opportunities available to them, they diminish their *collective* possibility for upward mobility. Increasing the supply of university certificates by churning out university degrees, without an increase in the economic demand for such degrees, means a self-defeating inflation. As long as access to a university degree was restricted to a relatively small and privileged class, university study could underpin the inheritance of social status from one generation to the next, but societal investment in "human capital" by establishing mass universities threatens the disproportionate appropriation of educational capital by a small number of socially elite families.

Differentiation within the system of higher education offered a compromise formula upon which liberals and conservatives could agree.

On the one hand, for the liberals, the universities remain socially open, although the possession of a degree from a mass university is clearly no longer a guarantee of finding a job; at best, university education becomes a value in itself. On the other, for the conservatives, degrees are provided from an elite sector, which do entail an "entitlement" that distinguishes those possessing them from their competitors in the labor market.

In his analysis of mobility studies conducted in the 1950's, Boudon (1973, p. 23) warned that educational expansion was leading to a drifting apart of the educational and social structures of the population. For example, a survey carried out in the United States in 1949 showed that 70% of respondents reported a higher *educational* level than their fathers, but that only 39% had a higher *social* status. A 1973 mobility study in the United States found *all* respondents (males) to have a higher educational level than their fathers while only some 37% had a higher social status (Featherman and Hauser 1978, p. 67). A gulf had opened between educational and social structures, one that threatened to widen with continued educational expansion.

Institutional differentiation of the educational system may lead to an amelioration of this discrepancy. In terms of the economic metaphor with which this section began, the introduction of such differentiation represents a "monetary reform," which devalues a proportion of the currency in circulation. It restores the relationship between occupational and economic systems; the educational system then once again performs the function of selection as it had before the educational expansion disturbed it. In this context Teichler (1974) speaks of a "need for social inequality" in the labor market which differentiated institutions of higher education can fulfill.

Grusky and Hauser (1984) reviewed a number of studies on social mobility from seven different countries (including the United States, Germany, France, and Japan) and concluded that the rise of the middle and lower strata during the 1960's did not come at the expense of the upper strata. Rather, the upwardly mobile were recruited to newly created positions in the service sector and government bureaucracy.[12] At the beginning of the expansion the educational system absorbed a large proportion of its own products. Many obtained education degrees and easily found jobs in the expanding secondary educational system. The early phase of expansion also coincided with opportune expansionary conditions in the government bureaucracy and private economy. This concealed the fact that the universities were turning out more degrees than could be accommodated in the long term.

With the beginning of economic recession, however, the continuing pressure of the prospectively upwardly mobile could no longer be met. The "new middle class," which had established itself in the public service sector (education, health) had gained its new position through educational certificates and sought by the same means to pass its new status on to its offspring. However, the rising demands for high-status positions could no longer be satisfied, especially by an economy now in downturn. The simultaneous educational expansion and economic recession intensified competition in the labor market. The lengthening queues of unemployed university graduates with formally comparable "entitlement" qualifications attested to the lack of synchronicity that had developed between the occupational and economic systems as a result of the educational expansion in recent years. Social mobility now became a zero-sum game, for when the number of higher status positions plateaus or declines, upward mobility by one social group is possible only against corresponding downward mobility of another.

Institutional differentiation can diffuse the conflict in such situations by introducing a new basis for selection where educational expansion had largely eliminated that which had existed previously. Such a response in education policy is in keeping with the values of the new middle class: the principle of (formal) equality of opportunity is maintained while access to an elite educational sector is introduced which is based on meritocratic criteria. This compromise does not halt educational expansion but does abate its inflationary effects.

Under the combined pressure of educational expansion and economic recession this policy of institutional differentiation becomes increasingly an instrument for "social closure" (Weber 1956; Parkin 1974). Students from the lower strata are effectively turned away from elite institutions by means of increased costs and stricter admissions standards. The preeducation required to meet acceptance criteria is made so rigorous as to eliminate virtually all but those who have followed a specifically university-preparatory secondary curriculum. As opposed to the undifferentiated mass sector (based on comprehensive schools), where selective procedures are postponed to a later stage in ones' education, the elite sector imposes them at ever earlier stages. In Japan this tendency is so extreme as to present a caricature, for there the decision as to whether a child will eventually gain access to an elite university is made with its enrollment in the appropriate kindergarten. In Japan it is possible to obtain elite educational certificates only if the child's parents have pursued a planned, *long-term* strategy.[13]

Differentiation at the level of higher education forces the institutional and curricular differentiation at biographically ever earlier stages. A public school in an inner-city ghetto of the United States is an obviously inauspicious beginning for an education which may, only theoretically, end with the attendance of an elite university. It is in effect only among the upper strata that the implementation of such long-term educational strategies can be pursued, due both to the requisite financial resources and to the cultural horizon (e.g., length of educational planning). Attempts at supplementing an originally underprivileged background can hardly overcome the headstart enjoyed by upper class children.

4.5 Structural Transformations in Higher Education

The educational system has not only witnessed a quantitative expansion over the past 30 years but has undergone a number of structural changes as well. Official statistics generally encompass only few of the important organizational criteria and therefore often fail to represent these changes accurately; nevertheless they do provide some indication of the extent and direction of changes which have occurred. The available data serve as the basis in this section for an analysis in particular of the institutional differentiation of higher education in various countries.

(a) Table 4.1 presents the differentiation that has taken place among the institutions of higher education over the past four decades in the *United States*, where one finds the greatest degree of change during this period. Whereas almost half (49.7%) of all students in 1950 were enrolled in a private institution, this proportion had fallen to 21.4% in 1992. The growth in the public educational sector was due largely to expansion of

Table 4.1: Percentage Distribution of Total Enrollment, by Control and Type of Institution, United States 1950-1992

	Public Institutions			Private Institutions			Total Enrollment in
	2-year %	4-year %	Univers. %	2-year %	4-year %	Univers. %	1000 (100%)
1950	7.3	43.0*		2.2	47.5*		2 296.6
1955	9.9	46.1		1.6	42.4		2.678.6
1960	10.9	48.2		1.7	39.2		3 610.0
1965	17.5	49.6		2.2	30.7		5.967.4
1970	24.3	50.6		1.4	23.7		8 649.4
1972	28.6	27.0	21.1	1.3	14.6	7.4	9 214.9
1975	34.3	25.7	19.0	1.2	13.4	6.4	11 184.9
1980	35.8	24.6	17.8	1.6	14.0	6.2	12 096.9
1985	34.9	25.1	17.5	2.1	14.5	5.9	12 247.1
1990	36.0	25.6	16.7	1.8	14.4	5.5	13 710.2
1992	37.9	24.7	16.0	1.6	14.4	5.4	14 491.2

* Separate time series for 4-year institutions and universities available only after 1972.

Rows add up to 100%. Sources: See Appendix I.

community colleges, with the proportion of students attending them growing from 7.3% in 1950 to 37.9% in 1992. In absolute terms the expansion was even more impressive: from an enrollment of 170,000 in 1950 to one of 5.5 million at its highpoint in 1992.

Between 1960 and 1972 the tertiary sector expanded by 5.6 million students, and between 1972 and 1992 by 5.3 million. During the former period the community colleges absorbed 40% of the growth and during the latter 54%. This absorptive capacity indicates the extent to which the community colleges were able to shield elite universities from the educational expansion. The greater the influx of students, the more those who were shunted away from elite universities sought access to mass institutions.

The proportion of students in the United States enrolled at private universities declined between 1972 and 1992 from 7.4% to 5.4%. The proportion attending public universities also declined during this period, from 21.1% to 16.0%.

There was thus an inverse relationship between expansion and selectivity: the more selective an institution (see Table 4.5 below), the less it participated in the expansion. Nevertheless, the absolute enrollment figures for private universities also grew during the 1960's. The 16 private universities with the highest academic prestige rankings showed a 29% increase in enrollment between 1960 and 1980. However, during the same period the overall increase in the tertiary sector was 235%.[14]

The educational expansion did not eliminate selection but only shifted responsibility for it to a higher structural level. With three-fourths of children completing high school, this institution cannot perform selection. As Labaree (1984, p. 559) has noted, passing children from one grade to the next has become merely an "administrative routine" and says little about their cognitive or social skills. This opens the tertiary sector to almost everyone; such openness and formal equality of opportunity constitutes essential features of the democratic ideology. On the other hand, however, they hide the fact that selection continues to be performed – within the tertiary sector.

The high percentage of school leavers who go on to begin university study is also deceptive, for approximately half of those enrolling in community colleges drop out within the first year. After the full two years offered at community colleges only 38% of those beginning study there receive the final certificate (the "associate degree"). By contrast, the drop-out rate at the elite institutions is under 5%.

However, the community college does have an important integrative function. Many may drop out of the community colleges, but these are nevertheless open to all who want to attend them; no one can feel in principle excluded from the opportunity of attending university. Furthermore, anyone who leaves the institution does so on his own, as it were, and not as the result of social discrimination or bureaucratic restrictions. This self-selection relieves the educational institutions of having consciously to conduct and to rationalize its own selection.

Another difference between the mass and elite sectors is in the respective proportions of part-time students. Their numbers increased between 1963 and 1992 from 30% to 39.2% among men and from 31% to 46.6% among women. However, part-time students are distributed disproportionately between the two sectors; at community colleges they make up 63% of all those enrolled but only 12% of the men and 24% of the women enrolled at private universities. Part-time matriculation allows only partial participation in the academic milieu, while job and family responsibilities make up the major focus of the part-time student's life.

A further indicator of the difference between mass and elite institutions is the ratio of full-time students (or the equivalent thereof) to full-time instructors (or the equivalent). At private institutions there are an average of 13 students per instructor and at public institutions 19.[15] While it is not possible in the data available to differentiate community colleges from other public institutions, one can presume that the figure is even higher at the former.

(b) The concentration of students in mass institutions while the elite sector remains set apart is also a feature of higher education in France and Japan. The relative proportion of all students who are enrolled at both the *grandes écoles* in France and the national universities in Japan has declined over the past 30 years. One can also observe in these countries an inverse relationship between the selectivity of an institution and its expansion.

In *France* the proportion enrolled at mass universities underwent an initial increase from 67.7% to 78.7%, only to decline again after 1970; in 1990 the figure stood at 64.6% (Table 4.2). By contrast, the proportion at the *grandes écoles* (engineering schools) declined from 6.2% to 2.4%. In the early 1960's the Instituts Universitaires de Technologie (IUT) were founded to absorb the expanding number of prospective engineering students and to relieve pressure on the other universities. As Table 4.2 shows, these polytechnics increased their proportion of students from 2.0% to 16.1% in 1990.[16]

The process of expansion and democratization in the overall system of higher education has had little impact upon the *grandes écoles*. Even the student revolt of May 1968 was not able to shake their predominance; on

Table 4.2: Percentage Distribution of Total Enrollment, by Control and Type of Institution, France 1960-1990

	Univer-sities %	Engineer. (IUT)** %	Teachers' college %	Grandes Écoles			Total Enrollment in 1000 (=100%)
				Engin. %	Other* %	Classes prép. %	
1960	67.7	2.0	6.3	6.2	8.5	9.3	300.8
1965	73.1	1.9	4.5	5.6	8.3	6.6	422.6
1970	78.7	5.8	2.5	3.2	5.6	4.2	764.4
1975	76.4	8.8	3.0	3.1	5.1	3.6	940.9
1980	75.8	10.7	1.9	3.4	4.5	3.7	1065.5
1985	73.9	14.7	1.5	3.7	2.3	3.9	1226.5
1990	64.6	16.1	0.9	2.4	12.0	4.0	1698.7

* Various (private) universities, such as "Ecoles normales supérieures"; "Ecoles juridiques et administratives"; "Ecoles supérieures artistiques et culturelles", etc.

** IUT = "Instituts universitaires de technologie"; figures include "Instituts universitaires de formation des maîtres."

Classes prépratoires: Special courses organized by universities and/or secondary school to train students for the entrance examinations of the "Grandes Ecoles."

Rows add up to 100%.   Sources: See Appendix I.

the contrary, these elite institutions emerged from this period with heightened prestige (Suleiman 1978, p. 74), for the inflation of university degrees from mass institutions has only augmented the exclusivity of a degree from a Grande École. The elitism of the *grandes écoles* and the development among their products of a self-consciously closed circle has been criticized, particularly by the political left, for over a century.

The attempt by the Socialist government in France in 1983 to facilitate the admission of labor union officials to the exclusive École Nationale d'Administration (ENA) elicited a storm of protest from alumni of the institution. Its anciens élèves are organized in a political lobby group that jealously guards the tradition of their alma mater.[17] The government's proposals for reforming the admissions procedures of the ENA transgressed the institution's sacrosanct principle of concours – a rigorous selection examination, with the number of students granted admission being established before the examination. This "guillotine" eliminates 60%-80% of applicants, regardless of their personal abilities or scores as only a fixed number of places is available each year.

Also in France there is the tendency to advance, in biographical terms, the selection time to the elite sector. Special two-year courses prepare prospective students for the admission examinations to the *grandes écoles*. These are offered principally at the elite lycées in Paris (e.g., Louis-le-Grand), and the prestige of the various lycées depends upon the proportion of their pupils who pass the examination. The percentages for the individual lycées are published each year in Le Monde.

The number of pupils accepted for these classes préparatoires is strictly limited. Between 1965 and 1981 the number enrolled in the preparatory class at the Louis-le-Grand Lycée rose from 880 to 937, that at Saint-Louis Lycée from 1027 to 1210, and that at Henri IV Lycée from 565 to 692. The proportion of females rose from 4.7% (1964) to 28.2%. This led to greater competition among the males, which concentrated even more those from the upper strata. Whereas 55%-65% were from the upper strata among those in the mathematics/science preparatory classes in 1967, the figure had risen to 70% in 1981 (Bourdieu 1981, p. 61; and Table 4.7 below).

In the United States the relationship between the public and private sectors of higher education is determined by market competition; the academic prestige ranking is therefore subject to change over time. In France (as in Japan), on the other hand, the elite universities are protected by a state monopoly, which encourages a very stable relationship between an educational institution and an employer – both the government bureaucracy and private companies. This monopolization explains how the *grandes écoles* have been able to maintain their elitist character, despite their lack of an outstanding reputation in either research or teaching.[18] They provide, in effect, merely the institutional setting for a form of self-fulfilling prophecy: they draw the best students from the secondary educational system because they guarantee them superior career prospects.

(c) A major feature of the system of higher education in *Japan* is the high proportion of students in the private sector, while elite universities are generally those in the national sector (Imperial Universities). Private institutions accounted for 62.3% of all male students enrolled in 1960 and for 68.7% in 1992, and the relative student enrollment in the public sector has seen a corresponding decline, particularly among women (from 21.4% to 12.2%; Table 4.3).

Between 1960 and 1992 the proportion of women enrolled in tertiary education rose from 20% to 40%. In absolute terms the increase was 1 million, 84% of which was at private institutions, especially two-year colleges. In Japan it is the private sector which protects elite (national) universities from an influx of students due to educational expansion. Furthermore, some 30% of all female students at two-year colleges study home economics, a subject that seldom qualifies one for an academic occupation. Women's degrees – in nonacademic subjects from two-year colleges in the mass sector – are therefore very often of a "second-class" nature and lack in social prestige.

While a number of outstanding universities are private, such as

Table 4.3: Percentage Distribution of Total Enrollment, by Control and Type of Institution, Japan 1960-1992

	Universities			Junior Colleges		Technical	Total Enroll-
	National	Public	Private	Private	National+ Public	Colleges	ment in 1000 (100%)
	%	%	%	%	%	%	
Men							
1960	28.9	4.0	62.3	2.8	2.0	*	568.5
1965	23.2	3.6	66.1	3.0	1.5	2.6	844.6
1970	20.3	3.0	69.6	2.6	1.0	3.5	1242.4
1975	19.2	2.5	71.8	2.3	1.0	3.2	1462.0
1980	21.3	2.4	70.6	1.8	0.9	3.0	1516.8
1985	23.2	2.5	68.5	1.7	1.0	3.1	1499.5
1990	23.7	2.5	68.2	1.8	0.8	3.0	1640.3
1992	23.4	2.5	68.7	2.0	0.6	2.8	1712.7
Women							
1960	21.1	4.2	35.2	35.2	4.3	*	142.2
1965	16.0	3.0	38.9	38.5	3.5	0.1	262.6
1970	12.3	2.5	38.8	43.4	2.8	0.2	471.9
1975	11.6	2.2	40.8	42.9	2.4	0.1	673.9
1980	11.4	2.0	41.5	42.1	2.8	0.1	736.5
1985	13.1	2.3	41.0	40.1	3.3	0.2	768.9
1990	12.7	2.2	41.9	39.8	2.9	0.5	1026.7
1992	12.2	2.3	43.4	38.8	2.7	0.6	1161.1

* Technical Colleges have been founded in the early sixties.
Rows add up to 100%.   Source: See Appendix I.

Waseda, these are the exception, and most of the institutions in this sector are very small and located in the suburbs. These are generally specialized schools such as business colleges. The discrimination against private institutions is seen in their funding: until 1976 they received no public support and depended entirely upon student tuition fees, whereas 80% of the financing at public institutions was provided by the government. The relative expenditure per student is also disproportionate between the two sectors (1,378,000 yen public versus 420,000 yen private), as is the student to instructor ratio (8.5 public versus 29.5 private; Ichikawa 1979, p. 40).

It is not surprising that there is great variety among institutions in the private sector, and that their heterogeneity is the basis for social selection. The distribution of students in terms of social background reflects the level of tuition at the various institutions; a student at a public university paid an average of 146,000 yen per year in 1977 while a medical student at a private university paid 1,727,000 yen (Ichikawa 1979, p. 56). Because of this great variation in the level of tuition charged by the universities and colleges the institutional differentiation between the public and private sector does not coincide with the social segregation of students in terms of social background and cultural capital (see Table 4.6 below).

Selection for the elite universities takes place long before formal application. A large proportion of applicants to them have attended elite institutions in the secondary system, which – in contrast to those in the tertiary system – are principally in the private sector. Most private elite schools were founded during the 1950's as the system of public education was undergoing a reorganization. Until this time parents had been able to send their children to the school of their choice, but the new education law restricted children to attending the school in the district in which they lived. This excluded many from prestige schools in the public sector, and the result was that private schools were founded to cater to the demand for elite secondary education. In 1983 about 30% of pupils in Japan were enrolled in private schools. Children must pass entrance examinations in both sectors, but whereas 90% pass in public schools, only 30% do so in the private schools. These elite institutions are marked by selection – not expansion. At the University of Tokyo in 1982, 48% of beginning students came from private schools, and the 15 highest ranking schools in terms of the proportion of pupils admitted to elite universities are all private (Rohlen 1983, pp. 21-22).

As a preliminary conclusion it can be said that in France as well as in Japan educational institutions have been founded to train students for the highly selective entrance examinations of the elite universities (classes préparatoires in France, "cram" schools in Japan). These preparatory institutions have themselves become selective, thus reinforcing the process of selection and shifting it back to earlier stages in the individual biography. A similar historical process of expansion and selection is observed in the United States: the comprehensive high school opened the tertiary sector to almost everyone. This enormous expansion had two (unintended) consequences: An increasing differentiation of higher education into elite and mass institutions and the reelevation of private high schools as preparatory institutions to qualify for the elite university (Coleman et al. 1982).

(d) In *Germany* there is no elite sector that can compare with the "ivy league" universities of the United States, the *grandes écoles* in France, or the "Imperial universities" of Japan. Table 4.4 presents the changing distribution of students at the different types of institutions for higher

Table 4.4: Percentage Distribution of Total Enrollment, by Type of Institution, (West) Germany 1960-1992

	Universi- ties %	4-year colleges %	Comprehensive universities %	Teachers' colleges %	Other colleges %	Total Enrollment in 1000 (=100%)
Men						
1960	71.0	21.4	*	4.6	3.0	207.2
1965	70.3	22.9	*	4.5	2.3	264.5
1970	67.2	25.0	*	6.0	1.8	363.3
1975	67.5	19.7	5.3	5.7	1.8	493.1
1980	67.3	21.0	7.1	3.0	1.6	584.2
1985	65.2	25.8	7.0	0.7	1.3	830.8
1990	63.2	27.0	8.3	0.3	1.2	973.7
1992	62.7	27.2	8.6	0.3	1.2	1004.6
Women						
1960	67.8	**	*	27.4	4.8	63.5
1965	70.3	**	*	25.8	3.9	80.3
1970	60.3	10.6	*	26.4	2.7	139.4
1975	61.2	11.7	4.8	20.0	2.2	250.1
1980	66.5	15.0	5.6	10.8	2.1	334.1
1985	72.8	17.2	5.3	2.6	2.1	505.9
1990	72.3	17.9	6.5	1.3	2.0	605.3
1992	72.0	18.1	6.8	1.1	2.0	635.4

* Comprehensive Universities (combination of universities and 4-year colleges) have been founded in 1972.
** Data not available.
Rows add up to 100%.   Sources: See Appendix I.

education in Germany. Between 1960 and 1992 the proportion of students enrolled at full universities fell from 71% to 62.7% while that at specialized colleges rose from 21.4% to 27.2%. Earlier plans to establish "comprehensive universities" as the standard institution of higher education have been dropped, and the size of their overall student body therefore did not grow substantially between 1975 and 1992 (from 5.3% to 8.6%, men). There was an increase of almost 800,000 male students during the period 1960-1992, and only 28.7% of this increase was absorbed by (specialized) four-year colleges (compared to 54% by the community colleges in the United States). Thus, it cannot be said that the four-year specialized colleges served as a *cordon sanitaire* for the universities in Germany.

As a result of the integration of teaching colleges into universities there has even been a de-differentiation in regard to female students. The proportion of women enrolled in higher education who attend a university has risen from 67.8% to 72% (1992). While, in addition, there has also been a sharp rise in the proportion attending specialized four-year colleges, these have absorbed between 1970 and 1992 only 20% of the educational expansion among women. One must also note that up to the early 1980's 42% of female students were enrolled in liberal arts subjects; this low level of collective diversification makes them particularly susceptible to unemployment in times of economic recession (see Chap. 6).

The structure of higher education in Germany (as in Italy) has seen very little structural change since 1960, although the number of students has grown from 270,000 to 1.6 million. One victim of the quantitative expansion has been the fiction of homogeneity within the university sector. The recognition of essential differences came first as the expansion of specialized colleges separated students into those receiving more "abstract" education (at universities) and those receiving more "practical" education (at colleges). In addition, the introduction of a *Numerus clausus* system limiting the number of students accepted in overfilled subjects divided the student body into an "elite" who gain admission to a *Numerus clausus* subject and the "rest" who are enrolled in "mass" subjects.[19]

(e) Universities in *Italy* present something of a special case. Of all the countries examined here, Italy has the least differentiated system of higher education. With the exception of a few private institutions, all students in Italy attend public universities, which enjoy formal equality with one another. (This does not rule out, however, a certain prestige ranking in specific disciplines; in economics, for example, the University of Milan enjoys a dominant position.)

Italian school authorities introduced comprehensive schools in the 1970's. Internally, however, these were not fully integrated, with the departments for different occupational tracks remaining separate. This reformed educational system soon showed substantial success in increasing the proportion of pupils receiving the school certificate that permits university study – for the class of 1985 the proportion was 85%. But what has been the effect of this lack of selection in secondary school on higher education? As Fig. 4.1 shows, one effect has been the very high drop-out rate – some 60% – at Italian universities. Less than 10% of a given year's cohort of school children now complete a university degree.[20]

The drop-out rate varies from discipline to discipline; it is higher in political science, sociology, psychology, and economics and lower in medicine, pharmacy, chemistry, and literature. In terms of the social background of students, departments with a higher percentage of students from the lower socioeconomic groups tend to show the highest drop-out

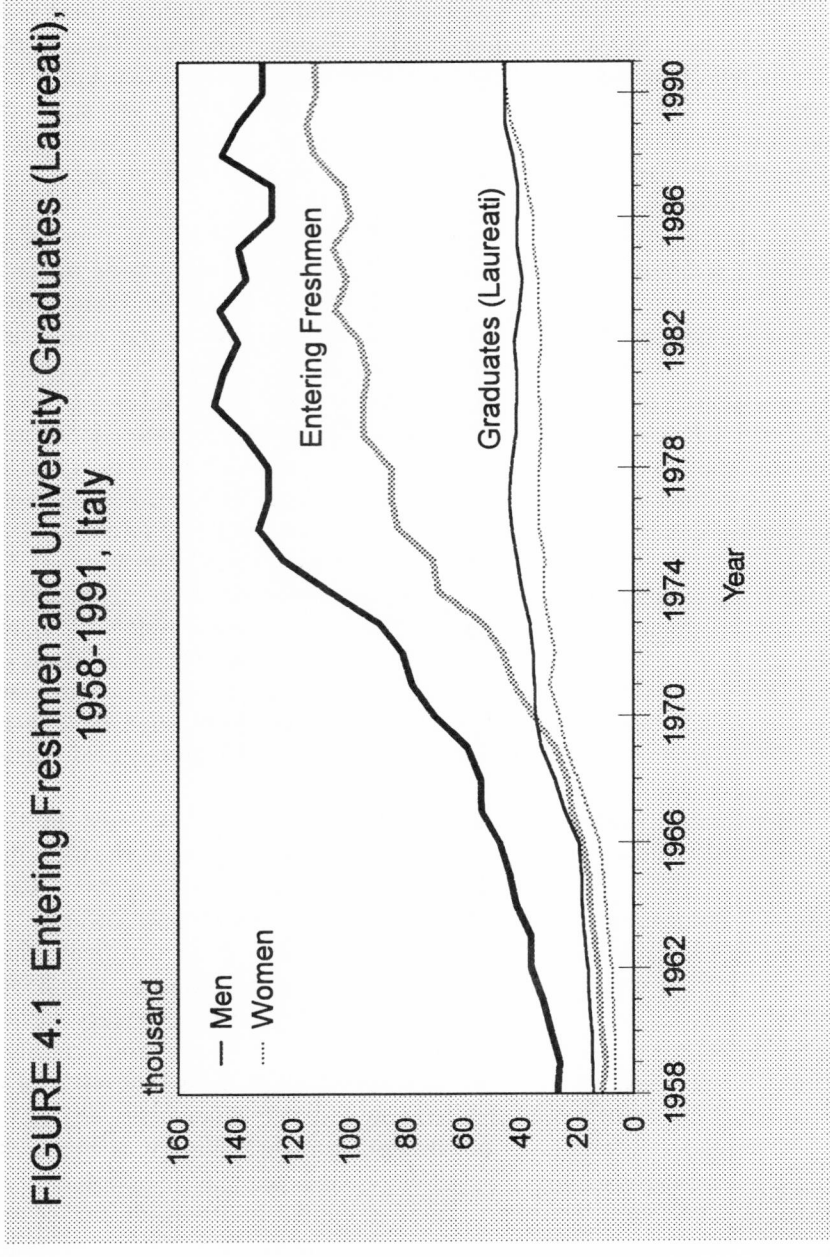

FIGURE 4.1 Entering Freshmen and University Graduates (Laureati), 1958-1991, Italy

rates. These students generally obtain their school certificate from a technically oriented comprehensive school (istituti technici); many hold full-time employment while pursuing their university study and attend classes only sporadically. Departments, on the other hand, in which the drop-out rate is particularly low draw students largely from the upper strata, who have obtained their secondary certificates from classical (noncomprehensive) elite schools, and who do not work during matriculation. Such students are also predominantly those who attend the few private universities in Italy (e.g., Bocconi in Milan).

For those with a secondary school certificate in Italy there is open access to the university. No *Numerus clausus* system sets a ceiling on the number of students enrolled in any subject, and although some universities have introduced entrance examinations (e.g., the Economics Department at the University of Milan), the results are not binding, and those failing the examination may nevertheless enroll. Selection at Italian universities is thus informal and consists principally of self-selection, i.e., the student's own anticipation of eventual failure. The student's choice of subject is also in large measure the determinant of his probability of obtaining a degree, and this choice correlates with individual characteristics such as social background and previous education. The Italian system therefore shows latent, or informal, differentiation. Although officially there is no selection and the universities are homogeneous, analyses of students' backgrounds confirm the role played by informal mechanisms of self-selection. As the data on drop-out rates in Fig. 4.1 show, the role of these informal mechanisms has become increasingly pronounced with educational expansion and impose an insurmountable barrier to a large percentage of students.[21] The figure clearly show that the drop-out rate is not stable over time but increases with increasing enrollment rates.[22]

At the beginning of this chapter it was argued that a necessary (although not sufficient) precondition for continued expansion has proven to be the differentiation of an elite sector. Of all the countries compared here Italy has the lowest degree of institutional differentiation in higher education. Nevertheless, Fig. 4.1 shows that the Italian university system has expanded considerably between 1970 and 1990, and so this case seems to contradict the argument. However, the figures also reveal that only enrollment rates have expanded, but not the "product." Since 1970 the annual growth rate in the number of university graduates is relatively low compared to other countries. Italian students attend university, but they do not graduate.

4.6 Social Differentiation in Higher Education

Differentiation of the system of higher education into mass and elite sectors exerts a considerable impact upon the educational opportunities of the different social groups at university. The social function of selection as carried out today by elite institutions is similar to that of European universities in the early 19th century. While equality of opportunity continues to be the official education policy, a side effect of the concomitant differentiation is inequality of opportunity.

In addition to individual performance, a number of ascriptive characteristics have always played an important role in selection to the elite sector, effectively discriminating against certain social groups. Women, for example, were excluded from the Universities of Harvard and Princeton until the mid-1960's and from the Polytechnique in Paris until 1972. In the 19th century university applicants in France had to submit a reference from the mayor of their city attesting to their political reliability (Shinn 1980, p. 49). Despite the bureaucratically highly regulated application procedure in France, the personal interview plays a crucial role in the granting of elite university admission (*grandes écoles*), with the applicant's personality and life-style constituting important selection criteria. Sons of alumni find admission substantially easier at elite institutions in the United States; during the Depression of the 1930's, for example, their proportion among the students at Princeton increased from 13.3% to 22.7% and at Yale from 13.5% to 29.6% (Karabel 1984, p. 19).

The following report on the admissions procedures at Harvard during the 1920's provides an example of the increased closure of private universities vis-à-vis those not from the traditional upper strata. Admissions procedures were reformed in the mid-1920's, with personality and character being added to the traditional selection criteria of school grades and entrance examination score. In the period 1906-1925 the proportion of Jewish students at Harvard increased from 7.5% to 27.6%. Virtually all the stipends awarded went to Jews. In a report to the Harvard Faculty in 1922 the chairman of the stipend commission, A. Lawrence Lowell, decried the "Jewish problem" and the "Hebrew invasion" and asked for a "Jewish quota" to reduce the number of Jewish students at Harvard (Karabel 1984, p. 13).

Anyone who had direct contact with Jews was not considered socially respectable, at least not at a private university dedicated to the social integration of the upper strata. Lowell feared that a high percentage of Jewish students would prevent the white Anglo-Saxon Protestant establishment of the east coast in the United States from sending their sons to Harvard, and this was precisely the traditional clientele of Harvard. Lowell proposed a gradual reduction in the number of Jews to be admitted, pointing out that their proportion had been held to under 5% at Princeton and Columbia.

Lowell's proposal was eventually rejected by the faculty because it too ostensibly violated the democratic principle of equality of opportunity upon which the reputation of Harvard rested. Lowell then shifted to a more subtle strategy. This was the intention of the admissions "reform" that extended the selection criteria. Applicants were required to fill out a questionnaire asking, among other things, the father's religion. "Life-style" was now regarded as a criterion, and various questionnaire items served as its operationalization. To avoid any uncertainty, a photograph of the applicant was also required (Karabel 1994, p. 14).

The admissions offices, which have the sole responsibility for the acceptance and the rejection of applicants, consider such factors as life-style, cultural breadth, and sports and political activities along with school grades and entrance examination scores as legitimate selection criteria for private universities, and such questionnaires continue to be a part of the selection procedure at private universities up to the present day.[23]

Admissions procedures were liberalized only in the 1960's, under pressure from the student movement and antidiscrimination laws. Affirmative action requirements have forced the admission of proportions of women and minorities corresponding to their relative size in the population. In many cases the courts have reviewed the selection criteria and admissions procedures of private universities, and such court cases bring the universities undesirable publicity (Manning 1977).

These reforms have led to substantial changes in the institutions. They have changed the "exclusive" universities – where life-style, social contacts, and sports activities played at least as great a role as classroom performance – into "elite" universities which train professional leaders for high-level positions in the meritocracy. This is the major difference to the highly selective institutions of the 19th century in which selection was based on wealth and family background. In the earlier "exclusive" institution the emphasis was upon social and cultural integration of the upper strata; in the modern "elite" institution it is upon academic excellence and technical virtuosity. Today, academic performance is undoubtedly the major consideration in admission. This change of emphasis in admissions criteria notwithstanding, however, today's elite universities remain as socially selective as they were in the 19th century. Admission requires a long and systematic preparatory school background, which is generally within the means only of the upper strata. And students from the upper classes usually do not feel embarrassed by filling "life-style questionaires."

(a) Table 4.5 presents the social backgrounds of beginning students at three university types in the *United States*: selective private universities,

Table 4.5: Social Background of Entering Freshmen by Type of Institution, United States 1982, Men

	Stanford	Selective Private Universities	Selective Public Universities	Community Colleges
	%	%	%	%
Parental income ($)				
less than 6,000	1.4	1.5	3.1	4.5
50,000-99,000	28.9	28.4	19.6	7.9
more than 100,000	11.1	15.6	5.3	1.3
Father's education				
college degree	28.2	31.9	31.4	19.8
graduate degree	49.8	43.9	24.4	10.3
Father's occupation				
Physician, dentist	10.7	10.4	4.3	0.8
Lawyer	5.7	6.4	3.1	0.7
College teacher	6.6	3.7	1.7	0.5
Skilled worker	3.3	3.8	7.3	16.1
Semi-/unskilled worker	4.0	2.2	5.1	10.8
Father's religious preference				
Jewish	12.0	15.6	10.6	2.0
Average grade in high school				
Percentage A or A+	64.8	40.9	15.8	3.0
Academic rank				
Percentage top 20%	97.6	84.0	60.3	22.8
Attended private high school	*	20.0	5.2	1.8
Miles from home to college				
more than 500	65.6	46.2	6.6	1.0
Mother worked full-time				
never	47.4	48.5	40.6	36.0

* Data not available.   Sources: See Appendix I.

selective public universities, and "open" community colleges. Data specifically from the (private) Stanford University are also available from a special study conducted there.

Recruitment to private universities and that to community colleges show considerable differences in regard to social background. In 1982 40% of students at Stanford University came from families with an annual income over $50,000, while only 9.2% of those at community colleges did so.[24] Compared to the 26.9% of students at community colleges from working class families, only 7.3% of those at Stanford showed such a background. The difference in terms of academic performance is even greater: only 3% of those at community colleges had an average Grade of A or A+ in high school – as opposed to 64.8% of those at Stanford. Also remarkable at Stanford is the high proportion of out-of-state students – 65.6%. As noted above, nation-wide recruitment is a major characteristic of elite institutions. A high percentage of students (20%) at selective private universities have also attended nondenominational private schools.[25]

The data in Table 4.5 demonstrate that students in such a segmented system of higher education are distributed according to social background. The hierarchical ranking of the educational institutions corresponds to the social differentiation of the students.

(b) A similar distribution of students by social background is also seen at universities in *Japan*. Table 4.6 distinguishes students at public and private universities in terms of parental income (20th percentile groups for the overall population).[26] Because of the high tuition fees at private universities the distribution of educational opportunities is more "skewed" toward the highest income class (52.9% in 1961). Comparison of the data from 1961 with those from 1976 show that the educational expansion has in fact not decreased but actually *increased* the relative discrimination against those from the lower socioeconomic groups: whereas 26.2% of students in the public sector were from the highest income group in 1961, the proportion had risen to 35.4% in 1976. Educational expansion may have opened the door to the university, but those who entered were principally from the middle and upper strata. The unequal distribution of educational opportunities is even more evident at the elite universities. Some 47% of students at the University of Tokyo in 1970 were from families in the highest third in the country in terms of income, and only 7.3% were from the lowest third. The concentration of the higher strata is even more extreme at the University of Keio, where 68% of students were from families in the highest third and only 2.2% from the lowest third.[27]

In their survey of 277 political science students at the University of

Table 4.6 : Percentage Distribution of Students by Parental Income, Japan 1961-1976

	National Universities %					Private Universities %				
	I	II	III	IV	V	I	II	III	IV	V
1961	19.7	20.2	15.4	18.5	26.2	6.4	9.2	12.3	19.2	52.9
1976	12.7	12.3	15.1	24.5	35.4	5.6	7.7	10.6	25.4	50.7

V = Top 20% income class; IV = second 20%; III = middle 20%; II = fourth 20%; I = lowest 20%
Source: Cummings (1980. p. 226).

Tokyo in 1984 Takashi and Ikuo reached similar conclusions. They found 90% to be males and 42% to come from families with an annual income of over 8 million yen (an income enjoyed by only 10% of the population), while only 16% were from families with an income under 5 million yen (62% of the population). The authors also showed the political attitudes of students in the early 1980's to be increasingly conservative. "Leftwing students at the University of Tokyo who led the protest movement in the 1960's have become a myth" (Takashi and Ikuo 1984, p. 28).

(c) A similar situation is found with universities in France. All the studies conducted since the Second World War have found that approximately half of the students at the *grandes écoles* are from families of the upper social strata (*cadres supérieurs*) while only some 5% are from the working class (Table 4.7). The "inheritance" of admission to the Polytechnique in Paris is particularly evident: almost one-fourth of its students have a relative who at some time also attended the institution. (In 1972 there were a total of 12,000 *polytechniciens* in France).

The distribution of students by university subject also shows a pattern that we have observed for other countries: in 1987, 50.9% of medical students were from the upper strata, 36.7% of law and economics students, and 22.3% of engineering students (Table 4.8). The representation coefficient[28] is a measure for the relative discrimination for or against individual social groups. In the overall student body, the proportion of those from the upper strata (professionals, high civil service; *cadres supérieurs*) was 4.7 times their representation in the population and those from the working class only 0.4. The relative discrimination declined between 1962 and 1987, principally as the result of an influx of children from the middle and lower socioeconomic groups in technical and social science subjects. Medicine and, to a lesser extent, law remain relatively "closed" subjects. The concentration of the upper strata in elite subjects as well as at elite institutions shows that these two forms of differentiation can exist beside one another, thus further increasing the degree of social closure.

(d) Social differentiation by university type and by the subject studied is also evident in *Germany*. As in other countries, medicine is a subject that is relatively "closed," while electrical engineering is the field with the highest percentage of students from the lower socioeconomic groups (Table 4.9). It is also the latter where one finds the highest proportion of drop-outs and of those switching to other subjects; only 40% of those beginning postsecondary education in this field eventually receive a degree. There is a strong correlation between the prestige rank of the university subject and the proportion of upper class students. At the top of the prestige hierarchy we still find the learned professions law and medicine, and these subjects have the highest proportion of upper class students enrolled; at the bottom of the hierarchy we find the technical subjects and the social sciences with the highest proportion of students from lower class backgrounds.[29]

The prestige order of the institutions of higher education also corresponds exactly to the proportion of upper class students enrolled: The proportion of students from the lower strata enrolled in specialized four-year colleges is almost twice that at universities (Table 4.10). Although the social differentiation at German institutions of higher education is less than at elite universities in Japan, France, or the United States, one nevertheless finds similar structures: The proportion of upper class students varies exactly with the prestige and selectivity of the university subject and the institution and both selectivity effects are cumulative.

A study by Titze (1981, p. 192) has documented the social differentiation at German universities as early as the 19th century. He found the highest proportion of students whose fathers were university graduates at the Universities of Marburg (34.2%) and Göttingen (31.4%) and the lowest at the University of Breslau. The further east the university was located in Prussia, the more "provincial" it was in terms of the background of its students. For the years 1908 and 1931 the social profile of different university subjects at German universities has been shown in Table 2.4. It seems that the prestige order of university subjects has not changed much over time and that the "learned professions" had been and still are preferred by upper class students.

(d) Conclusion: Regardless of whether admission to elite universities is regulated by a government bureaucracy (as at the *grandes écoles* in France) or by the individual universities themselves (as at the private institutions in the United States), the result is virtually identical. While the various social categories in Tables 4.5-4.8 vary due to nationally specific characteristics, the tendency is clear throughout these data that while mass universities have opened themselves to the lower strata, the elite universities have managed to resist democratization. Inflation in their numbers has meant a devaluation of degrees from mass institutions, but a degree from an elite university has retained its market value. The differentiation among institutions of higher education entails a number of benefits for society: it upholds the democratic principle of formal equality of opportunity, preserves the social openness of universities, institutes an "internal," performance-based competition, and lessens the struggle over distribution of jobs in the labor market.

The rigorousness of the selection, upon which the prestige of elite institutions is based, increases the market value of a degree from one of these institutions, as the following example shows. By the end of the 1980's the (then expected) declining number of young persons of university age threatened the financial solvency of some universities in the United States, forcing them to consider either closing or merging with

Table 4.7: Social Background of Students at French Elite Universities (Grandes Écoles)[30]

	Ecole National d' Administration (ENA)		Ecole Centrale Paris(Engineer.)		Ecole Normale Supérieure*	
	1947-62 %	1963-69 %	1961/62 %	1990 %	1961/62 %	1990 %
Lawyers, Physicians, High Civil Service***	50.0	54.6	47.0	47.3	51.0	56.6
Manual Workers	1.6	1.0	2.0	5.6	3.0	3.3

	Polytechnique Paris		Classes Préparatoires** Mathematics Humanities	
	1961/62 %	1979 %	1967/68 %	1967/68 %
Lawyers, Physicians, High Civil Service***	57.0	65.0	56.5	63.0
Manual Workers	2.0	5.4	3.5	4.0

* Ulm et Sèvres, Paris   ** taupins, khâgneux   *** Cadres supérieurs
Source: See Appendix I.

others (Mingle 1981). The two traditional rival universities in Florida responded with opposite strategies: Florida State University became an "open" university, lowering admission requirements and relaxing curriculum standards, while the University of Florida became more selective, raising the necessary examination scores, demanding foreign

Table 4.8: Social Background of Students by University Subject, France 1962-1992

		Physicians, Lawyers, High Civil Service %	Middle Manage-ment %	Employ-ees %	Self em-ployed %	Farmers %	Manual Workers %	Other %
Medicine	1962	43.7	16.1	9.6	21.0	4.6	3.9	1.1
	1977	51.1	16.7	7.8	12.0	3.8	7.8	0.8
	1982	52.0	17.8	7.1	10.6	3.8	8.0	0.7
	1987	50.9	19.4	6.4	9.6	3.4	8.8	1.5
	1992**	42.6	16.6	6.4	7.2	2.7	6.2	17.3
Law,	1962	33.6	20.0	11.6	20.8	6.6	5.9	1.5
Eco-	1977	37.1	17.9	10.8	13.2	6.3	13.0	1.7
nomics	1982	34.8	19.9	11.2	11.2	5.8	15.3	1.8
	1987	36.7	21.1	10.4	10.4	4.5	14.8	2.1
	1992**	33.3	19.0	10.6	9.3	2.7	11.0	14.1
Huma-	1962	28.7	26.2	6.8	21.5	6.7	8.2	1.9
nities	1977	32.2	20.6	11.5	12.2	5.6	16.4	1.5
	1982	32.3	21.4	10.9	11.2	5.3	16.7	2.2
	1987	30.5	22.2	11.2	10.1	4.4	18.4	3.2
	1992**	26.1	21.7	10.6	7.9	2.9	13.4	17.4
Engi-	1974	16.2	17.2	11.8	12.9	12.5	26.9	3.5
neering	1982	18.7	21.5	11.2	11.9	9.5	24.8	2.4
	1987	22.3	23.8	10.4	10.5	6.9	23.8	2.3
	1992**	24.9	23.7	11.3	9.7	4.3	16.7	9.4
Coeffi-	1962	8.2	2.6	0.7	1.9	0.4	0.2	***
cient of	1977	5.4	1.4	0.6	1.6	0.8	0.4	***
Represen-	1982	4.7	1.4	0.5	1.4	0.9	0.4	***
tation (all	1987	4.7	1.5	0.5	1.3	0.9	0.4	***
subjects)	1992	*	*	*	*	*	*	***

* Data not available (Data of Population Census 1992 published after this table was created.)
** Data for 1992 are not strictly comparable with other years because the categories of social background have been changed.
*** Residual category for which a coefficient of respresentation cannot be computed.
Rows add up to 100%.   Sources: See Appendix I.

language skills, and increasing the level of performance demanded of students. The result was, that the University of Florida attracted more student applications, while the traditional rival Florida State University lost a considerable number of students (Riesman 1979, p. 348).

A similar relationship between a university's selectivity and the market value of its degrees is reported by Schwartz (1983, p. 42) in France. The traditional method for granting admission to most subjects at French universities is the seniority principle: first come, first serve. In June 1981 the University of Paris VII tested a new method based upon entrance selection, taking school grades as the criterion. The result was a dramatic rise in the number of applications.

The normative conflict between a demand for selectivity and for democratization reflects a certain conflict of interests on the part of students. On the one hand, surveys confirm that students – collectively – oppose selectivity and support university opening and the relaxing of admission requirements. On the other, however, to improve their individual marketability they seek admission to selective universities and subjects. This normative conflict lies at the root of many of the "self-contradictions of the mass university" (Jarousse 1984). The worse the conditions in the labor market become, the greater are these contradictions.

Table 4.9: Social Background of Students by Selected University Subjects, West Germany 1981

	Class I %	Class II %	Class III %	Class IV %
Medicine	38.1	24.7	24.9	12.3
Law	27.5	27.7	24.5	20.3
Biology. Chemistry. Pharmacy	21.2	29.0	26.5	23.3
Humanities	18.5	26.5	31.5	23.5
Psychology	18.4	16.8	30.4	34.4
Architecture	14.9	22.9	31.0	31.2
Mathematics, Computer Science	12.5	21.6	32.4	33.4
Social Sciences	8.2	34.1	30.3	37.7
Electrical Engineering	8.2	19.5	30.6	41.7
Percentage of each class in the sample	17.7	25.7	29.2	27.4

Class I: Upper class; Class IV: Lower class

N = 10.108   Rows add up to 100%.   Sources: See Appendix I.

Table 4.10: Social Background of Students by Type of Institution, West Germany 1981

	Class I %	Class II %	Class III %
Technical Universities	25.8	54.6	19.6
Universities	22.5	55.9	21.6
Comprehensive Universities	9.2	56.1	34.7
4-year Colleges	7.0	53.3	39.7
Percentage of each class in the sample	18.3	55.2	26.4

Sources: See Appendix I

5

From Patronage to Meritocracy

5.1 Meritocracy and Educational Expansion

The constantly rising demand for educational qualifications and the unrivaled expansion of higher education over the past century would not have been possible to such an extent if a university degree had not been associated with professional opportunities and thereby the chance for upward social mobility. While noneconomic motives do play a role in the choice of the subject studied, and university study can have a certain intrinsic value (if only for the lack of other prospects), the educational expansion over this period without doubt stems from the anticipation that academic degrees carry an economic value that can be cashed in on the labor market. Those who have called for equality of educational opportunity have done so in the expectation that a degree will improve the prospects for a professional career and for a rise up the social ladder. Parallel with educational expansion has come meritocracy – the distribution of economic responsibilities on the basis of formal qualifications. Educational expansion and meritocracy are complementary processes of the progressive bureaucratization and rationalization of Western industrial society (Meyer 1978; Schluchter 1979).

However, opposition arose early and in a number of social strata to the principle of meritocratic status allocation. Max Weber compared this principle to that of aristocratic birth in feudalistic society; an academic degree took the place of noble heritage as bourgeois society used the university to "refeudalize" the class structure. Weber at the same time pointed out, however, that modernization of the state administrative structure is impossible without a trained set of civil servants, and that meritocratic forms of status distribution constitute an unavoidable consequence of bureaucratization (1956, p. 736).

As the processes of production were made increasingly subject to scientific principles, and the functions of state administration became ever more complex, there was a growing demand for qualified personnel. Possession of a university degree became a major criterion for such personnel, both in the private economy and in the government bureaucracy (Pierenkemper and Tilly 1982).

This development in the labor market, however, is not sufficient by itself to explain the success of which meritocracy has enjoyed in Western countries. In addition, there was also a causal effect in the opposite direction: the rising numbers of unemployed university graduates made it possible to limit recruitment to formally highly qualified job seekers. In reference to Italy at the end of the 19th century, Barbagli describes the pressure which unemployed university graduates[1] exerted through their political "patrons" (i.e., legislative deputies) to find them positions in the government bureaucracy, regardless of how modest. The bureaucracy followed the principle of patronage rather than that of market rationality and recruited unemployed university graduates even for positions requiring little or even no formal qualification.[2]

Over the course of the past century the distribution of positions on the basis of birth, family connections, and corruption has gradually been replaced in Western industrialized countries by that based on the possession of a university degree. Meritocratic principles were adopted first in the government bureaucracy, for it was only here that a central authority commanded sufficient power to enforce uniform selection criteria and recruitment procedures for the filling of positions. By the end of the 19th century, however, these meritocratic principles were being introduced in the private economy as well.

This chapter limits itself to the consideration of this process in the government bureaucracy. The success of meritocratic principles in the state administrative apparatus made this apparatus a model for the politically democratic and economically rational distribution of opportunities for employment and social ascent. Meritocratic hiring policies, as will be pointed out, made headway first not in those countries that were in general more progressive and democratic but rather in those with more patriarchal-autocratic governments (e.g., Germany and Japan). In the United States – the most "democratic" country at the time – political parties strongly opposed the introduction of meritocratic principles. The analysis below examines the types of resistance that were mobilized against the introduction of meritocracy and the strategic importance which its introduction had for the control available to the state bureaucracy.

5.2 Symbiotic Relationships

(a) The number of civil servants in Germany totaled 204,000 in 1870, 460,00 in 1913, and 1,100,000 by 1932. The increase in the number of public employees in the United Kingdom between 1861 and 1921 was from 72,000 to 383,000. Despite its antibureaucratic tradition, the United States witnessed a comparable growth in the civil service during this time – from 100,000 civil servants in 1881 to 655,000 in 1920. By the late 19th century the government bureaucracy had grown to become the largest employer in the economy. With this growth in the size of the civil service the state was developing in many countries from one based on the traditional privileges of an established elite to one based on social welfare for the masses, and in doing so it was taking over many of the social functions which had earlier been fulfilled by the market or by family relations. Particularly in the areas of health and education the state was beginning to take on entirely new responsibilities. It is therefore not surprising that the number of public employees should also have risen.[3]

The state bureaucracy was often able to exploit the tensions among government, parliament, and political parties so as to augment its own power. With frequent changes in the constitution, for example, in France in the 19th century, and frequent electoral swings in the relative standing of political parties, the state bureaucracy became a source of stability and continuity (Hattenhauer 1980, p. 314). The expansion in the size and power of the bureaucracy often also led to new constitutional problems of its own, however, as the administrative apparatus of the state managed increasingly to elude parliamentary control and to pursue its own interests.[4] The famous constitutional lawyer, Lorenz von Stein (1876, p. 51), observed in the late 19th century that, "the era of drafting constitutions is essentially over, and all large civilized societies are embarking upon the era of administration."

With the growing political power of the bureaucracy came increasing social prestige of those making up its elite. The structure of public administration became an important ladder to social status, and government bureaucrats who rose to the highest positions in the civil service belonged to the upper strata of society. The nature of the selection criteria for the hiring and promoting of civil servants determined to a considerable extent the "openness" or "closure" of the society. In the 19th century those of aristocratic birth enjoyed an advantage in selection for the highest positions in the bureaucracy, and the filling of vacancies by patronage and nepotism was common. Before the demise of the German Empire in the First World War, members of the Social-Democratic Party

(SPD) and labor union functionaries were excluded from public employment; the only avenue for social mobility open to them was that of the party or union.[5]

In almost all Western countries political parties and organizations were being formed by the end of the 19th century that sought the reform of the government bureaucracy. These challenged recruitment structures based on aristocratic birth and the sale of state positions and called for their replacement by a "rational" bureaucracy based on personal qualification. In the United States "civil service reform associations" and in France the *Union pour la Verité* were founded to oppose patronage, nepotism, and corruption in the civil service. The more the government bureaucracy expanded, the less it was able to rely on patronage and nepotism, and the greater was the opposition to the awarding of sinecure jobs to idle aristocrats. Its further expansion required modern administrative procedures and rational standards of efficiency and autonomy.[6]

In a number of countries it is possible to pinpoint fairly clearly the transition from feudalistic to meritocratic bureaucracy. In the United Kingdom, for example, the Northcote-Trevelyan Report of 1854 led to reform of the civil service. In Japan an examination procedure was introduced in 1883 modeled on the Prussian example, emphasizing legal and economic training; every applicant for a higher position in the state administration had to pass this examination before receiving the status of "imperial" civil servant. In other countries, such as France, the process of bureaucratic reform was stretched out over a period of up to 50 years. It was only in the period before the First World War that examinations became the basis for hiring and promotion of bureaucrats in France (Legendre 1968).

In the United States, on the other hand, the acceptance of meritocratic principles in the government bureaucracy took a different course. There the bureaucracy was still controlled by political parties in the late 19th century, and the Democrats or the Republicans awarded public offices ("spoils") to their supporters after each electoral victory. The parties thereby commanded the most important organ for enabling their successful applicant to carry out his mandate. The rivalry between President and Congress over control of the federal bureaucracy was the basis for a continual constitutional struggle in the United States (Nelson 1982). Enactment of the Pendleton Act in 1883, finally, cleared the way for the establishment of meritocratic principles for the bureaucracy.

(b) The reform of government bureaucracy would not have been possible without an expansion of the universities, for it was only through these that personnel could be trained to carry out the responsibilities required of a modern, rational, efficient administration. In addition to providing the skills needed of bureaucrats, however, universities also played an important role in the selection of those who were to become bureaucrats. In some cases the specifically technical features in the prospective bureaucrat's education were of relatively secondary features. In the United Kingdom, for example, students aspiring to higher positions in the public administration attended Oxford or Cambridge, where they studied the humanities. This study was surely not considered to impart technical knowledge that the bureaucrats would later need in performing their public office but served instead a principally selective function. Here, as in other countries, the selection carried out by the university took the place of feudal privilege in the recruitment of persons to administer the state, and this selection was based not solely upon qualification but also included such characteristics as social background, political persuasion, and life-style. With this common university education behind them, an *esprit de corps* developed among the new bureaucrats which transformed the civil service into a new closed, homogeneous class. Its social homogeneity and *esprit de corps* were features that were as crucial for the growth in bureaucratic power as was its qualification-based recruitment.

The universities accelerated the process of bureaucratic institutionalization and exerted a strong influence upon the internal structure of the public administration. The hierarchy of positions in the state bureaucracy mirrored the hierarchy in the educational system,[7] and the development of career regulations and status relationships almost always oriented itself to the educational system. The more differentiated and hierarchical the educational system, the more differentiated and hierarchical the bureaucracy tended to be (Lutz 1979, p. 665). The "entitlement" system tied the university and the bureaucracy to one another and made them mutually dependent.

The symbolic power of the university was carried over to the bureaucracy. University education socialized the future public officials and fashioned them as representatives of the dominant social culture. To the political power of the bureaucracy was thus added the symbolic power of specialized training, culture, and life-style. Bureaucrats were not merely public employees but also served as representatives of a certain quasi-aristocratic style. The university degree imbued the official positions of bureaucrats with the power and prestige of cultural "goods" and legitimized their bureaucratic authority.[8]

In his study of the "German mandarins" Ringer (1969, p. 86) analyzed the role of humanities education for the bureaucrat. He showed German idealism to be an ideology specific to the traditional upper strata and particularly of the civil service. The bureaucrats' counterpart to the political power or economic capital of other elites was their education. For them the role of education provided by the *Gymnasium* and the university was less a source of professional training than a source of this symbolic authority, and the ideology justifying this authority explains the bureaucracy's isolation of itself into a self-conscious class. Its humanistic education delivered, in its own eyes, the truest legitimation for class privilege and political power. As a result, the civil service allied itself neither with democratic political parties, appealing to the uneducated masses, nor with industrial-commercial interests, pursuing only a crass materialism (see Chap. 5.5).

This form of political power cannot be legitimized by either elections or the market. The type of political functions which the bureaucracy saw itself as performing could only be threatened if subjected to the vagaries of electoral majorities and could not be measured by market success. In many countries one of the central goals of the reform movement was in fact the removal of the bureaucracy from influence by political parties (e.g., in France and Japan). The performance of state administrative functions was to be made stable over the long term, and thus decoupled from the vicissitudes of electoral outcomes, by guaranteeing bureaucrats professional life tenure and independence from political forces. Thus bureaucratic power was legitimized by *symbolic* forms of competence. The most important source of this legitimation was the bureaucrat's specialized training and qualification – represented by the university degree.

The need to underpin this legitimation explains the meticulous observance of rituals in meritocratic selection procedures. An analysis of the employment examinations in the United Kingdom or of the *concours* in France would show the educational features that were demanded to have generally little to do with the set of responsibilities which would later have to be carried out by the bureaucrat. Possession of a university degree and the strenuousness of the selection procedure – particularly that of the *grands corps* in France[9] – served not only as a surrogate legitimation for the civil servants' power but also as a defense against demands for any form of performance evaluation. Their "merits" lay in a purely symbolic form of performance, and their education and examination score protected them from political influence and from evaluation of their performance in office.

(c) In the symbiotic relationship between university and bureaucracy the former is not a mere servant to the latter. As described above, the expansion of the university depended upon the expansion of the bureaucracy; however, the reverse was also the case: the bureaucratization of politics and many other areas of social life enabled institutions of higher education to attain an invulnerable position in society. The societal role of the university rested less on its education of an entrepreneurial or political elite than on that of a bureaucratic elite. There is a close affinity between the educational and socialization processes of the university and those of the bureaucracy. The aura of power, political influence, and stability which surrounds the bureaucracy carries over to the university.

It was crucial to the university that its selection criteria and its definition of culture, ability, and life-style correspond to those of the bureaucracy, and that the latter accept its preselection. Only in such a symbiotic relationship could the university stabilize its political influence, and this influence would wane to the extent to which this relationship was jeopardized.

Both the development of a professionalized civil service and the continual expansion of university are aspects of the modernization process. Bureaucracy and university have grown since the 19th century to become "organs" of the modern state. The following sections describe the critical *transition phase* in the change from feudal, patronage-based state administration to the modern, meritocratic bureaucracy. As is seen, this transition took very different forms in the various countries examined. A major theme here is the consequences which the reform process had for both the bureaucracy and the university. It is argued that the way in which patronage was overcome, and the extent to which the university was involved in this, had lasting consequences for the bureaucracy and for the university. In France, for example, the dominant role of the *grandes écoles* can be understood only in the context of their role in overcoming patronage in the state administration.

The first country analyzed below is the United States, where development of a state bureaucracy was faced with the task of overcoming the spoils system. In contrast to virtually every European country, where the university degree and tested ability of bureaucrats served as the basis for an autonomous bureaucracy, the American bureaucracy remained in the control of local party bosses. Its "detour" through the radical-democratic spoils system prolonged the establishment there of a meritocratic bureaucracy. The analysis of this detour illustrates the conflict between radical-democratic and meritocratic principles for the distribution of positions of status.

5.3 The Spoils System: Domination of the Bureaucracy by Political Parties

(a) Until the late 19th century the United States remained, as it were, a "stateless" state. The bureaucracy was underdeveloped, and the definition of political institutions was still in flux. Tocqueville was one of the first observers to acquaint Europeans with this aspect of the American political system; it has remained the subject of controversy ever since. Many argue that immigrants to the United States were hostile to government in general, and that the antibureaucratic politics of the country grew out of their experiences with closed, arrogant bureaucratic castes in the Old World.[10] There did of course exist government institutions, but the relationships among them were less firmly established than in European countries at the time. Since the constitutional jurisdiction of the organs of state was less clearly defined, a constant, if latent, struggle existed among them.

The spoils system – the domination by political parties of the bureaucracy – must be seen as the attempt to reconcile two opposing forces. On the one hand, the need was growing in the United States as in other countries for government performance; on the other, the opposition on the part of the political parties prevented the creation of a professional bureaucracy. The time that the country could continue simply "muddling through" came to an end more or less with the War Between the States in 1865. A compromise was found according to which patronage was left in the hands of the political parties, and the frequent rotation in appointive offices prevented the formation of a closed bureaucratic caste. The price which the state administration paid for this strategy, however, was incompetence, corruption, and instability.

As regards the development of political institutions, events in the United States and in Europe at the end of the 19th century were tending in largely contrary directions. While in European countries democratic parties were being founded that opposed the political dominance of the executive and the bureaucracy, in the United States it was the power of political parties that had to be broken if a rational bureaucracy were to be built upon the basis of a competent, qualified civil service. The conditions under which this would be possible were also those for the creation of a symbiotic relationship between the university and the bureaucracy. The spoils system of political patronage had to be replaced by a meritocratic system of rational civil service before the government bureaucracy could take its place in the job market for university graduates.

(b) The defenders of the spoils system quoted the doctrine of "due participation" as propounded by Thomas Jefferson (President, 1801-1809): no political party and no social group is intrinsically entitled to offices of public trust; in principle, every citizen has the right to hold public office. However, Jefferson recognized the dilemma inherent in this radical-democratic conception: "If a due participation of office is a matter of right, how are vacancies to be obtained? ... Can any other mode than that of removal be proposed?"[11] It was the concept of rotation in office that provided here the crucial formula for avoiding the greater evil of an arrogant bureaucratic caste. The Tenure of Office Act of 1820 specified a number of public offices that could be held for a maximum of only four years, and the list of such offices grew over the years until a high percentage were subject to the rotation principle.

Andrew Jackson (President, 1829-1837) developed the principle further: "There are, perhaps, few men who can for any great length of time enjoy office and power without being more or less under the influence of feelings unfavorable to the faithful discharge of their public duties. ... Office is considered as a species of property, and government rather as a means of promoting individual interests than as an instrument created solely for the service of the people. ... Offices were not established to give support to particular men at the public expense. No individual wrong is, therefore, done by removal, since neither appointment to nor continuance in office is matter of right."[12]

Conflict was inevitable between the rotation principle, on the one hand, and the need for adequate qualification of administrative personnel and continuity of governmental processes, on the other. Long before Taylor rationalized industrial production by fragmenting the production process, Jackson proposed a form of "Taylorism" for dealing with this conflict: "The duties of all public officers are, or at least admit of being made, so plain and simple that men of intelligence may readily qualify themselves for their performance; and I cannot but believe that more is lost by the long continuance of men in office than is generally to be gained by their experience. I submit, therefore, to your consideration whether the efficiency of the government would not promoted, and official industry and integrity better secured, by a general extension of the law [= Tenure of Office Act, P.W.] which limits appointments to four years."[13]

Jackson's optimism, however, has not been confirmed by historical experience. The notion of "due participation" degenerated over time into a battle between the political parties – and to the principle of "to the victor belong the spoils of the enemy."[14] After each election which the incumbent party lost, the victorious party reaped the personnel spoils of the battle by dismissing the previous officials and replacing them with persons from its own clientele. Thus the one evil of bureaucratic arbitrariness and impenetrability was banned only by sanctioning the contrary evil of party-political corruption. It was the responsibility of the political parties to oversee and administer the rotation principle.

Many officials were in fact entrusted with no actual bureaucratic responsibilities but were merely rewarded in this way for helping in the successful election campaign. It was common in every constituency that the roll of appointed public officials included the names of several party functionaries who were concerned principally, or even exclusively, with party-political work. It was also common that bureaucrats who thanked their jobs to "spoils" appointments were assessed between 5% and 8% of their salary by the party as a form of "job fee;" its nonpayment spelled dismissal. This feature of the spoils system provided the major source of financing for political parties as late as the First World War.

When Max Weber (1956, p. 1076) visited the United States he observed: "American workers, responding in 1904 to the question of why they allow themselves to be governed by politicians whom they profess to despise, answered: we would rather have bureaucrats that we can spit on than, like you, a bureaucratic caste that spits on us. That has been the traditional standpoint of American 'democracy.'"

Compared to 19th century political parties in European countries, which were only beginning to form, those in the United States enjoyed a wide organizational network of activists and were much more integrated into the everyday political life of the nation. The Jacksonian definition of bureaucratic responsibility – keep it simple enough that anyone can hold office – was an important precondition for the eventual appointment of even uneducated first-generation immigrants to positions of public trust.

This form of political patronage was eventually to fall into general disrepute, but not solely because of the corruption inevitable in it, for it also handicapped the state in fulfilling important government functions. Key (1962, p. 388) recites the following incident which illustrates the contradiction between the rotation principle and the need for government performance. "A Chicago building inspector, appointed through party channels, inspected a water tank atop a building. The 40,000-gallon tank later collapsed and fell through six floors of the building, killing five men and injuring six others enroute. The inspector's testimony before the coroner's jury follows:

Question: How long have you been a building inspector? *Answer:* Nine months.
Question: What were you before that? *Answer:* I was a malt salesman.

Question: When you were made a building inspector did you know anything about the work? *Answer:* No. I didn't know anything about it.

Question: When did you inspect the building and the tank? *Answer:* It was in January.

Question: Did you find anything wrong with the tank? *Answer:* No. It looked all right to me.

Question: Are you in a position to know whether it was all right or not? *Answer:* No, I'm just the same as you or anybody else who might inspect it.

Question: Did you inspect the anchor plates? *Answer:* Well, I looked at them."

The logic behind this system can be seen in the career of George Washington Plunkitt. Arriving as a penniless immigrant in New York City, Plunkitt in a relatively short time became boss of the city's famous Tammany Hall political machine and eventually won election to the United States Senate. In the following quotation from his memoirs Plunkitt formulated the secret to his success and imparted advice to the next generation:

I guess I can explain best what to do to succeed in politics by tellin' you what I did. ... Did I offer my services to the district leader as a stump-speaker? Not much. The woods are always full of speakers. Did I get up a book on municipal government and show it to the leader? I wasn't such a fool. What I did was to get some marketable goods before goin' to the leaders. What do I mean by marketable goods? Let me tell you: I had a cousin, a young man who didn't take any particular interest in politics. I went to him and said: "Tommy, I'm goin' to be a politician, and I want to get a followin'; can I count on you?" He said: "Sure George." That's how I started in business. I got a marketable commodity – one vote. Then I went to the district leader and told him I could command two votes on election day, Tommy's and my own. He smiled on me and told me to go ahead. If I had offered him a speech or a bookful of learnin', he would have said, "Oh, forget it!" That was beginnin' business in a small way, wasn't it? But that is the only way to become a real lastin' statesman. I soon branched out. Two young men in the flat next to mine were school friends. I went to them, just as I went to Tommy, and they agreed to stand by me. ... And so it went on like a snowball rollin' down a hill. ... Before long I had sixty men back of me, and formed the George Washington Plunkitt Association. What did the district leader say then when I called at headquarters? I didn't have to call at headquarters. He came after me and said: "George, what do you want? If you don't see what you want, ask for it. *Wouldn't you like to have a job or two in the departments for your friends?*"[15]

The key to obtaining public office was possession not of a university degree but of a "marketable good." A person's power was measured by the number of votes he could command at election time. The ability to deliver 60 votes seemed sufficient to secure appointment to some position.

The postelection distribution of the "spoils" – the offices available for filling – followed a simple pattern. The precinct managers of the winning party were allotted a number of appointments on the basis of the party's relative electoral success in the respective precincts; these local party bosses could then distribute the offices allotted to them as they pleased, and they were awarded to those activists who had delivered the "marketable goods" when they counted – on election day. Those in possession of these "goods" were unable to cash them in only in the event that their party lost the election.

The way in which the spoils system worked to the disadvantage of the middle class businessman can be illustrated in a case from the harbor of New York City. A high proportion of tax revenue stemmed from customs duties in New York harbor, and political party competition was therefore intense for control of the customs office there. An election victory would bring the winning party command of hundreds of highly sought-after jobs; the harbor was therefore also the most important source of income for the local political parties. The efficiency of the customs office was very limited, and the paperwork on some incoming shipments sometimes lasted weeks. The customs officials did not carry out the work themselves but contracted it out to others, for they themselves were engaged exclusively in the political activities for which they had received their official positions. Similar conditions were common in the postal system, which at the local level was also an important resource for the spoils system. Often it was the case that hundreds of postal bags were piled high in post offices as a result of laxness or the lack of organization (Skowronek 1982, pp. 61-62, 72-73).

In the late 19th century a movement arose calling for reform of such malpractice in machine politics. This self-styled "progressive movement" was supported not by blue-collar workers or immigrants but by the upper and middle social strata. Those most disadvantaged by "spoils" politics were the entrepreneurs of the then-consolidating capitalist class, and these formed an alliance with the new middle class of graduates from the rapidly expanding universities who, by virtue of their educational qualifications, viewed the government bureaucracy as their personal domain. The clear aim of the progressive movement as regards the state bureaucracy was to change the way in which government operates so that it would better resemble an industrial enterprise. A merit system was to be introduced so that those holding office in the public bureaucracy would be hired and promoted on the basis of qualification and performance, evaluated in terms of competence and impartiality.[16]

The bitterness of the struggles over reform of the bureaucracy were the result not only of its mismanagement, corruption, and incompetence. It also involved the *political-constitutional* question of who controls the administrative structure of the state. At the federal level the conflict pitted the President – generally in alliance with the reform movement – against the Congress – the traditional bastion of political party power. Here the issue was ultimately over the extent to which Congress was willing to authorize the President to expand the government bureaucracy – which was also an instrument for extending the power of the executive branch.[17]

The reform movement scored its first victory over the spoils system with enactment of the Pendleton Act in 1883, which placed certain areas of the bureaucracy under the protection of a merit system that required applicants for public office to pass an initial examination. A provision in this law empowered the President to extend the merit system gradually to an increasing number of offices.

The Pendleton Act was aimed not only at improving the performance of the civil service but also at breaking the power of party bosses, who were dependent upon the proceeds (assessments) from spoils appointments. Without this financing they would be unable to keep their party machines in operation. Upon his inauguration as President in 1889 Benjamin Harrison lamented over the power of the party machine: "When I came into power [1889] I found that the party managers had taken it all to themselves. I could not name my own Cabinet. They had sold out every place to pay the election expenses."[18]

Of the 131,208 positions in the federal bureaucracy in January 1884 the Pendleton Act placed 13,924 (11%) under the provisions of the merit system. This number was extended in subsequent years, and in January 1900 there were a total of 208,000 positions – 94,839 (46%) filled by merit system appointments and 113,161 (54%) by spoils appointments. Thus, despite the growing proportion of jobs covered by the merit system the overall expansion of the bureaucracy still left the spoils system considerable scope (Skowronek 1982, p. 69).

The Pendleton Act proved surprisingly successful. By 1913 some 71% of federal positions were filled by appointees who had passed the required examinations. To some extent this success was due to political party competition. Presidents facing probable defeat in an impending election often used the opportunity to deprive the other party of some of their anticipated spoils – and spoils-based financing – by extending the merit system before leaving office. During the Depression of the 1930's, however, the number of federal offices filled by merit appointments declined from 76% to 59%, as the high unemployment figures placed politicians under pressure to provide additional jobs. In the years 1950-1970 the proportion of merit positions in the federal bureaucracy varied between 82% and 86%. In 1971 the Postal Reorganization Act removed postal employees from the coverage of the merit system, and the proportion then fell to 67.7%. In 1985 the figure stood at 61%.[19]

The reform proceeded much more slowly at the local than at the federal level, and many of these positions are still being filled with spoils appointments today. The classical example of an urban political party machine is that of Chicago. The city is divided into precincts with approximately 70,000 voters each, and in each there is a precinct manager in charge of maintaining the machine. In one of these, for example, the precinct manager Connors in 1952 had between 350 and 500 jobs that he could fill as he saw politically fit.[20]

The spoils system was an institution of the urban lower classes – immigrants, workers, minorities, and lower level white-collar employees who enjoyed few of the benefits of the industrialization process. They were less interested in the efficiency and neutrality of the state bureaucracy than in social contacts, community solidarity, and personal dependability. For these persons the party precinct manager appeared as something of a social worker: he arranged jobs, helped in getting around bureaucratic regulations, and could sometimes even provide cover for those evading police investigations.

The reform movement, on the other hand, espoused the values of the enlightened middle class; here social relationships were based on competition rather than on solidarity. Entrepreneurs, attorneys, professors, and physicians were interested in an efficient civil service based upon qualification and performance. Only a government bureaucracy oriented toward these values could offer university graduates career opportunities. Thus, the conflict between patronage and "neutrality" in the civil service was not only a power struggle between President and Congress; it was also a struggle between conflicting political value orientations. Wolfinger and Field (1966, p. 307) argue that this conflict may be understood "as a clash between middle-class admiration of efficiency and the working-class' desires for representation of their interests." The working class was excluded from university study before the 1930's, and for them extension of the merit system in government employment meant an immediate threat to their jobs.

Particularly university graduates had an interest in the reform movement. While the public bureaucracy remained a system of nontenured, spoils-dominated positions, it offered them little prospect of lasting employment, career, or social mobility. When an incumbent political party lost an election, some 80% of public employees were fired and replaced by supporters of the winning party. Under these conditions a stable relationship could not develop between the university and the government bureaucracy. Employment in the private sector offered much more secure and lucrative career possibilities. Before becoming President, Theodore Roosevelt had served as Chairman of the Civil Service Commission empowered with overseeing enforcement of the Pendleton Act; Roosevelt remarked that "the civil service is not looked to as a career by anyone. Very few young men come into the service at Washington with any idea of remaining more than a few years; often merely long enough to support them through a course at a professional evening school. This feeling will continue until promotions ... are based upon merit, and a check put upon unjust removals."[21]

The coalitions that developed included business, university, and government authorities, on the one hand, and political parties, immigrants, and Congress, on the other. The former styled themselves "progressives" in opposition to backward, corrupt party politics; support for the latter was found principally among the urban lower strata. A meritocratic bureaucracy appeared as the savior of the citizen against the forces of corruption.

Ultimately, the spoils system died of its own internal contradictions. As early as the beginning of this century the political parties encountered growing opposition on the part of public officials to the arbitrariness of dismissals purely on the basis of party-political motivations. Labor unions began to organize public employees, and – at least for a time – were loyal allies of the President in the struggle against the spoils system: The Pendleton Act promised job security. Those who did enjoy the protection of the merit system could not be dismissed on political grounds, and this generally meant de facto life tenure.

(c) Why was the political struggle to replace patronage by meritocratic standards in the government bureaucracy waged several decades later in the United States than in Western Europe? In answer to this question Epstein (1967, p. 110) points out that the democratic political party system of the United States is much older than its counterparts in Western European countries; in the latter, in fact, political parties were founded only *after* reform of the civil service had begun. Shefter (1977) generalized this observation to the following hypothesis: a spoils system could not develop in countries in which political party activists were excluded from holding public office and therefore depended for power upon the ideological mobilization of the masses. An example is the SPD during the German Empire: party members were barred from the civil service, and the party – therefore unable to mobilize supporters by offering material incentives – was forced to rely upon the socialist ideology and the building up of an organizational structure outside of government. Even after the SPD became successful in gaining electoral office it still could not offer its voters the corruptive spoils of appointive office in the bureaucracy. Wallerstein (1974) has pointed out that historically the development of a spoils system was frustrated by the existence of strong government. Wherever a bureaucratic caste had developed – with special privileges, entrance restrictions, and class consciousness – *before* the bourgeois revolution took place, the civil service was strong enough to rebuff any attempts of political parties to usurp power over the state administrative institutions – and personnel.

A further factor influencing the development of a meritocratic bureaucracy was the stability of the political system. Three periods can be distinguished in the history of the American bureaucracy in the 19th century. The first was that from 1800 to 1840, during which political parties were relatively underdeveloped, and access to appointive offices was generally controlled by politicians labeling themselves Democrats. Particularly in the federal bureaucracy there was virtually no party-political rivalry. While it was not free of all forms of patronage in the filling of offices (Hoogenboom 1968), there was no corruption involved, and it did operate efficiently – leading to its being held up as an example in the Northcote-Trevelyan Report in the United Kingdom (Finer 1952; Hart 1972). In the period 1840-1875 power changed hands frequently; in fact, between 1875 and 1896 there was a change of party in the White House or of party majority on Capitol Hill almost every two years. This was the heyday of the American spoils system. All Presidents elected between 1896 and 1912 belonged to the Republican Party, and this Party was able to establish its power over several legislative periods. It was also during this period that the federal bureaucracy was reformed, with the merit system being extended to an ever growing proportion of public offices. Generalizing from the course of these events, one could hypothesize that times of political instability and frequent change in legislative majorities are particularly favorable to the development of the spoils system.[22]

It is important to note, however, that the expansion of the educational system is a necessary, albeit not sufficient, condition for the introduction of meritocratic standards in the civil service. The system of higher education began to expand particularly early in the United States and was larger than that in European countries by the end of the 19th century. In spite of this, however, no stable relationship developed between the bureaucracy and the university. American universities prepared their students principally for jobs in the private sector, as the government bureaucracy gave only a poor image of itself and offered industrious young university graduates little in the way of attractive career opportunities.

(d) Opponents of the Pendleton Act in the United States had argued that the creation of a merit system would foster a privileged caste of parasitic bureaucrats – a repugnant state within the state. To meet this objection the Pendleton Act stipulated details of the type of entrance examination that was to be administered to applicants for public office. Such examinations in the United Kingdom included questions which applicants could answer correctly only if they had studied literature at Oxford or Cambridge. The American counterpart, on the other hand, was to be oriented specifically to the nature of the work which would be expected of a successful applicant; if the job, for example, demanded nothing more of the employee than that he or she be able to read and write, then nothing but literacy could be tested. Anyone could apply for any position; rather than only promotion "up through the ranks" the hiring of "outsiders" for higher positions was particularly encouraged.

Such specialized examinations were common for the American civil service until the late 1930's. In 1936 President Franklin Roosevelt appointed a commission to review civil service hiring policies, and this commission found that these examinations were too specialized and led to the hiring of persons with only very narrowly defined areas of expertise and ability. As a result, the nature of the examinations was changed so as to test general knowledge and intelligence, which increased their attraction to graduates of the expanding universities. Thereafter the percentage of university graduates in the American civil service grew steadily. After 1984, however, there was a swing again toward antimeritocracy and favoring specialized demands for the position.[23] Statistical studies carried out by antidiscrimination groups have shown that in many cities the application examinations entail a systematic disadvantage to those from ethnic minorities (Hays and Kearney 1984, pp. 28-29).

The various changes in civil service examination standards reflect the history of political trends over the years. The practical, specialized type of test was supposed to prevent the development of a European-style caste of university-trained bureaucrats. However, those hired on the basis of this test lacked sufficient general knowledge, and emphasis was shifted in the 1930's to possession of a wider general education, thus benefiting university graduates. This, on the other hand, disadvantaged ethnic minorities, and in the 1980's the movement was away from meritocracy, presumably in a way to provide "affirmative action" toward lower socioeconomic groups and ethnic minorities.

The analysis in the following section shows in the case of France to what extent the nature and content of the examination (*concours*) affects the socioeconomic composition of the civil service.

5.4 The *Grandes Écoles* and Government Bureaucracy in France

There are few countries in which the selection for leadership positions in both the public and private sectors is so dominated by educational institutions as in France. The *Grandes Ecoles* and the universities are instruments of the state that restrict and regulate the circulation of elites. Suleiman (1978, p. 12) therefore speaks correctly of a state-sanctioned elite which thanks its legitimation to educational certificates of elite institutions. The *Grandes Ecoles* and the entrance examinations form virtually insurmountable barriers protecting the bureaucratic elite from the lower social classes. The personnel at the highest level of the French bureaucracy have survived meritocratic selection at various points in reaching their position. Below we examine the way in which selection at the educational institutions and through the meritocratic entrance examination creates a socially homogeneous civil service.

The way in which high public officials are selected and appointed is a delicate political/constitutional issue in every country. The recruitment procedures for the bureaucratic elite in France were altered over the course of the 19th century along with the frequently changing constitution. The switching back and forth between monarchy and republic brought with it a political instability that until the end of the 19th century handicapped efforts to carry out the sort of administrative reform that was seen at that time in United Kingdom and Prussia.

The French Revolution ended the practice of venality of offices and the feudalistic right of aristocrats to sinecure positions. In 1791 the National Assembly made all public offices subject to election: "Administrators are to be *elected by the people* for a term of office in order – under the supervision of the king – to carry out the administrative function of the state."[24] This rule soon led to mismanagement and anarchy, and it did not survive the revolutionary years. Napoleon restored the procedure of the *ancien régime*: bureaucrats, in particular the heads of the regional administration (*préfets*), were selected and appointed by the central government. The principle was thus: "The state must be master of its servants" (Kessler 1978, p. 6). This policy was interpreted by the various governments during the restoration years (1814-1930) as they pleased. Patronage and nepotism once again became rife; the judiciary was not independent of the executive, but judges were selected from among the leading "notables" in their communities (Legendre 1968, p. 271).

The changes of government in France during the 19th century represented not merely the alternation in office by opposing political parties within a given constitution (as in the United States), but the repeated fundamental rewriting of the country's constitution. As a result, the hostilities of the ousted elites after such a change of government ran deep: Although judges enjoyed life tenure in office under any given constitution, their seats were often pulled out from under them as a new government assumed office. In 1810, for example, 15 out of 32 judges at the High Court in Paris were dismissed. After the Restoration some 300 judges were purged. The incoming government under the new Third Republic cloaked a similar action of its own with the mantle of legality by temporarily suspending the permanence of judiciary appointments, removed 614 of them from the bench, and then reinstituted life tenure for those who had survived. In 1830 François Guizot dismissed 636 out of 764 prefects in a single move. Such a "clean sweep" is referred to in French as *coup de balai* ("coup of the broom") or *épuration* ("cleaning out").[25]

While such actions strengthened the individual regime's hand at the time, in the long term their repetition only added to the nation's political instability. As Hintze (1963, p. 40) points out, the resulting masses of former civil servants who had been dismissed in such political purges nurtured a hostility toward the culprit regime which not only diminished the regime's public legitimation among an important segment of the population but also often made these former government officials willing agents in attempts to oust it.

Numerous attempts were made to replace the corruption, patronage, and arbitrary dismissals of these practices by adoption of a rule-abiding and nonpartisan personnel policy for the bureaucracy. Examinations were introduced in 1853 for some diplomatic positions, but these became universally accepted in the foreign service only in 1880. This was similar in the case of judges, for whom examinations were first administered in

1875, although it was 1908 before a combination of university degree and passing examination scores were definitively established for appointments to the judiciary (Legendre 1968, pp. 241, 271). These reforms remained limited to only a number of government positions before the First World War, and in 1914 de Jouvenel could still speak of a *république des camarades*. Family connections and patronage still took priority over university degree and examination scores.[26]

The Polytechnique, which had been founded in 1794 as an engineering school, became an important model for the meritocratic selection of civil servants. This institution reached the height of its political influence in the late 19th century. Its success derived from three principles. First, in contrast to the universities, which demanded the *baccalauréat* certificate from a secondary school for admission, the Polytechnique required applicants to pass an examination. This *concours* thus represented selection explicitly on the basis of ability rather on that of previous educational degrees. Only 200 applicants per year were accepted, and since the *baccalauréat* did not suffice for admission, special two- or three-year courses were offered to prepare applicants for the examination.[27] In the 50 years between 1830 and 1880 only 1.3% of those admitted did so immediately after the *baccalauréat*, and all others had attended a preparatory course (Shinn 1980, p. 70).

Secondly, all students at the Polytechnique were required to live in a special boarding school where very strict supervision and discipline was maintained. The institution thus attempted not only to impart technical knowledge to the students but also to instill in them an identity as belonging to an elite. It was a conscious, if unspoken, policy of the Polytechnique to create an *esprit de corps* among the students that was part of the "hidden curriculum" of the institution and united the students into a closed elite of French society (Kosciusko-Morizet 1973). The *esprit de corps* fostered by this common background led to a formal association among its former students *(anciens élèves)* which resembled the conservative associations of professionals in Germany during the Empire. Its members formed a close-knit, elite network in society that was closed to "outsiders." When at the end of the 19th century liberal education ministers attempted to abolish the boarding-house requirement at the Polytechnique, they met vociferous resistance from its board of directors, who claimed that this was an essential aspect of the students' education as it spared them the "anarchy" prevalent at universities (Shinn 1980, p. 134).

Thirdly, at the end of the two-year course of study at the Polytechnique students took a final examination, their scores on which remained crucial for their entire subsequent career. Those who had scored among the top ten of their class were free to choose among the top positions of the French bureaucracy.

The Polytechnique experienced a varying fate at the hands of the different regimes that ruled France during the 19th century. During the revolutionary years it was republican-democratic in nature and dedicated to the goals of the Revolution, supervised by a civilian administration and providing a predominantly practical-technical education. The institution was militarized under Napoleon, who was suspicious of its republican nature, and who planned its eventual dissolution. It was only under considerable pressure from his generals, mindful of the needs for the training of future military officers, that Napoleon relented to its continued operation. The price that he demanded was introduction of the boarding-school provision, accompanied by mandatory military service by its students after completion of the course there. With the Restoration the Polytechnique became frankly elitist; the admissions examination required knowledge of classical languages, and tuition fees were charged. In 1816 Marquis de Laplace carried out a far-reaching reform of the school's curriculum; priority was given to mathematics and theoretical geometry over practical training, with laboratory work disappearing almost completely. A "symbolic" qualification of the elite thus took precedence over its practical training.

Between 1830 and 1880, 63.5% of students finishing the Polytechnique joined the military, 25.2% took up a career in the civilian administration, and 11.3% went into private industry. Those with the top examination scores, who could choose their career path freely, entered the civilian administration. Although the majority of the school's students initially chose a career in the army or navy, military service proved unattractive to many, and some 36% left it within ten years (Shinn 1980, pp. 80, 167).

The Polytechnique had a lasting influence upon the French administration. As early as the revolutionary period the school pursued a policy that was later to become a model for the entire government bureaucracy in combatting the abuses of patronage. The system that was eventually established combined specialized educational institutions with *concours* procedures that allowed only as many to pass as there were vacancies in the administration. This reform, however, took years to be fully implemented. During the 19th century there was a lack of the necessary continuity of political institutions as well of political will. No uniform, consistent policy was possible as long as the basic public ideology was being shifted constantly between monarchial, revolutionary, and republican forms of government.

A further hindrance was the preference of the bureaucracy to form a symbiosis with the elite institutions rather than to make use of the universities for the purposes of preselection and qualification of its personnel. In the 19th century only few elite schools were founded, and these – being specifically for the elite – admitted only a limited number of applicants. The directors of the Polytechnique, and later those of the ENA, scrupulously avoided any spill-over to their institution of the expansion that was taking place in the universities. Such "Malthusian" thinking was always a feature of the ideology of the French elite, who feared that a democratic opening of their elite institutions would mean a decline in their standards of excellence (Suleimann 1978). The resulting lack of potential personnel handicapped reform of the administration; it was therefore possible to carry out such reform only gradually, beginning at the highest levels.

In 1848 Hippolyte Carnot, Education Minister of the revolutionary government, attempted to establish an ENA that would train bureaucrats in a way similar to that in which engineers were trained at the Polytechnique. His plan to require higher level government bureaucrats to have been trained specifically for positions in the state administration was defeated, however, and France had to wait until 1870 for such a institution to be founded. Upon his country's defeat in the Franco-Prussian War, Boutmy, a professor at an architecture school, founded a private institution for the training of administrators. He seized the historical opportunity and set up a corporation, seeking donations from politicians, writers, and bankers, and with the funds that he collected he founded the École Libre des Sciences Politiques. In July 1872 this school opened its doors with an initial class of 84 students; tuition was 70 francs.

Whereas the ten top students in each Polytechnique class were free to apply for the highest positions in the bureaucracy, this school for administrators concentrated on preparing students for the application examinations given by the various ministries. After the three-year course of study here students stood a good chance of passing these examinations. This approach guaranteed the autonomy of the bureaucracy, for each ministry designed its own examination in terms of the specific qualifications needed for the responsibilities which it fulfilled, and applicants' performance on the examinations was evaluated by representatives of the ministry itself. The bureaucracy thus retained supervision of the selection while the selection criteria and demands became to some extent standardized.

By the time of the First World War most ministries in the French government had come to accept this procedure. An exception remained the appointment of prefects of the regional administration who were considered to be too politically sensitive to be selected on the basis of academic examinations. Over the years the school for administration adjusted its education ever more to the structure of the bureaucracy, tailoring its courses specifically to the demands of the various ministries. A study conducted in 1936 found that a majority of those hired for higher level positions between 1900 and 1930 had completed this school as shown in Table 5.1 (Kessler 1978, pp. 22-23).

The figures illustrate that the school was able within only a few decades to assume a virtual monopoly over recruitment for leadership positions in the French bureaucracy. Patronage and nepotism were thus replaced by meritocratic recruitment criteria. A symbiosis developed between the school for administration and the state administration itself. As Kessler (1978, pp. 21-22) has remarked, the school and the bureaucracy became mutually dependent, as the accommodation of the school's programs meant that the two had become wedded to one another. Because of the close attention of the school's curriculum to the *concours* of the various authorities, the academic courses offered, for example, by law schools at the universities were unable to compete. The universities, rather, held fast to their traditional curricula and concerned themselves little with the new qualification demands in the expanding welfare state.

The establishment of the school for administration in 1872 had shown the way of the future regarding the training of civil servants. The school was finally closed in 1945 and replaced by a public institution, the ENA. In the same year the Institut d'Études Politiques was founded in Paris to provide students a preparatory course leading to the admission examination of the ENA. Since 1945, therefore, the educational path for future civil servants has had three steps: completion of the *baccalauréat* at a secondary school; study at the (university level) Institut d'Études Politiques in preparation for the ENA admission examination; and a three-year course of further education at the ENA. In the 1960's there were generally some 4500 students enrolled at the Institut d'Études Politiques.

Table 5.1: Appointments of High Civil Servants (1900-1930)

	Appointments in absolute numbers	Graduates of Ecole Libre des Sciences Politiques
Council of State (Conseil d'Etat)	117	96.6%
Finance Ministry	211	95.7%
Auditing Office	92	89.1%
Foreign Ministry	280	87.8%

The number of students admitted annually to the ENA has varied between 81 (1947) and 127 (1974). Approximately 75% of the students passing the ENA admission examination between 1947 and 1969 had obtained a previous degree from the Institut d'Études Politiques (Bodiguel 1978, pp. 206). This Institut therefore has a similar function for the ENA as the preparatory courses for the Polytechnique: it is directed specifically at the type of knowledge and skills that are required for the ENA while also serving as an early selection and socialization for its students.

The adoption of meritocratic selection, however, has not lessened the social homogeneity of the bureaucratic elite; rather, the long socialization period has only increased the extent of the common academic background among civil servants. Bureaucrats do not begin to develop an *esprit de corps* only after having served in the administration for some time, but rather they emerge from the ENA or Polytechnique already conscious of belonging to an elite. The Institut d'Études Politiques was initially established to combat this homogeneity by helping students from lower socioeconomic groups gain admission to the ENA. It was affiliated to a university and was intended to provide the requisite knowledge and abilities needed at the ENA to a broad spectrum of students. However, this has not proven to be the case.

A study in the 1960's of higher level civil servants in the three arms of the *grands corps* (Council of State, Finance, Auditing) found that 65%-80% in each were from the upper social strata, regardless of whether they were of the older generation (from the former school for administration, or through patronage) or the younger (ENA). The rigorous admission examination for the ENA is thus a selection filter which only few from the lower strata manage to pass (Darbel and Schnapper 1969, vol. 2, p. 105).

An important innovation, however, has been made regarding the ENA admission examination: this has been divided into two, one for "normal" students ("external") and one for bureaucrats seeking promotion from the lower levels ("internal"). The proportion of seats reserved for the latter declined between 1947 and 1974 from 44% to 38%.[28] The social backgrounds of the two groups differ markedly. Between 1963 and 1969, 37.5% of the "normal" students were from Paris as opposed to only 18.5% of the bureaucrats; 63% of the former came from upper class backgrounds compared to only 24% of the latter.

Social selection is therefore less strict in the "internal" competition. Most of the bureaucrat-students do not have a previous university degree. After ten years' experience in the civil service and upon the recommendation of their organizational superior, bureaucrats above a certain level may attend a course preparing them to take the ENA admission examination. The substantive demands of this "internal" examination of the ENA, however, are no less selective than those of the "external" examination. The proportion of those passing the internal examination between 1945 and 1974 was 12%, compared to 9% in the external examination.

The application examination for civil servants (*concours fonctionaire*) opens to those of lower socioeconomic status a career that may even reach to leadership positions in the bureaucracy. In fact, this is the only such avenue that is generally available to them. It is noteworthy that the proportion of seats allocated to "internal" students at the ENA has been reduced over the years.

During the 1970's there were calls from the Socialist Party and some labor unions (in particular the CFDT) for abolition of the ENA and the training of higher civil servants at universities. The proposals were for the various ministries to hire persons, upon passing the appropriate application examination, directly from the university. These new employees would enter the civil service not at the higher levels but at lower levels and would have to prove themselves in the internal labor market of the ministry and thereby gain promotion step for step up through its ranks. This plan would therefore have substituted practical on-the-job training for the three-year course of study at the ENA. Kessler (1978, p. 107) criticized this proposal with the following argument: "The foundations of bureaucratic society [*société administrative*] would thereby be put into question. The principle of the *concours* is to be retained, but selection is stretched out interminably, and the access to the *grands corps* is delayed. Such a slow rise could only deter gifted university students, and this would completely alter the character of the public administration."

At the end of the 19th century, when a large proportion of bureaucrats obtained their positions through political patronage, the meritocratic principle of the *concours* gradually gained ground. In the meantime this principle has been fully institutionalized, and we can now review the results. It is remarkable here that the altered selection procedures for the state bureaucracy have had very little effect upon the overall social profile of the civil service. Those who obtained their positions by corruption, cooptation, or exerting personal pressure upon public officials differed little in this respect from those who have survived the rigorous examinations in elite schools and the ENA. This finding becomes somewhat less surprising, however, when one examines more closely the selection procedures of the *concours*.

The long educational path of students emerging from the ENA

represents a cumulative selection process. The probability of attending a Paris *lycée* is small. The probability of obtaining a degree from the Institut d'Études Politiques – considering the high drop-out rate – is likewise not very high. The probability of passing the ENA admission examination is 10%, whereby one must consider that many students anticipate their failure in this examination and therefore do not even take it. At every point along this selection process there is a filter which discriminates in favor of students in command of the cultural and intellectual code of the upper strata.[29]

The remarks by Marceau Long, Director-General of the French Central Administration, provide an "inside" view of the application examinations: "There is a healthy but sometimes misguided competition among the various ministries. This competition leads to an ever higher educational standard being expected of those taking the examination. The system misleads one into overestimating the educational level which is actually required of a civil servant." About the examination itself Long observed: "It appears as though any *concours* that does not contain at least three written and three oral examinations deserves complete scorn. For example, the *concours* for the position of assistant technician in a mine works (preeducation approximately that of a *baccalauréat*) contains six written and five oral examinations. The individual departments are tending to 'seal off' certain positions by erecting barricades around them that are as high as possible."[30] The strategy here seems to be: since a difficult test imbues those passing it with the aura of an elite, each department tries to make its own tests as difficult as they can in order to heighten the prestige and standing of the ministry.

The following description of a *concours* in the Finance Ministry in 1914 illustrates the atmosphere surrounding such occasions (Sadran 1977, pp. 92-93): "The applicants appeared on the day of the examination in formal attire [*habit de soirée*]: white tie, white gloves, silk hat. The chairman of the jury thanked the applicants for the attention accorded him and the other members of the jury. He invited them to 'make themselves comfortable' for the course of the examination. But this still meant: frock, velvet waistcoat, transparent spats. The suit could not be put permanently away thereafter, however, for it would be needed again for the oral examination. Those who were lucky and passed the examination expressed their thanks to the members of the jury and then visited all department members, even those who were retired."

The entrance examination for the ENA also includes an oral and a written part, which together last several days. The written part consists of an essay on a very general topic of politics, law, or administration. What is judged of the applicants is not their detailed knowledge of the subject but rather the spontaneity of their thoughts, the nature of their argumentation, and the brilliance of style. Sadran (1977, p. 94) notes that, "The higher in the hierarchy the *concours* is, the more important that one shows composure and appears to stand 'above it all.'" Similar criteria are important in the oral examination. An examiner rejected an applicant because he was "grumpy, sullen, and tense," with the justification: "What if the high civil service and the *grands corps* were to become a rendezvous for sad figures, overloaded with factual details but incapable of representing a happy France...?"

In this context it is interesting to note that applicants from the provinces almost always score better on the written than on the oral examination.[31] Sadran points out that the most successful applicants come from Paris and have attended the Institut d'Études Politiques, where a number of the instructors are themselves high civil servants. The students here thus have role models and the opportunity to copy their bearing, style of thought, and value judgements. As Sadran (1977, p. 99) continues: "The evaluation during the examination is based very essentially on a 'mirror effect.' The applicant must present his examiner with the image which the examiner is seeking for a position to be filled. In the case of the *concours* for a leadership position, this image is essentially the self-image of the examiner."

While this procedure purports to value only substantive qualifications, personal characteristics as personality, life-style, and intellectual flexibility become redefined in such a way as to determine ultimate success or failure. Nevertheless, this system is not entirely closed. Over the past century a fairly constant proportion of 20%-25% of the students at the elite institutions have come from the lower social strata. However, it is unlikely that these "outsiders" have a lasting, innovative effect; rather, one could expect them – as an insecure minority particularly at the higher levels – to tend to *hyperconformity*.[32]

The bureaucratic elite remains in control of the selection process for bureaucrats. Most instruction at the ENA is carried out by part-time staff whose principal function is in the bureaucracy itself. The school's board of directors has 19 members: seven from the upper levels of the bureaucracy (including the Vice-President of the Council of State and the Director of the Central Administration), five university professors, five who are not public employees, and two representatives of labor unions. Thus, counting the professors, 12 of the 19 are high-level civil servants (Kessler (1978, p. 49). The *concours* given after studies and upon entrance to the civil service is conducted exclusively by high-level bureaucrats from the hiring agency. The examiners in the oral examination are recruiting for similar positions as they themselves have.

That there is a political character to selection at the ENA is demonstrated by the fact that almost every change of government over the past 20 years has been accompanied by a "reform" of the procedure. The Socialist government in 1983 instituted a "third" path to the ENA for outstanding labor union representatives.[33] Several union representatives have gained entrance to the ENA by this means and gone on to assume high-level positions in the state administration. When the conservative government of Jacques Chirac came to office in 1986, the Secretary of State for Public Administration, Hervé de Charette, announced a new "reform": the Socialists' "third" path violated the principle of equality and was therefore to be abolished.

De Charette furthermore accused the Socialist government of patronage: they had illegitimately appointed party members to civil service positions from outside the normal channels (*tour extérieur*), that is, they had neither studied at the ENA nor competed on an internal labor market for the position. When the Socialists had come to power in 1981, they had too few highly trained personnel who could meet the meritocratic standards of the bureaucracy, and some means had to be found to compensate for this. By the end of their term in office the relationship was three applicants from the ENA or from within the bureaucracy for every one from the *tour extérieur*. De Charette claimed that "respect for the neutrality of the public administration must be a sacred duty of every government" and declared the end to this "abuse."

De Charette was determined drastically to reduce the number of students at the ENA. Enrollment at the school had risen so sharply during the 1970's that the conservative government regarded its character as an elite institution to be threatened. A total of 81 students completed the course in 1947, and the figure had declined to 51 in 1959. However the numbers rose in the 1970's, and 166 were admitted in 1985. Chirac's government decided to reduce the figure to 132 in 1986 and to 80 in 1987. De Charette argued that expansion of the school "had led to such an extraordinary heterogeneity in terms of age, preeducation, and attitudes of the students that the school authorities were facing virtually insurmountable pedagogical problems. Excessive recruitment of former ENA students has led to the progressive devaluation of the leadership positions which ENA students are taking up. The quality of the positions and the responsibility associated with them has suffered. Therefore as of 1987 the ENA will not admit more than 80 students."[34]

The thinking behind these changes in education policy is evident: a school which doubles its size within 40 years ceases to be an "elite" school. The educational expansion jeopardizes the elite character of institutions that have a key role to play in the government bureaucracy. The increase in size to 166 students per year seemed to the conservatives seriously to threaten the homogeneity of the French civil service.

5.5 The Crisis of the Prussian Bureaucracy

Its public servants selected on the basis of merit and proven competence, the Prussian bureaucracy served as a model of nonpartisan administration in the 19th century, and it was often to Prussia that reformers in the United Kingdom, United States, and Japan turned for an example against which to measure the efficiency of their own administrative structures. The renowned historian and student of public administration in the German Empire Otto Hintze (1963, p. 27) proudly praised this bureaucracy in 1911 when he observed that, "Overall, the German civil service is by far the best in all of Europe, which is to say, in all the world." There is no doubt that, compared to the spoils system of the United States, the Prussian administration certainly did represent exemplary standards of efficiency and rationality.

The bureaucracy had formed a close relationship with the universities in Prussia as early as the 18th century. As a result of this relationship not only did the country enjoy a progressive bureaucracy but the "entitlement" system also became strongly entrenched. The highly hierarchical organization of the government bureaucracy mirrored the hierarchical organization of the educational system. Every educational degree entailed "entitlement" to a position at a particular level in the bureaucracy, and there were strict entitlement regulations for all educational institutions, from public gardening schools to universities (M. Müller 1931).

However, a look at the inner workings of this bureaucracy would have mitigated the foreigner's respect for its putative efficiency and nonpartisanship, for it combined a strong element of feudalistic tradition with its proudly progressive sides. Although the Prussian authorities had very early carried out reforms designed by Cocceji (1748) to base recruitment to its bureaucracy upon meritocratic principles, in practice these principles continued to be wedded to a form of patronage. In fact, the Prussian bureaucracy has been described as a "synthesis of spoils system and merit system" by Rosenberg (1958, pp. 75-76), who continues: "There existed a congeries of cues, of coexisting but often contradictory criteria that were used to judge the qualification of applicants for positions. 'Qualification,' as defined by the King, meant very different things: prominent family background and influential social contacts; the ability to obey but also to lead and to dominate; the cleverness to bluff, goad, intrigue, and to sell his own personality; the ability and the willingness to make cash payments; and last but not least, individual distinction in terms of learnedness, intellectual insight, and outstanding professional skill and mastery."

After lawyers of bourgeois background largely replaced aristocrats in the higher levels of the bureaucracy in the 18th century, the latter began to win back much of their lost ground in the 19th by obtaining university degrees and thus the "entitlement" which enabled them to compete in the meritocratic bureaucracy with the middle class. The proportion of aristocrats filling upper positions in the Prussian civil service increased between 1820 and 1841 from 25% to 33%. By the middle of the century they occupied between 75% to 90% of the various leadership positions in the Prussian bureaucracy (Hattenhauer 1980, p. 256). Things had changed little by the turn of the century, at which time 55% of county executives (*Landrat*) were aristocrats.[35]

Rosenberg (1958, p. 80) refers to this type of recruitment as one of "limited competition." While in theory all positions in the civil service were open to any citizen of the country, the redefinition of class privileges as personal "qualifications" restricted the actual extent of competition for these positions. Thus an aristocrat who possessed a minimum of university education would be awarded a position over a lawyer of bourgeois background.

The Prussian civil service combined absolutistic deference, class solidarity, *and* professional independence. First of all, the bureaucrat swore his oath to the King, and this bound him to *loyalty* – in a way that was juridically similar to that of the feudalistic vassal to his lord. Secondly, cooptation by those of one's own class was an essential requirement for one's entry into and promotion within the civil service. As Eschenburg (1961, p. 39) has pointed out, "Anyone who was fit for military duty but was not a reserve officer could never obtain a higher level position, much less appointment as a diplomat. One must not forget that a condition for receiving a commission as reserve lieutenant was his acceptance by the officer corps of his local militia district. The criteria for this acceptance corresponded the societal image of the upper class and stressed political reliability – in the sense of unconditional acceptance of the political system."

Thirdly, the Prussian civil service valued *qualification* and professionalism. University law study was not regarded as a sufficient guarantee of competence among the lawyers in the bureaucracy – as a result of their "dissolute life-style" law students had a particularly poor reputation (Jarausch 1984, p. 60) – but what was important was that they had endured a rigorous practical training in the state administration and the courts. Those who survived this training belonged to the elite of the legal profession.[36]

It would also be very misleading to portray the Prussian bureaucracy as embodying the precepts of value neutrality and "blind justice." Its success rested instead upon a combination of contradictory principles, often in conflict with one another, for traditional class values permeated the civil service as much as did modern standards of professionalism. The loyalty oath was a relic of the feudal era and bound the bureaucrat to the King, while cooptation bound him to his fellow bureaucrats. These traditional features of his professional role distinguished the Prussian civil servant from his counterparts in the United Kingdom and the United States.

Seldom were there bribery scandals in Prussia, and Eschenburg (1961, p. 40) points out a reason for the probity of its bureaucrats: the social homogeneity of the civil service "placed a high moral standard upon them in order to maintain their class authority. Their arrogance protected them from petty corruption." In their immunity to corruption, therefore, Prussian bureaucrats were merely following their own class interests. The acceptance of bribes would have been a senseless means to pursue these interests in view of the social privileges which they already enjoyed. Class solidarity promised far better rewards.

The British student of public administration Finer (1927, pp. 8-9) wrote in the 1920's: "[W]hen we in England hear the word 'bureaucracy' we imagine a vast body of officials, wielding great power, imbued with so definite and particular a tradition and view of their calling, that it separates them, and makes their ways of thought and behaviour strange and alien from the rest of society. We imagine that the living bureaucracy is exactly what the word itself implies – government by officials; that they form a special caste or estate. We think that this body attempts when it is old and big enough to be sure of itself, to claim its identity with the State and, avoiding direction by the people, aims at directing them. ... But in the continental sense, England has no bureaucracy."

It is an open question as to whether United Kingdom does not have a 'bureaucracy' in the sense described by Finer, and it is also controversial whether his description of the continental (Prussian) bureaucracy is correct. Important for the present argument is that some aspects of the Prussian bureaucracy were progressive, modernized and in accordance with "due process of law" (*Rechtsstaat*) while others were backward and preserved feudal relics. The Prussian bureaucracy combined features of modern public administration with relics of traditional absolutism. Down to the First World War it had experienced none of the crises which the bureaucracy in other countries had gone through, such as the reforms initiated by the Pendleton Act in the United States (1883) and the Northcote-Trevelyan Report in the United Kingdom (1853[37]) or the purges to which the French bureaucracy was continually subjected by the country's periodic constitutional upheavals.

The synthesis of feudal deference and modern neutrality in the Prussian bureaucracy is seen in the county executive (*Landrat*), a crucial figure in the country's civil service. At the end of the 19th century most of those county executives were still aristocratic *Junker* and thought in feudalistic terms; however, many had studied law and were fully versed in the principles of civil constitutionalism.

It was only with the First World War and the Revolution of 1918/1919 that this labile synthesis of modernity and traditionalism broke asunder. When the Emperor abdicated and a republic was declared, a critical question for the new state was the likely response of the country's civil servants, sworn to loyalty to the no longer reigning monarch. However, this proved only a formal problem, for the Emperor from his exile in the Netherlands issued the following statement: "I herewith release all civil servants of the German Empire and of Prussia from the oath of loyalty which they have sworn to me as their Emperor, King, and Commander-in-Chief."[38]

This declaration by the deposed Emperor may have erased their legal allegiance to the monarchy – but not their ideological allegiance to it. The leaders of the revolutionary government were well aware that the German bureaucracy was by no means a neutral, nonpartisan instrument of the state, dedicated only to its professional ethos. Therefore one of the first actions of the new President, Friedrich Ebert, was to call on the nation's civil servants:[39] "I know it will be hard for many to work with the new men who have taken over the leadership of the nation, but I appeal to their love of the people of our country. A failure of the nation's organization in this difficult hour would condemn Germany to the direst misery. Join with me now in brave and unflagging perseverance, everyone remaining at his post, to help our country, *until the hour of relief*[40] *has come.*"

In this context, one must ask what Germany's civil servants understood by the "the hour of relief." They had already become "leaderless" in their own eyes, and the thought of "relief" could only have filled them with the added anxiety of dismissal from office and thus also of income and prestige. For this reason the new government quickly dropped any plans for a radical change in the personnel of the bureaucracy, for such a "clean sweep" would surely have spelled total chaos for the country. The organizational capacity of its bureaucracy was already being seriously questioned as a result of the military defeat, but without its continued performance of a planning function mass famine would surely have ensued. Their dismissal would in any case have been legally problematic, as the civil servants enjoyed life tenure. In addition, it would have too starkly contradicted the patriarchal tradition of Germany. A "clean sweep" of public officials – their mass "relief" – as was common after an electoral victory, for example, in the United States was not an effective possibility for the leaders of the fledgling Weimar Republic.

The question of how the republic could go on being administered by a functionally necessary but constitutionally hostile bureaucracy had to be answered if the new state was to survive. A historically portentous compromise was reached. The bureaucracy was shunted ostensibly into political neutrality – into a theoretical "no-man's land" which in practice did not exist. In November 1918, immediately after the Revolution, the civil servants were told that they were expected to continue meeting their public responsibilities – "regardless of their personal opinions." Whether they continued in public service as monarchists or as republicans was up to them so long as they fulfilled their official duties.

Although this maintained the fiction of a nonpartisan bureaucracy, it was clear to the leaders of the new government that the majority of higher civil servants were still monarchists, and that this fact would not be without consequences for the running of the new government. As Hattenhauer (1980, pp. 306-307) has observed: "In contrast to tradition, the civil servants were given freedom of political opinion. In other words, with one stroke of the pen the conventional concept of bureaucratic loyalty was replaced by mere fulfillment of function. The basic moral concepts of duty and loyalty which had bound civil servants personally to the monarch paled before the new freedom. An era of the civil service had come to an end." The words of the historian Friedrich Meinecke capture the mood among those at the higher levels of the civil service when he wrote in 1919: "I remain, toward the past, a monarchist in my heart, but I shall be, toward the future, a republican in my head."[41]

The Prussian state had enjoyed the advantages of a civil service based on the principles of competence, loyalty, and life tenure. However, the disadvantages potential in these same principles came to haunt the Weimar Republic, and to exacerbate its crises. The German bureaucracy never experienced a "clean sweep" of the bureaucrats after a change of government or a change of constitution. Whereas in the United States the adoption of life tenure for civil servants had represented a significant advance over the spoils system in terms of modernization, in Germany it now proved a dangerous handicap for the new democracy.

The compromise which the SPD government entered into with the monarchist bureaucracy demonstrates the true strength of the latter, as well as the degree to which it had become a state within the state. The calamity of the War and the upheaval of the Revolution had been able to sweep away the monarchy. For the bureaucracy, too, this was a time of one of its most serious challenges; however, in the end it proved to be stronger than the forces attempting to sweep it away as well. It is telling, in fact, that the SPD could count it a victory when it was able merely to get some of its own members into the bureaucracy. The social strata which the SPD represented lacked the formal qualifications to assume leadership positions in the civil service, but it was less their modest educational certificates than their political affiliation which closed the door to their gaining bureaucratic positions of their own.

In 1911 Hintze (1963, p. 71) had justified their exclusion in crystal clarity: "Any civil servant who is active as a Social-Democrat violates his oath to duty. If the state were to give in on this, it would mean denying its faith in its own justice." During the course of the Weimar Republic the SPD continued trying to appoint its members to positions in the bureaucracy, which led to accusations of illicit patronage from the "monarchists in their heart," and it was indeed the case that the SPD often violated the law on bureaucratic recruitment. Only at the end of the Weimar Republic era was the SPD able to present supporters of its own who also possessed the formal qualifications required for a normal civil service career.

The struggle for control of the bureaucracy during the Weimar Republic shows the extent to which educational degrees can represent a *political* weapon. Few SPD members could boast of a university degree, and this degree was the *cordon sanitaire* with which the bureaucracy insulated itself. The specialized training of the bureaucrat was the basis for the organizational power of the bureaucracy, and against this the democratic political parties were ultimately impotent.

The Revolution had shaken the self-image of the bureaucrat, but his class-based power remained largely unassailed. How could the republican government reproach recruitment to a civil service which, with its demands for formal qualifications, observed demonstratively meritocratic standards, and which in fact rebuked the democratic political parties themselves for violating these standards? As early as the late 19th century the conservative political parties of the day had recognized the danger in allowing working class children to attend the university, and the use to themselves of university graduates who were from their own class.

5.6 The Japanese Examination System

While the bureaucracy in the United States remained for decades a political football in the competition between political parties, the Japanese bureaucracy at that time presents an example of state administration in which parties were excluded from any influence at all. The Japanese examination system for higher level civil servants represents the opposite extreme to that of the spoils system. Recruitment and selection lay completely in the hands of the government, and this allowed the bureaucracy to be used by the state as an instrument in its modernization policy. The Constitution of 1889 placed the hiring and promotion of higher civil servants clearly outside the jurisdiction of Parliament (Spaulding 1967, p. 142) and specified the passing of the appropriate examinations as the only avenue to positions in the upper levels of the bureaucracy. The express aim of this reform was to abolish both class-based privilege and, especially, political party patronage in the filling of civil service positions.

The basic bureaucratic structure that still exists in Japan is that which was created between 1880 and 1910 by combining national traditions with features of European models. Japanese politicians visiting Europe were impressed in particular by the Prussian bureaucracy. Similarly as the Prussian bureaucracy had been a driving force in the modernization and centralization of that country, the Japanese hoped that their own bureaucracy – still relatively underdeveloped by European standards – could eventually play a leading role in Japanese modernization.

While, on the one hand, this modernization required an expansion of educational institutions, it was, on the other, the reform of the government administration which sparked the expansion of Japanese universities. The relationship between bureaucracy and university that developed in Japan was even more symbiotic than that in Prussia, and can be compared only to the role which the *grandes écoles* played in the development of the French administration. The analysis below is restricted to the system of examinations which was introduced in 1883 and continued its use until 1940.[42]

Until the Meiji Restoration in 1868 some structural features of the social system in Japan resembled that of feudalistic Europe. Public offices were monopolized by the warrior caste of Samurai; these offices were inherited, and access to them by the bourgeois strata of society was possible only in exceptional cases. The core of the modernization process was the reform of the state administration, which began in 1868 and modeled itself on the systems of France, the United Kingdom, Prussia, and to some extent the United States. In 1874 two French legal experts were given positions at a newly founded law school to teach the first courses offered in law there. One of these was Émile Boissonade de Fontarabie, who in October of that year was commissioned to draft the first codification of Japanese laws. This was enacted into law, largely unchanged, in 1882.

The reform of the state bureaucracy oriented itself almost entirely on the Prussian model. A leading proponent of reform was Ito Hirobumi, one of the most prominent Japanese politicians at the end of the 19th century. With other members of the Japanese government he visited Europe in 1871-1873. This delegation was especially taken by the reforms of the Prussian bureaucracy. Several months were spent in Vienna with Prof. Lorenz von Stein, an immigrant from the German state of Schleswig-Holstein. Stein, an expert on constitutional issues and administrative reform, had taught between 1842 and 1855 at the University of Kiel but had been dismissed over his support for the political independence of his state. Between Ito and Stein there developed a particularly friendly relationship, and Ito attempted to convince Stein to come to Japan. Stein proposed instead that a number of Japanese civil servants concerned with questions of administrative reform be sent to study in Vienna.

The basic features of the Prussian administrative system regarding the training and selection of civil servants are briefly summarized here because the Prussian system served as a model for the bureaucratic reform in Japan:

(a) After completing the study of law at a university and passing the first state examination, the person being hired for the civil service received a one-year period of initial training in the court system. This training was the same for future judges and for future administrators. The trainee, at least 20 years old, had be able to support himself financially, for during the training period he received no salary.

(b) After this year came the second examination in law; those who passed had the status of "junior lawyer." They then served a three- or four-year period as apprentice. At this stage the training of judges and that of administrators were separated; future judges remained in the court system while future administrators transferred to the bureaucracy. Also during this apprenticeship no salary was paid to the trainee.

(c) Upon finishing this apprenticeship the trainee took the third examination, which was given only in Berlin; those who passed had the status of "assessor." At this point the trainee was qualified to fill a vacancy in the civil service, for which he finally received a salary. However, as a result of the relative scarcity of vacancies there were generally hundreds of "assessors" who had been waiting years for a position (Hattenhauer 1980, pp. 253-254).

(d) In the state administration there was a monopoly on the part of lawyers. Law study was regarded as the mandatory educational path for all higher positions, for it was the job of the bureaucrat to "apply the law." Homogeneity throughout the bureaucracy was thus the product of a common university study and, more particularly in fact, the common training which future civil servants underwent after completing university study. The 5 years of training not only ensured homogeneity among civil servants, however; it also provided the bureaucracy an extended period during which it could observe and, ultimately, select among the potential applicants for positions. Both the chronic scarcity of vacancies and the need to support oneself during this long period furthermore ensured that the hopefuls for civil service appointments would not harbor republican attitudes.

In the years after his trip to Europe Ito was, with varying success, a major proponent calling for the adoption of this approach in Japan. One feature that made this approach – a bureaucracy based upon bureaucrats selected by qualifications and competence – particularly attractive in Ito's view as a model for Japan was the way in which it created a monarchist-conservative *esprit de corps* among civil servants (Spaulding 1967, p. 49).

The Prussian system, however, could not be adopted directly in a cultural context with traditions and values so different from those in Prussia. A serious drawback initially was the lack of sufficient university capacity to produce enough of the needed law students. Since the few state-run law schools that existed in Japan were unable to provide the formal qualifications to enough potential civil servants, these schools were united and expanded into an "imperial" university, Todai University. In later years other "imperial," i.e., state, universities were founded.

In contrast to Europe, where universities existed prior to the expansion of the bureaucracy, in Japan *the two systems were developed parallel to one another*. At least in the early years it was the bureaucracy which dictated the rate of university expansion, and under these conditions it is therefore not surprising that the universities were clearly "servants" of the bureaucracy. The curriculum, duration, and overall capacity had to conform to the needs of the bureaucracy. Since Japan adopted the Prussian civil service system, with its lawyer monopoly, law schools were the first institutions of higher education to be founded there, and until the Second World War they remained the dominant colleges within the state universities.

One way in which the Japanese bureaucracy departed from the Prussian model was that civil servants were not recruited directly from the university. A complicated system of examinations was instituted for the various branches of the administration, and it was a basic principle in Japan that civil service applicants had to pass these examinations. Controversy continued from the reform of 1880 until the Second World War over how these examinations were to be organized, what they should include, who was to do the testing, and, most particularly, whether certain university graduates may be allowed direct access to the civil service *without* taking the examinations. The debate over these questions is not presented in detail here; rather, we consider only the fundamental features of the Japanese examination system.

Without a unified system of higher education it was not possible originally to establish standards that would provide automatic entitlement to the civil service. In addition, there also existed no unified system of secondary education, and most of the students enrolled at universities had not attended proper high schools. In most cases those from the bourgeois upper strata had, following a lower level secondary school, completed a one- or two-year preparatory course at the university which qualified them for full matriculation. Study at the law college of a state university then lasted another 3 years.

Most students did not take such a preparatory course, however, and these then studied at private law schools. These schools received no financial support from the government and were therefore dependent upon the tuition fees charged of students. There was a clear difference in the quality of legal education provided by the state universities and by private schools, and this difference continued even after the First World War, when some private schools were permitted to call themselves "university" (e.g., Waseda).[43]

Since the educational system had not yet actually been developed into a "system" as such (Archer 1979), civil service examinations were instituted as a substitute for the standardization which university selection would otherwise have provided. Any Japanese male could take an examination, *regardless of his previous education*. However, higher level positions required the higher level examination, and this corresponded to a state law examination.

In time it was seen that some students without a breadth of general education managed to memorize and "cram" enough of the subjects in these examinations to be able to pass them; as a result, a preexamination was required of those who lacked the usual educational certificates. This included principally those from the private law schools, who had not completed the special preparatory course for university study (corresponding to the *Abitur* in Germany or *baccalauréat* in France) and in many cases had not even obtained a certificate from a lower level secondary school.[44]

Examinations were differentiated horizontally in terms of the specific branch of the bureaucracy for which they were given – general administration, judges and public attorneys, and diplomats – as well as vertically – for the various levels in the civil service. Regarding their historical adoption, most examinations originated in the period 1887-1893; these generally remained in use until the Second World War. In 1936 there were approximately 155 different civil service examinations, and the overall infrastructure involved in the testing procedures had become a major sector of the economy, with private preparatory classes, boarding schools, and publishing companies. On the black market it was also sometimes possible to obtain the answers in advance. Although the testing system underwent numerous controversial changes between 1887 and 1941, its basic principles, those deriving from the Prussian model, were not changed. Table 5.2 lists the years in which the various types of examinations were given; for general administration and the diplomatic service no examination was required after the training period (Spaulding 1967, p. 189).

Theoretically it was required of every applicant that he pass the higher examination for the branch to which he was applying. There were, however, exceptions. The chief among these were graduates of Todai University, who were not only accepted directly for civil service training but were in fact given priority in hiring. Only when vacancies were left

Table 5.2: Entrance Examinations in Japan, 1894-1941

	General administration	Judges and public attorneys	Diplomatic service
Preparatory examination (=high school level)	1894-1943	1906-1912 1923-1943	1894-1941
Higher examination (=university level)	1887-1890 1894-1943	1885-1943	1894-1941
Posttraining examination (=for "assessor")	-	1893-1945	-

after Todai University students had all been placed were graduates from other universities considered. Passing the examinations posed a very high hurdle. Of the 13,939 persons taking the higher examination between 1897 and 1912 only 1005 (7%) passed it; of the 43,095 taking it in the years 1928-1943 only 4466 (10%) passed. Between 1925 and 1945 a total of 22,833 took the preparatory examination, and of these only 2027 (9%) passed. One applicant is reported to taken the preparatory examination every year from 1921 to 1941, and failed each time, principally due to the required knowledge of a European language; in 1941 the Justice Ministry finally exempted him from having to pass the examination (Spaulding 1967, p. 265).

Anyone could, in principle, take one of these examinations, and in fact had the constitutional right to do so. As the low percentages of those passing indicate, on the other hand, hardly everyone stood a hope of success in doing so. Effectively a condition for this success was having survived a long, highly selective educational path. The questions on the examinations were largely based upon the curriculum of Todai University.

The examinations did not lead to the awarding of a formal educational certificate but were purely selective in nature, that is, they were intended exclusively for the purpose of filling vacancies in the government administration. The performance level required to pass was not fixed before the examination but was raised or lowered in terms of the number of vacancies to be filled at the time. This meant that those scoring lower than just that number of higher scoring applicants needed to fill the momentary vacancies stood no chance. As a result, for these the examination imposed in effect a "guillotine," similar to that in France with the *grands concours*.

Many attempts were made between 1880 and 1940 to abolish the automatic preference enjoyed by Todai University graduates. Although Parliament's jurisdiction explicitly excluded issues pertaining to civil service recruitment, numerous petitions were submitted demanding that graduates of Todai, as those from all other universities, be required to pass the examination. Often these gained the support of leading jurists and administrators. When reform laws were in fact approved by the lower house of Parliament, however, their fate was inevitably to be buried in committees of the upper house.

Between the Wars opposition to Todai students' exemption grew so great that all applicants, including those from the Todai university, were required to take the examination. Still, the latter's probability of success remained high, with some 40%-50% passing. This reform provided a common standard for judging the quality of the various law schools, and this only emphasized the difference between state universities, particularly Todai, and private universities – thus consolidating the role of the former as elite institutions. A graduate of Todai University was as good as assured of a career in the civil service, provided only that he sought one. Graduates of private universities, on the other hand, seldom managed to pass the examination. The obvious success of state university students in finding acceptance in the civil service increased the public recognition of their superiority and strengthened the differentiation between the "elite" state sector and the "mass" private sector in Japanese higher education.

An analysis conducted by Kubota (1969) concerning the preeducation of those employed in 1949-1959 in the three highest salary levels of the civil service found that 55.1% had attended one of the "big eight" secondary schools, and that fully 25.8% were graduates of the "number one" school in Tokyo.[45] Among those holding such leadership positions 92.4% had completed their studies at one of the "imperial" universities – 79% at Todai University in Tokyo. The analysis also found that the average age of these civil servants was 41 in 1949 and 45 in 1959. This means that most of the leaders of the Japanese bureaucracy had either passed the prewar examination or attended Todai University and were thus exempt from it.

After the Second World War the American occupation authorities attempted to reform Japanese civil service recruitment, in particular to break the monopoly enjoyed by Todai students. A number of studies have shown, however, that their initial success had been counteracted within 10 years, and that the recruitment conditions returned to those obtaining before the War. In 1949 graduates of Todai University comprised 58.7% of civil servants in the highest salary level; by 1959 their proportion had returned to its prewar level of 95%. The force of the country's tradition thus overcame the effects of occupation innovations, and its traditional practices resumed in the 1950's.[46]

Thus the educational path of a high ranking imperial civil servant began at one of the "big eight" elite schools before the Second World War and continued through an Imperial university, preferably at Tokyo. Here he studied law, where the curriculum corresponded in detail to the demands of the higher examination for acceptance into the government bureaucracy. Imperial universities were the key to this system. Their exclusivity guaranteed a bright career, even if no vacancies were available in the year in which the examination was taken.

Kubota (1969, p. 71) has argued that "the intellectual quality as well as the degree of homogeneity of the Japanese higher bureaucracy was extraordinarily high. Thus in their common background at Tokyo Imperial

University we find one of the most important sources of both the cohesiveness and the potential strength and effectiveness of this remarkable body of bureaucrats." The state bureaucracy was (and still is) the driving force behind the modernization process in Japan. Its homogeneity in terms of intellectual training and value orientation is "produced" by a few highly selective elite institutions.

Nevertheless, many graduates from state universities chose a career in the private economy, where they enjoyed substantial prestige, earned a higher salary, and were subject to a less strictly regulated life. The total number of Todai University alumni numbered 9443 in 1923; of these only 30% had positions in the civil service, and the rest were employed in the private sector (Spaulding 1967, p. 280): 18.7% in the state administration, 11.1% as judges or public attorneys, 9.2% as private attorneys, 32.4% in banks and large firms, and 28.6 in other positions.

The real center of power in Japan was the *government bureaucracy*. Parliament and political parties played only a minor role before the Second World War. Since the Meiji Restoration the influence of the aristocracy had also been largely eliminated. It was through the bureaucracy that the conservative political elites exercised power – essentially the commercial/industrial upper strata and the large land owners.[47] Recruitment to the bureaucracy consisted of a rigid selection system that was controlled by the bureaucracy itself. Within the bureaucracy this selection system augmented the effect of the long socialization of those who gained entry to it.

The bureaucracy and the university stabilized one another in their respective positions in the political system of Japan. The President of Todai University was almost always one of the 26 members of the Privy Council – the leaders of the conservative establishment who played a key role in the government bureaucracy. For the bureaucracy the university furnished the selection, socialization, and formal qualifications of its personnel; in return it was imbued with an aura of power and influence. Gaining admission to a university played a critical role in a person's life; being refused a degree (which seldom happened) ended his career. The certainty of a bright career which came with a degree from an "imperial" university legitimized this institution to impose its curriculum and value orientations upon the student body. Democratization of this system would have broken the symbiosis and threatened the power of both the university and the bureaucracy.

The system of examinations provided the selection procedure with the appearance of democratic openness. In formal terms it actually was more democratic than the Prussian system upon which it was modeled;

everyone enjoyed the right to take any examination that he wished, regardless of social and educational background. However, the failure rate of 90%-95% on these examinations demonstrates the sham of this democratic openness, especially when one considers the minority of the population who even attempted to pass them. At least into the postwar period civil servants were recruited directly from Todai University, without even taking an examination.

In the United States the Japanese system was held up for scorn by opponents of the Pendleton Act. They saw in the American spoils system more than merely a corrupt and inefficient administration; for them it was the best guarantee against an arrogant and hegemonic bureaucracy that thwarted the will of the people as expressed in their political parties. A bureaucracy which had to fear loosing its personnel every four years was not in the position to offer long-term career prospects, and few university graduates therefore considered looking for a job with the government. In Japan, on the other hand, the political elite took for granted a career in the bureaucracy; this self-assurance in their political position would never have been possible under the spoils system.

6

Expansion in Higher Education 1960-1990

This chapter concentrates on more recent trends in higher education in the different countries. It is not possible to provide a complete report of the expansion which has taken place during the past three decades. Rather, this chapter focuses on a few selected topics which are discussed in previous chapters and are analyzed in more detail here. In the first part (Sect. 6.1) the gender gap in higher education and the different patterns of expansion for men and women are discussed. The following section (6.2) analyzes the choice of university subject, and it is argued that the student's choice of subject may be interpreted as a secondary adaptation to changing labor market conditions. Finally, we ask to what extent have the different patterns of expansion influenced the social background of students (Sect. 6.3). Did the social composition of students change in the late 1980's?

6.1 The Gender Gap in Higher Education

From a comparative perspective one can see that enrollment rates in higher education over the past three decades have followed different patterns of expansion in the various countries. In Japan enrollment rates for men increased rapidly during the 1960's and 1970's; after 1980 they first declined and then remained at approximately the same level for the rest of the decade. In the early 1990's they were still lower than in 1980, which was a turning point for university enrollment in Japan (Fig. 6.2). A similar pattern is found for men in the United States, with enrollment rates increasing until 1974, declining in the following years, and increasing again although at low growth rates until 1991 when the rate was still well below the peak of 1974 (Fig. 6.3).

A different pattern is found in Germany (Fig. 6.1), where enrollment rates have continuously increased, despite the worst economic recession since the Second World War and rigid bureaucratic regulations introduced to control university enrollment (*Numerus clausus*). A similar pattern of continuous expansion is found in France during this period (not shown here). Thus, in the period 1960-1990 we find a pattern of decline and stasis in the United States and Japan (for men), and a pattern of almost unbroken expansion in Germany and France (for men and women).

The enrollment of women increased in all countries between 1960 and 1990, and women can certainly be regarded as the "winners" in the expansion and the liberalization of educational policies, particularly in the European countries (Castles and Marceau 1989). Again, however, we find remarkable differences in the pattern of expansion between men and women in the different countries. Enrollment rates of men and women in Germany expanded more or less similarly, but without changing the relative position of men and women. A higher proportion of women attend universities, but a still higher proportion of men are enrolled. Social inequality between men and women – as far as this is expressed in participation rates in higher education – has been reproduced on a higher level; their relative position remained by and large unchanged.

In Japan the absolute difference between men and women in enrollment rates did not decline, but increased between 1960 and 1990.[1] More and more women attend four-year institutions of higher education in Japan, but they have been unable to catch up with men during the period considered here. Thus, the "modernization gap" between Japanese men and women has widened, and men have been successful in defending their privileges – at least as far as higher education is concerned. Fewer than 10% of young Japanese women obtain a *qualified* academic education, compared to more than 40% of men (1991).

A different pattern of expansion is found in the United States. In 1990 the majority of students at all institutions of higher education were women. The United States is the only country in which the relative position of men and women was reversed between 1960 and 1990. The number of women surpassed that of men not only at community colleges but also at state universities, despite a deep economic recession and deteriorating labor market conditions. It has already been argued that there is a close correspondence between participation in higher education and the relative power position of different social groups in society. Those who are excluded from university are subsequently excluded from high-status positions in the state bureaucracy and corporate business (Chap. 2). The exceptional pattern of expansion, as shown in Fig. 6.3, suggests that the role of women in American society has changed more

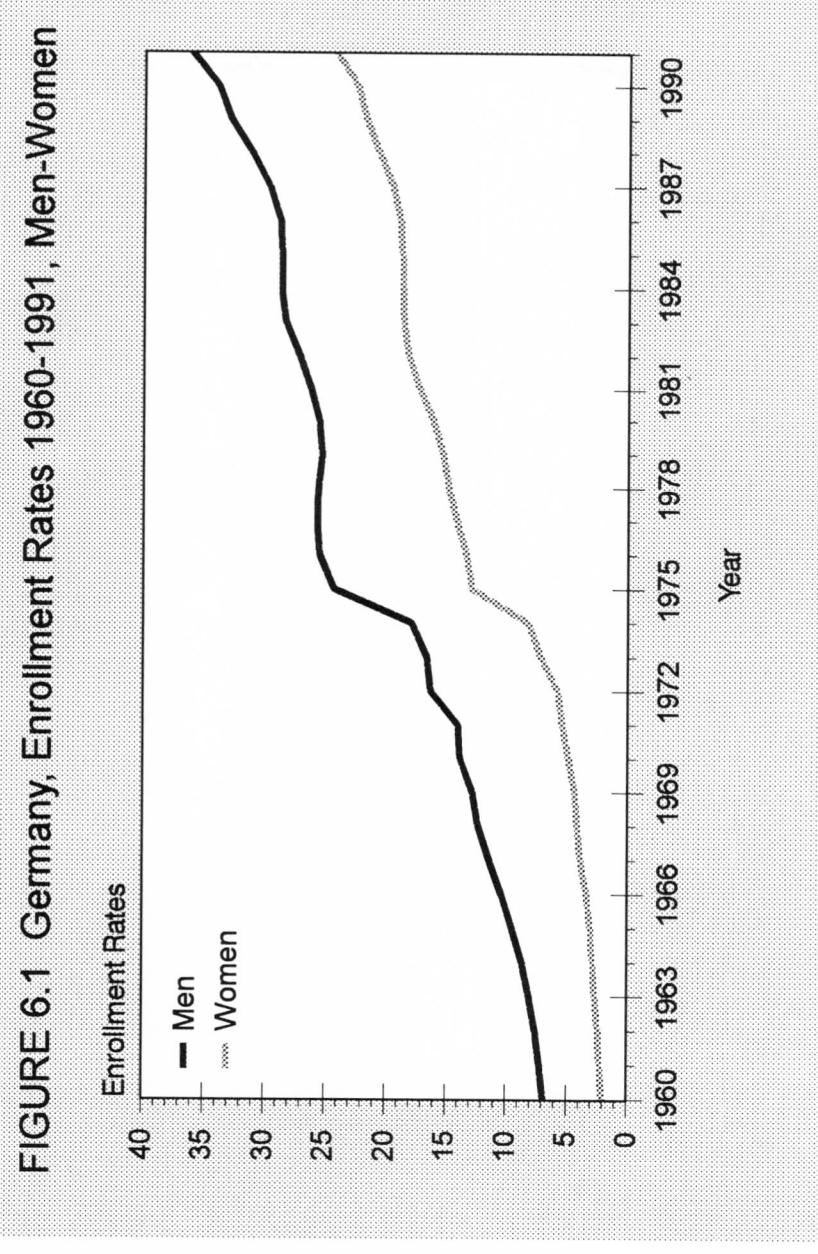

FIGURE 6.1 Germany, Enrollment Rates 1960-1991, Men-Women

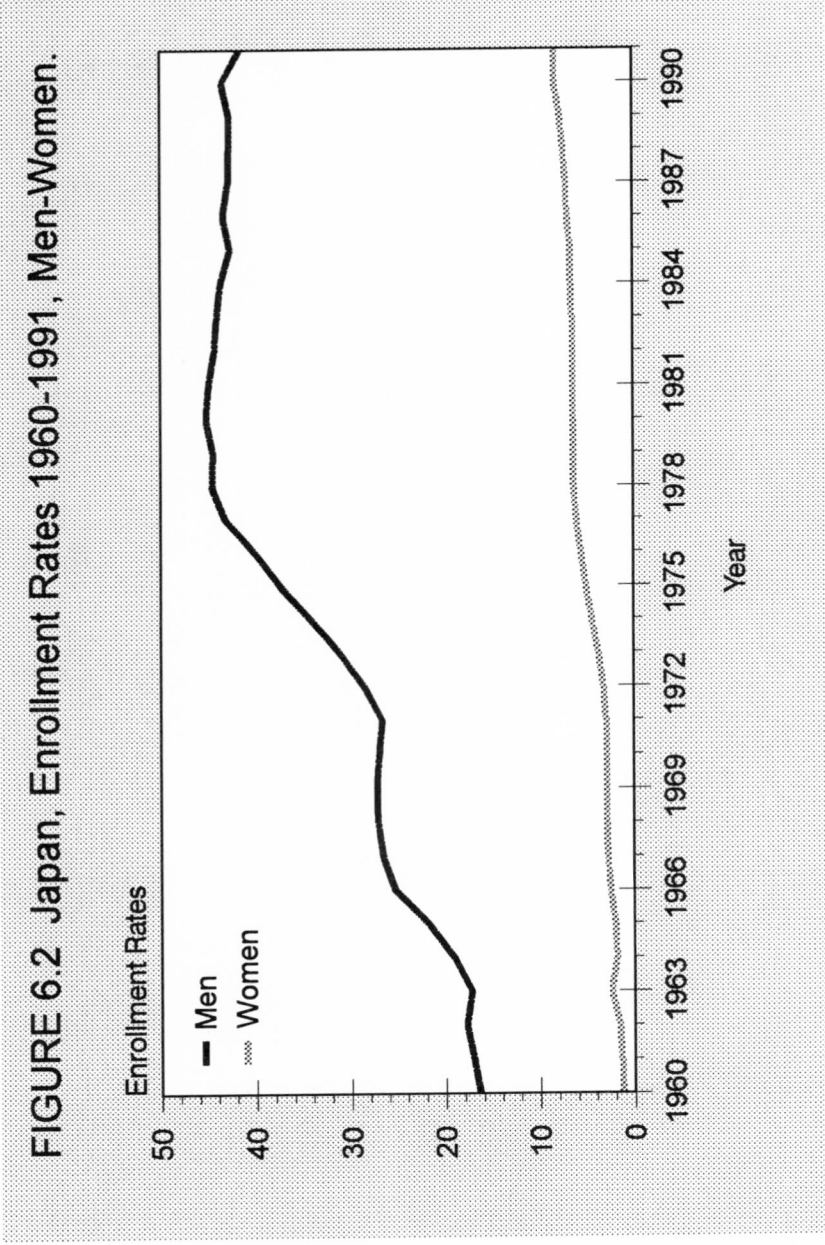

FIGURE 6.2 Japan, Enrollment Rates 1960-1991, Men-Women.

FIGURE 6.3 United States, Enrollment Rates 1960-1991, Men-Women

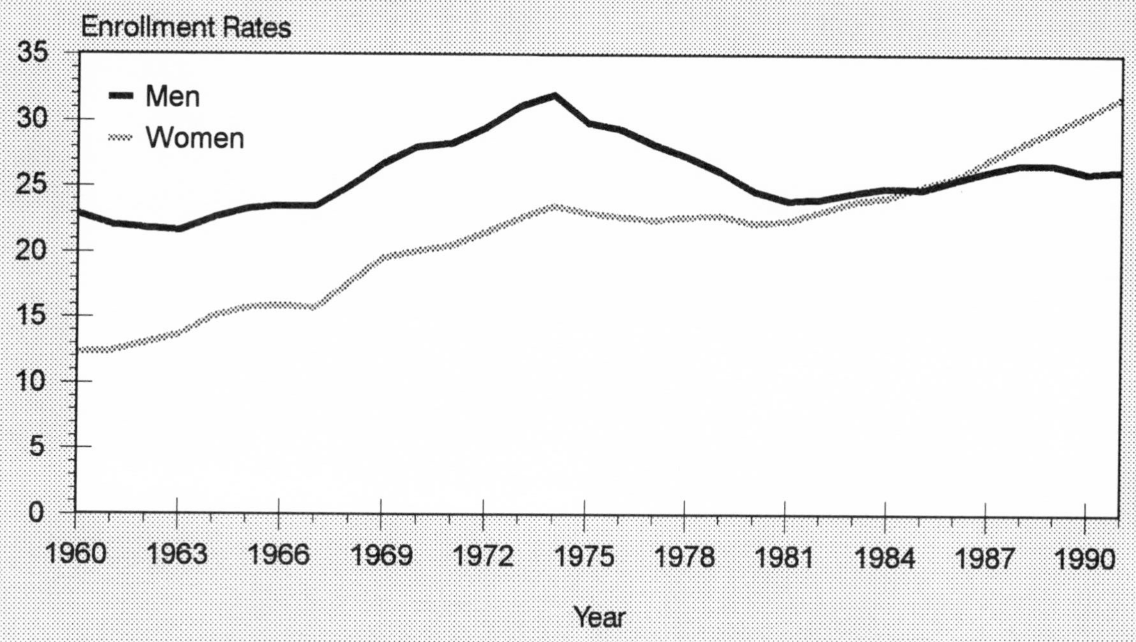

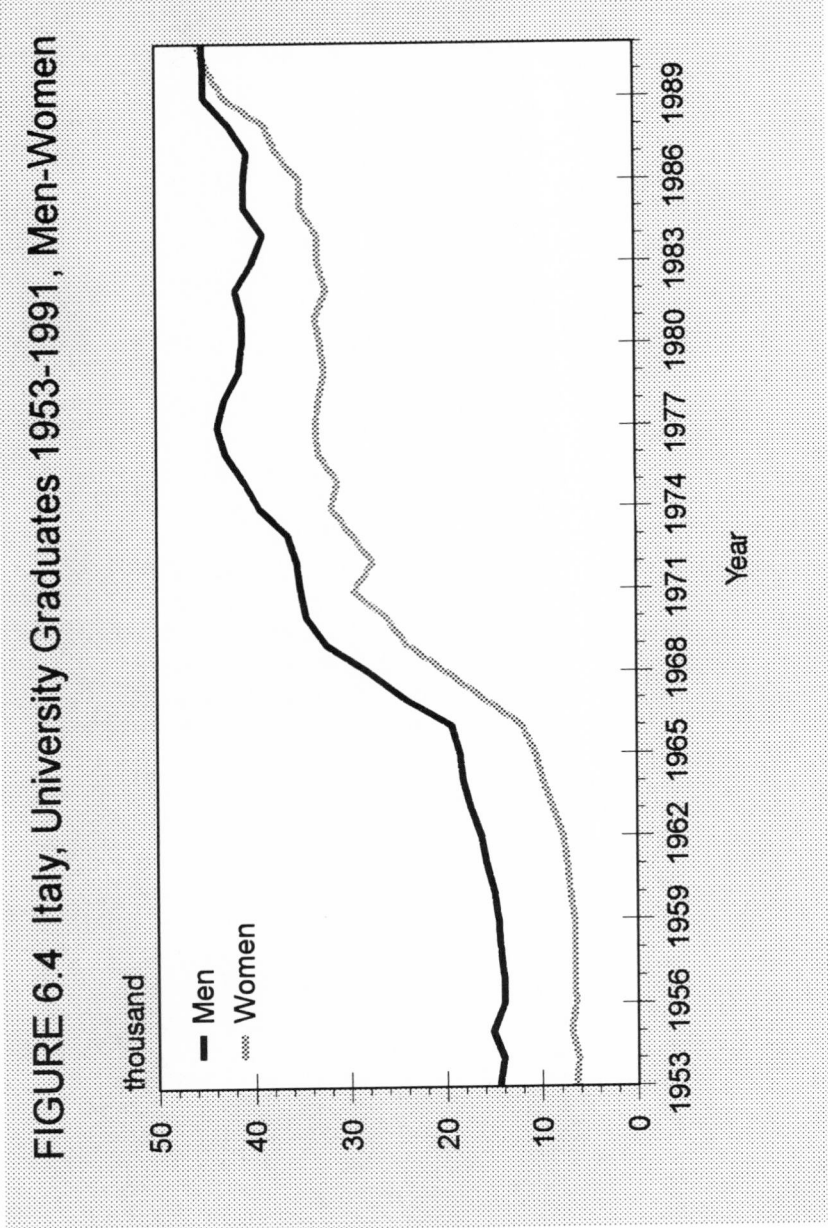

FIGURE 6.4 Italy, University Graduates 1953-1991, Men-Women

fundamentally than that in any of the other countries compared here.

In Italy we find still another pattern. Enrollment rates of men are still slightly higher than those of women,[2] but because of the lower drop-out rates of the latter the number of female university graduates (*laureati*) was as high as those of men in the early 1990's (Fig. 6.4).

Thus, in these four countries we find four different patterns of expansion for men and women. In Germany men and women increased their participation in higher education *pari passu* without changing their relative position; in Japan the gap in enrollment in four-year institutions widened between 1960 and 1990; in the United States women surpassed men in higher education; and in Italy women caught up with men, and their graduation rate is now as high as that for men.

How can we explain these different patterns of expansion? Why did enrollment rates for men remain constant for almost a decade in Japan and the United States, while they strongly increased in Germany and France? Why is it that only in the United States the enrollment rate for women is higher than that for men, while the difference between men and women has remained approximately constant in Germany but increased in Japan?

The technological and economic conditions have been similar in each of these countries. After 1975 there were worldwide economic recessions, and the oil crises and microelectronic "revolution" forced structural change and adaption of the national economy which led to high unemployment rates in all but one of the countries (Japan). Why have men reacted to changing labor market conditions in some countries, but not in all? Why have women increased their enrollment rates regardless of economic recessions and high unemployment?[3]

The explanations that have been offered by educational sociologists and economists refer almost exclusively to individual preferences. This is true for the proponents of the human capital theory as well as for those of Boudon's thesis (1977) of "perverse effects": individual preferences for social mobility, higher income, and status are the driving forces behind the expansion. In Boudon's model the unbroken expansion is the paradoxical effect of individual status competition, for each individual follows a simple rule: the more the better. The human capital theory assumes that individual actors gear their decisions to the economic conditions in the labor market: enrollment rates increase and decrease directly with the rates of return during the business cycle.

Some of the patterns of expansion shown in Figs. 6.1.-6.4 are compatible with Boudon's model of "perverse effects," others with the human capital theory, and still others with neither of these. One could argue that the human capital theory explains the decline and stasis of enrollment rates in the United States and Japan: with the decline in economic growth rates the demand for university graduates also decreased, and hence a smaller proportion of each cohort decided to attend university.[4] However, we expect similar reactions to the labor market in Germany as in the United States, and the theory does not predict that women should behave differently from men.

Boudon's model might explain the unbroken expansion in Germany and France. With rising unemployment the competition for the few remaining vacancies increases, and students try to improve their competitive position by acquiring more credentials. This model, however, fails to explain the pattern of expansion in the United States and Japan. In the United States only women continuously increased their enrollment rates, while men reacted differently.

It is argued here that enrollment rates are not only the aggregate outcome of individual preferences and aspirations but are also strongly influenced by the institutional background in each country, the political ideology, and changing recruitment practices of companies and the state. Cohorts which entered university in the early 1960's were strongly encouraged by the then prevalent political ideology that more education means more economic growth and more technological progress. American politicians were shocked by the loss of scientific and technological superiority (the "sputnik shock") and the loss of the dominant economic position of the United States in the world market. Politicians in the European countries worried about the relative backwardness of their countries in comparison to the American world power. Ten years later, in the mid-1970's, Freeman (1976) wrote his influential book on the "Overeducated American." His simple message – that there are too many students – was reinforced by deteriorating labor market conditions and may have discouraged many young men from attending university.

The decisions of individuals belonging to successive cohorts are influenced by contingent political, economic, and ideological circumstances which change over time and may have countervailing effects on their preferences for higher education. Moreover, different institutional and political arrangements may shape the reaction to the labor market in the various countries in different ways. For instance, in many European countries, particularly in Germany, a high proportion of the costs of higher education are paid by the state, whereas in the United States and Japan students (or their families) spend a substantial proportion of their income on university fees. We may assume that the higher the proportion of expenses for higher education to be paid by students or their families, the more strongly they react to the business cycle. Conversely, the higher the proportion of expenses for higher education paid by the state the less "elastic" are enrollment rates with respect to the labor market. In Germany and at most state institutions in France students can afford to attend university regardless of high or low unemployment because state universities do not charge fees.

Taking these institutional and economic constraints into account, the different patterns of expansion during the period 1960-1990 may be explained by a combination of factors which coincided in the different countries:

Since the mid-1970's Japan and the United States were hit by declining economic growth rates (oil crisis) and less favorable labor market conditions. A more conservative political and ideological environment discouraged the younger generation from participating in higher education ("overeducation"). In the United States a rising national debt, substantial cuts in the government budget for education, and growing unemployment rates among college graduates are additional constraints which may explain the decreasing enrollment rates for men in the late 1970's. Germany and France faced similar conditions, but here higher education is something of a "public good." The children of the middle class may attend university almost as long as they wish, and they prefer the status of a student as a "cheap" alternative to unemployment.[5]

This may be a cogent explanation for the pattern of enrollment rates for men, but certainly not for women in the United States. Women suffered from the economic recession as well as men, and they must pay the (sometimes exorbitant) fees of American universities as well as do their male counterparts. Nevertheless, American women increased their participation rate in higher education despite rising costs for education and gloomy prospects in the labor market. The number of women surpassed that of men at American universities during a decade characterized by economic depression, a declining position of the American economy in the world market, and a shift towards more conservative educational policies. The more recent increase in enrollment rates cannot be explained by a catch-up effect because their numbers surged ahead of those for men in higher education as early as the mid-1980's.

One might argue that poor job opportunities and a depressed economy are irrelevant for women's decision to enroll in higher education. Their attitudes are shaped by a political movement and the political struggle for emancipation, equal rights, and nondiscrimination.[6] Therefore women chose to go to university regardless of whether unemployment is low or high, and regardless of whether they are encouraged to do so or not.

Moreover, higher education is attractive even for those women who do not actively identify with the women's movement. The aspiration for higher education and a university degree does not conflict with the traditional attributes of the female role in society. In meritocratic societies a university degree allows women to compete with men on an equal standing.

Again, however, this explanation may be plausible for the pattern of university enrollment for women in the United States and perhaps in Italy, but not in Germany, and certainly not in Japan. Neither German nor Japanese women were successful in overcoming the gender gap in higher education. Moreover, German women pay a lower proportion of costs for higher education than American women, i.e., they could have achieved their emancipation at lower private costs than did American women.

We began with economic variables to explain the enrollment patterns of men in the United States and Japan, but the explanation failed when applied to women's pattern of enrollment in Italy and the United States. Next, "political" variables were added to take into account these deviant cases, for instance, the women's movement for emancipation and equal rights. Even this enlarged model, however, failed to explain the enrollment pattern of women in Germany, and certainly that in Japan. One could enlarge the model again to include culture as a *passe-partout*, but these ad hoc amendments to the model after it has failed to account for specific historical developments in different countries are, of course, unconvincing.

Both the concept of human capital and Boudon's model of status competition are "universalistic" models in that they seek to explain the pattern of expansion of higher education in all advanced industrialized countries. The human capital theory expects individuals to react to labor market conditions with rising or declining participation rates in higher education regardless of the institutional background. Similarly Boudon's concept of "perverse effects" predicts that individuals react to gloomy prospects in the labor market by more ruthless competition. However, again, this model does not take into account whether education is expensive or a quasi-public good, whether successive cohorts are supported by a liberal educational policy, or whether they are discouraged by conservative ideologies.

One need not argue that it is "culture" which prevents German or Japanese women from closing the gender gap in higher education. A careful analysis of institutional variables is required to explain the different patterns of educational expansion between men and women in different countries. Affirmative action in the United States is a political institution[7] which has forced companies to open professional careers for women – an institution which is not strongly developed in Japan or in Germany. For American women it pays to attend university because their job opportunities in the corporate world are better than those for women in German or Japanese companies. Comparison of the different divorce rates in the United States and Japan shows that American women are forced to invest in their education because they face a higher probability of having to care for themselves and their children later in life. It is beyond the scope of this chapter to analyze institutional differences between the various countries in detail, but it is evident that simple universalistic theories of higher education do not suffice to explain the complex patterns of expansion shown in Figs. 6.1-6.4. There are different paths to "modernization" and even those countries which have achieved similar levels of economic and technological development have, nevertheless, preserved traditional institutions and educational systems.

Trow (1974) has suggested that the expansion of higher education follows a "three-stage model": from elite to mass education, and from mass education to universalistic education. For secondary education this model proves correct in some but not in all countries. In the United States and Japan secondary education was offered only to a minority before the First World War (fewer than 10% of a cohort); it reached the level of mass education during the interwar period (50% of a cohort) and finally moved to the universalistic stage after the Second World War (up to 90% of a cohort). Higher education moved from elite to mass education, but in no country in the world has enrollment in higher education reached the "universalistic" level (more than 75% of a cohort). One might speculate as to whether the long period of decline and stasis in enrollment rates for men observed since the mid-1970's in the United States and later in Japan indicates an absolute ceiling for university education which no country is able to pass – for whatever reasons.[8] I shall not speculate on the idea of a ceiling for higher education but shall return to this problem in Chap. 7, where cycles of higher education are analyzed over a long period of time.

In the next section we observe that enrollment in some university subjects fluctuates strongly over time, and these fluctuations may be interpreted as a secondary adjustment to changing labor market conditions. Students may go to university regardless of the actual labor market conditions, but they take into account future job opportunities by the type of subject they choose.

6.2 Choice of Major Field of Study

The fact that variations in the economic cycle and the high unemployment figures have had little obvious effect upon educational expansion in some countries may indeed indicate a decoupling of the educational system from the labor market, but it does not mean that students completely ignore the altered opportunities which this entails for pursuing a career. Their response may be to select a different subject than that which they would otherwise have chosen rather than deciding not to study at all. Among the trends suggesting this are the decline in the number enrolled in subjects leading to a career in teaching and the growth in the numbers studying business and management or computer science – a trend which could be observed in the United States during the 1970's and 10 years later in Germany.

Beneath the surface of a relatively stable expansionary course for the *overall* university, enrollment in the individual subjects show strong cyclical variations. The regularity of the overall expansion and the strong cyclical variations in individual university subjects suggests that the process of choosing one's educational career falls into two phases. The first is to *whether* to study, and this decision is made fairly independently of economic considerations in regard to the business cycle or labor market conditions. For those who do decide to enroll in a university, the second question to be answered is *what* to study. It is at this point, in the choice of subject and not over matriculation per se, that factors related to labor market conditions may play a role. Many students do react to such economic signals, but they do not let gloomy economic predictions discourage them from seeking a university degree in one field or another.

One implication that government education authorities can draw from this is that university enrollment rates cannot be influenced substantially by political measures, whereas efforts may indeed prove successful which aim at guiding students to certain subjects by advertising the relative employment prospects in different fields.

Nevertheless, any success which this means of adapting to market conditions might have can only be temporary. This is not only because long-term predictions about future personnel needs in the various fields often prove incorrect, but also because such predictions themselves may – through their very success in influencing students in a certain direction – alter conditions in a way that lead to under- or oversupply in fields other than in those as predicted. The most recent example of such a catch-22 in predictions about future occupational vacancies is that of business and management studies, which recently seemed a subject of such promising prospects that an influx of students into it may within a few years outstrip the ability of the economy to accommodate all the new graduates with university degrees in the field. The expansion of this subject in many countries over recent years demonstrates the way in which the requirement of university education can, in effect, become trivialized. If all administrative employees become "managers," and all managers must be trained academically, the job prospects of those so trained will remain bright for only a while.

The employment prospects of all university graduates have suffered during the 1980's by the coincidence of several socio-economic changes: First and most important is the rising unemployment. Second, the growing national debt seriously constrains the ability of the government to hire additional civil servants. This factor is particularly important for Germany where a high proportion of university graduates have traditionally been hired by the civil service (see Chap. 5). At the beginning of the 1970's the government still hired some 70%-80% of university graduates in Germany, but today the figure has shrunk to only 10% in some fields. Services in the public sector have already expanded to their economic and political limits. Health services are under pressure to rationalize and will not be expanding in coming years. The educational system, until recently itself one of the major employers of its own products, is not even hiring enough personnel to fill its existing vacancies, due to the declining birth rate. In Germany educational experts have warned that because of the declining numbers of pupils in the schools it is possible that no teachers will be hired before the year 2000. The nation's birthrate has fallen so sharply that even with such a bar to new hiring the teacher to pupil ratio would still rise.

Conditions are just as dismal for jobs in the government administration. In Germany some 30% of all law graduates formerly found jobs here, but by 1984 the proportion had fallen to only 2%-3% in some states. Private law practice has also lost its former attractiveness, as the number of attorneys rose from 23,600 in 1970 to almost 47,000 in 1984. The competition has become discouraging especially for those just leaving university.

Once all fields reach the saturation point, the choice of subject may as well be random, as far as employment prospects are concerned, and an individual's studies can no longer be oriented to the relative occupational prospects that await him or her after obtaining a degree. Everyone could just as well study whatever they please, and there are in fact some signs that this attitude is gaining ground among students. However, the majority of students do behave "rationally" and are aware of the job prospects that they can expect. In general, there has been a trend away from subjects leading to employment in the *public* sector and to those for the *private* sector. Fewer students are enrolled in the study of German, English literature, and other teaching subjects, and more in business and engineering subjects.

Whether such a strategy on the part of "rational" students brings the expected success cannot be foreseen. In any case, a growing hoard of university graduates will be pouring into the private sector - due both to the high birthrates of earlier years and to the reorientation of today's students. Many who would formerly have chosen subjects in the humanities in the anticipation of finding employment in schools and in the civil service are now hoping instead with a degree in business, law, or engineering to find a position in the private service sector.

(a) The following tables portray the shift in student preferences regarding the subjects studied at university. For *Germany* a consistent time series is not possible due to the integration of specialized colleges (*Fachhochschulen*) into the overall university system. The left side of Table 6.1 shows the change in subject preferences from 1960 to 1972; the right side shows the change between 1977 and 1992.[9]

Aside from shifts between relatively minor subjects, two major trends can be seen in the first period. The proportion of men beginning study in engineering decreased from 20% to 13% while that in teaching increased from 7% to 12%. Natural sciences also expanded, from 16% to 20%, many of which students would also become teachers (*Gymnasium*). The proportion of women in medicine declined from 18% to 8%, while the number in teaching subjects rose from 34% to 37%. Thus the concentration of women upon a profession in which they have traditionally been dominant did not weaken in this period of expansion but rather strengthened. More then two thirds of female students were concentrated in only two subject groups: humanities and teaching. This low degree of diversification in the choice of subject increased their risk of becoming unemployed in later years (see Table 6A in the Appendix to this chapter).

The shifts during the expansionary years can be explained by the increased demand within the educational system itself, for the expansion was possible only by the hiring of additional personnel for the schools and universities. The students have therefore reacted here in their choice of subject and future career in terms of the employment prospects available. In the second phase, however, when the expansion slowed and fewer new personnel were needed, the shift was once again away from teaching subjects.

Table 6.1: Graduates by Major Subject, Germany, 1960-1992

	Period I				Period II							
	Men		Women		Men				Women			
	1960	1972	1960	1972	1977	1983	1992	1992*	1977	1983	1992	1992*
	%	%	%	%	%	%	%	%	%	%	%	%
Business, economics social sciences	25	25	10	10	26	28	28	30	20	26	30	35
Engineering	20	13	1	1	26	26	30	34	4	5	7	7
Humanities	18	17	29	30	17	14	12	10	41	35	32	30
Mathematics, natural sciences	16	20	6	10	17	16	18	18	16	14	14	15
Medicine	10	11	18	8	7	8	6	3	6	8	7	4
Arts	0	1	1	1	4	4	3	2	8	7	7	5
Education teaching	7	12	34	37	+	4	+	+	+	13	+	+
All Students (in 1000)	131	293	49	141	544	696	1004	168	280	437	635	110

Period I (1960-1972): Only university students (excluding students at specialized colleges);
Period II (1977-1992): All students (including students at specialized colleges).
+ Data not available. * Only first-year students in 1992. Columns do not add to 100% because
only particular subjects are presented. Sources: See Appendix I.

Between 1977 and 1992 students left subjects for which the public sector had offered the principal employer: This is particularly evident in the last column of the Table (1992*) where the subject choice of the *beginning* students are shown. The proportion of men in humanities subjects fell from 17% to 10% and that of women from 41% to 30%. The total preparing for a career in teaching stabilized at the end of the 1980's at about 4%-5% for men and 13%-14% for women. Those enrolling in medicine decreased from 7% to 3% among men and from 8% (1983) to 4% among women.

The proportion of men enrolling in engineering rose from 26% to 34%. A major shift among women is seen to economics and the social sciences, with their proportion here rising from 20% to 35%; more women were choosing to become managers, judges, or attorneys, and fewer teachers and physicians. The effective closing off of civil service paths had forced these changes.

Between 1977 and 1991 the total number of (beginning) students increased by 96%, but this overall increase was not distributed evenly between the sexes or across subjects. The greatest increases were among women in the subjects of economics/business and management (+ 523%) and law (196%), while the increase in men studying law was below average (+ 36%).

Due to women's traditional orientation to teaching jobs the decline in new positions in the educational system itself had a greater impact upon them than upon men. Since the beginning of the 1980's women have chosen economics and law rather that engineering, as these have a closer affinity to their traditional areas of interest. In 1977, 4% of women had chosen engineering, this proportion rose to only 7% in 1992. Because of the high influx of women into business and law competition in the legal profession and among managers can be expected to increase in coming years.

(b) Similar data for the *United States* are presented in Table 6.2, which shows the proportions obtaining a bachelor's degree in the various years. Among the "losers" in the competition for students are the subjects of teaching, humanities (letters), and social sciences, while the "winners" include those of business and management, computer science, health (nurses), and communication (journalism). The proportion of female students obtaining a teaching certificate declined from 46% in 1960 to 15% in 1990; during the same period the proportion obtaining a degree in business and management rose from 3% to 21%, compared to the increase among men from 21% to 27% (Jacobs 1995). By 1975 the proportion of men receiving an engineering degree had declined from 16% to 9%, only to rise again thereafter (to 17% in 1987). Particularly in this regard one sees that students try to respond to that which they perceive as "signals" from the labor market and orient their choice of subject in terms of likely income and career prospects. Figures in Table 6.2 also illustrate the cyclical character of enrollment in many subjects over the 30-year period (e.g., in social sciences and engineering).[10]

The reorientation among women in regard to careers in law and medicine is striking. Whereas in 1960 only 240 women obtained a first professional degree in law, 15,400 did so in 1990. During the same period the number receiving a first professional degree in medicine rose from 420 to 10,000; the interest organizations for physicians are particularly strong (Starr 1982), and this may explain their relatively modest increase – vis-à-vis law – in this subject. Although women made up 40% of the American student population even before the Second World War, they were admitted to the legal and medical professions only in the early 1960's.

A number of differences are evident between the distribution of students in the United States and that in Germany. In the United States 15%-17% of males study engineering as opposed to 30%-34% in Germany. In the United States 27% of men and 21% of women receive degrees in business and management, but only 15% of men and 13% of women enroll in business and management in Germany. A number of analyses have shown that these differences are not due to technological factors (e.g., product or production technology) but to different forms for the organization of production. Cultural and nationally specific factors exert a substantial impact on the form that the division of labor takes in various countries, and thereby on the job prospects of different occupations.

A substantially larger proportion of the overall workforce in American companies than in their German counterparts are employed as "managers." If two companies were chosen of similar size and producing a similar product with a similar technology – one company in the United States and the other in Germany (matched pairs) – we would find different organizational structures and a different division of labor in the two countries; among other structural differences the American company would likely employ a significantly higher proportion of managers and a

Table 6.2: Bachelor's Degrees by Major Field of Study and First Professional Degrees (law, medicine), United States, 1960-1990

	Men						Women					
	1960	1965	1970	1975	1980	1990	1960	1965	1970	1975	1980	1990
	%	%	%	%	%	%	%	%	%	%	%	%
Education	11	10	10	9	6	5	46	43	36	29	18	15
Engineering	16	12	10	9	14	15	-	-	-	-	2	2
Business and management	21	20	22	22	27	27	3	2	3	5	16	21
Social sciences	16	20	21	17	12	13	12	13	16	12	10	7
Letters	4	6	7	6	4	3	12	16	16	11	7	6
Health sciences	-	-	1	2	2	2	5	5	5	9	13	9
Physical sciences	6	6	4	4	4	2	1	1	1	1	1	1
Communication	1	1	1	4	3	4	-	-	1	2	4	6
Computer sciences	-	-	-	1	2	5	-	-	-	-	1	2
All Students (in 1000)	231	280	476	508	470	490	139	213	364	423	465	557
Law* (in 1000)	9.0	12.8	16.1	26.1	24.6	21.1	0.2	0.5	1.2	6.2	11.8	15.4
Medicine* (in 1000)	9.9	10.3	11.8	16.4	16.3	18.4	0.4	0.5	0.9	2.4	4.6	10.0

* First professional degrees.   Columns do not add to 100% because only particular fields of study are presented.   Sources: See Appendix I.

significantly lower proportion of manual workers compared to their German counterpart.[11] The division of labor and the assignment of work tasks and responsibilities to managers and employees varies from country to country and is anticipated in the "preferences" of students for particular university subjects.[12]

The interesting question from a causal point of view is of course: Do more American students choose business and management as their university major because there are more managerial jobs in the United States (compared to Germany); or are there more managerial jobs in the United States because more students have been trained in business and management? If the latter is the case, then the educational system exerts considerable influence on the division of labor and the organization of work responsibilities: the demand for qualified labor is conditioned in advance by its supply. This point cannot be elaborated here in more detail and the reader is referred to the relevant literature (Maurice et al. 1986). However, it should be clear that national differences in the distribution of students over different university subjects is not "accidental"; mutual adaptation processes between the education system and the organization of work tasks have shaped this distribution over time.

(c) The data on choice of university subject in *Japan* (Table 6.3) indicate, first of all, the great stability in its distribution over the period 1959-1992. No genuinely significant change is seen among men between 1971 and 1992. It is striking in the Japanese data that about one-third of Japanese men enroll in economics/business – even in relation to the figures for the United States a very high proportion.[13] The choice among male students thus shows little diversification and little variation over time.

Certain shifts did take place in the 1960's; these have since stabilized. The proportion in teaching (including the humanities) decreased, while engineering underwent an above-average expansion. The changes resemble those in the United States and Germany, except that the trend to subjects relevant particularly to the private sector has been even stronger in Japan. For women we observe a similar historical trend: they left education departments and enrolled in economics or business and management.

Japanese students, as their counterparts in other countries, are influenced in the choice of their university subjects not only by labor market prospects but by cultural values, and they show remarkable stability across phases in the business cycle. In a study of Japanese and German universities before the First World War Bartholomew (1978, p. 259) observed: "The percentages of students in the applied sciences of

Table 6.3: University Graduates by Major Field of Study, Japan, 1959-1992

	Men						Women		
	1959 %	1971 %	1975 %	1982 %	1987 %	1992 %	1982 %	1987 %	1992 %
Social sciences*	47	48	49	47	46	47	14	17	23
Economics/business	*	33	34	33	32	33	6	7	12
Law, politics	*	12	12	11	11	11	4	4	6
Sociology	*	2	2	3	3	3	5	5	5
Engineering	17	26	26	25	26	26	2	2	4
Humanities	13	7	7	8	7	7	35	36	35
Health sciences	4	3	5	6	6	5	9	9	8
Education	9	4	4	5	5	4	18	16	12
Natural sciences	2	3	3	4	4	4	2	2	2
Home economics	+	+	+	+	-	-	9	7	6
All Students (in millions)	0.5	1.1	1.3	1.3	1.4	1.5	0.4	0.5	0.6

Figures include only students at 4-year institutions (2-year colleges excluded).

Columns do not add to 100% because only particular fields of study are presented.

Figures for women are available only after 1980.

+ Figures not available. * "Social sciences" include economics, business and management, law, politics, sociology.   Source: See Appendix I.

engineering, agriculture, and medicine were virtually identical – 50.4% in Germany, 51.6% in Japan. But the differences in the figures for basic science and the humanities (or letters) were striking. The year World War I began, 13% of German university students were enrolled in basic science, but only 4.4% of Japanese university graduates had chosen a science major; similarly, the humanities had attracted 21.2% of the German students, only 8.5% of the Japanese students." While the percentages have changed in the meantime, Bartholomew's observations about the culturally specific pattern of subject choice are still valid. Only 4% of Japanese male students enroll in the natural sciences and 7% in the humanities.

While this historical summary does not present a systematic comparison of national differences, it does demonstrate the way in which the choice of subject among university students is influenced by nationally specific traditions and patterns of the division of labor. It shows which subjects are dominated by men and which by women, and the varying importance in social functions that an "academic" degree can have.

The stability of the choice of subject in Japan reflects the success which Japanese universities have had in insulating themselves from the influence of market forces. In contrast to the two-year colleges, which are open to largely all who apply, four-year universities receive more applicants each year than they can admit. Universities enjoy an effective monopoly which allows them, independently of changing labor market conditions, to expand or contract the size of their departments in terms of the needs or policy of the universities themselves. The relative distribution of students by subject indicates that the competition among departments has led to all of them participating roughly equally in the expansion that has occurred since 1971.

In the preceding sections it has been shown that patterns of educational expansion differ between countries; it has also been argued that the distribution of students over major fields of study varies between Germany, the United States and Japan. In the following section we ask whether patterns of social inequality have been changing during the past two decades.

6.3 The "Iron Law" of Social Reproduction

Research on elites and mobility has long felt the influence of the seminal thinker in the field, Vilfredo Pareto, and his concept of the circulation of elites. Pareto began with a simple two-class model of society: a ruling elite and the ruled masses. Between these two there existed for Pareto the possibility of exchange, as persons from the masses who are of outstanding ability climb up into and are assimilated by the upper social strata. "Because of the circulation of elites the ruling elite is constantly in a state of transformation. It flows like a river that today is never what it was yesterday. From time to time there occur sudden and violent eruptions. These revolutions always take place when in the ruling class – whether because of inadequate circulation or other causes – decadent elements collect which are no longer able to muster the force necessary to hold onto power and are too pusillanimous to use violence. In the meantime, persons of particular ability have gained power within the lower class who command the forces needed to carry out government functions, and who are prepared to use violence."[14]

Pareto's view of social mobility was not one founded simply on social justice; rather, he regarded it as an essential condition for stability in any society. Only by coopting and assimilating "new" elites emerging in the lower class can the ruling class legitimize and defend its position of power over time. To Pareto the circulation of elites is, as a rule, a violent and revolutionary process, and this explains the central role which the concept of violence plays in his theory. Because the ruling elites hold on to their power and deny new elites of the lower classes access to higher status positions the circulation process is usually enforced by violence and revolution.

Over the past century the "circulation of elites" has been tamed in modern industrial societies, and what previously occurred as "sudden and violent eruptions," appears today as social reform and peaceful evolution. A continual process of circulation through institutionalized mobility channels has replaced revolutionary upheavals. In modern democracies the educational institution, and in particular the university, provides the most important avenue of upward mobility. The selection processes of the university and the government bureaucracy determine the rate of exchange mobility (circulation) in a given country. This can be accelerated or slowed by a relative "opening" or "closure" of educational institutions, changes in selection criteria, or the introduction of selection procedures (e.g., entrance examinations). From the point of view of the "circulation of elites" one can analyze a country in terms of whether an exchange is taking place, the extent to which government institutions regulate the exchange, and the role of universities in determining the rate of exchange.

However, the expansion of universities cannot necessarily be taken as a factor facilitating the circulation of elites. Bourdieu and Passeron (1964), for example, have shown that ruling elites can use the university to protect their power and to restrict the circulation. In this case the upper strata monopolize the university and attempt to legitimize their political and economic position by means of academic certificates. The university thus becomes an instrument for the *social reproduction* of the ruling class. Bourdieu's provocative argument is that higher education does not accelerate the circulation of elites, but increases their power by legitimizing their dominant position. The ruling elite adds to its economic and political power the symbolic power of university degrees which transform their dominance into certified superiority: the ruling elite is not only powerful but intellectually superior.

The educational system serves as an instrument for social reproduction. The outcome of selective processes at the university shows that the "educational capital" can be handed down to the next generation as well as the "economic capital." Children of the civil service enter the civil service after graduating from university, and the *nouveaux riches* transform their economic capital into educational capital and bequeath both resources to the next generation.

In Chapter 2 the role of the university in the reproduction of social classes was analyzed for the period 1870-1939. It has been shown that before the First World War the German aristocracy acquired university

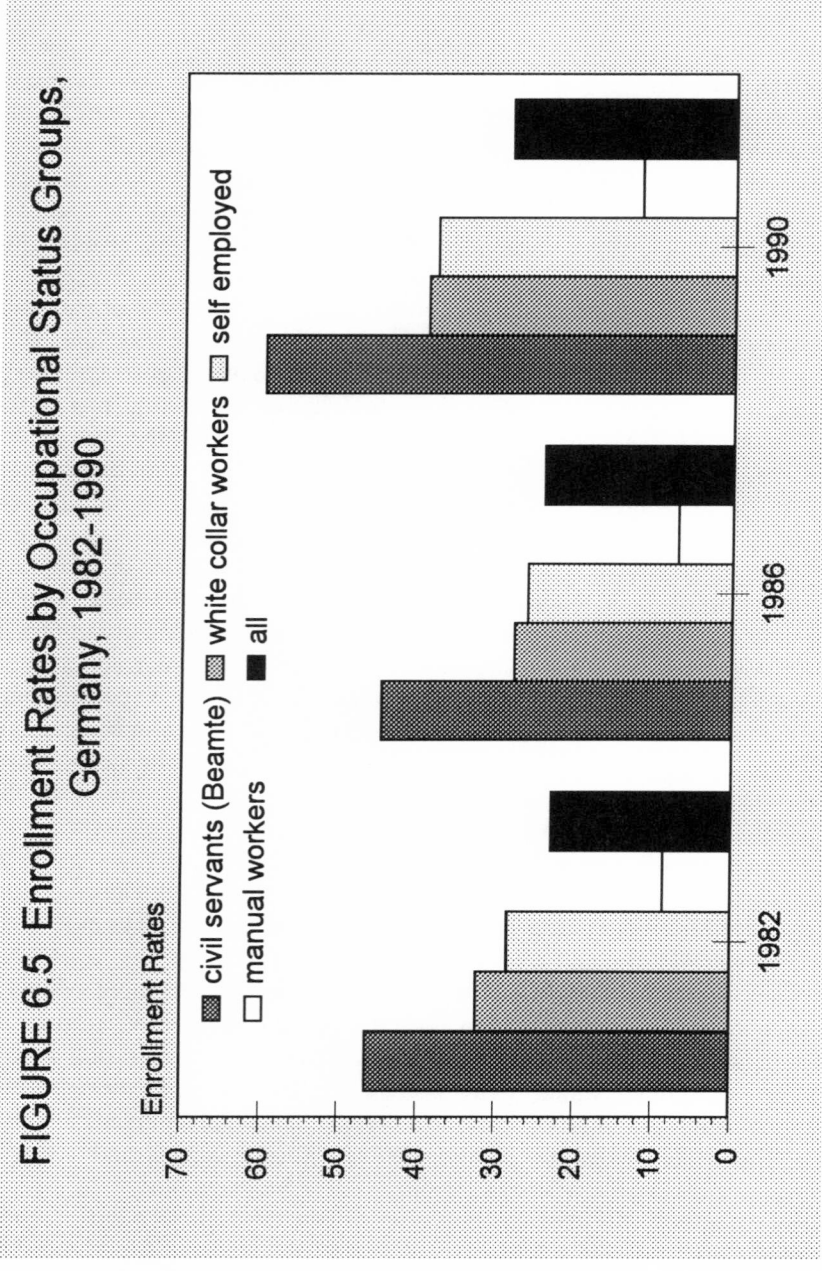

FIGURE 6.5 Enrollment Rates by Occupational Status Groups, Germany, 1982-1990

degrees to regain lost terrain from the bourgeoisie, and in the interwar period the bourgeoisie used university degrees to monopolize their class position and to exclude the working class from economic and political power. In this chapter the question is asked whether the rapid expansion of higher education in the late 1980's in Germany had any influence on the relative position of social classes in the universities. We also compare the social origin of German students with social background variables of students in the United States.

Figure 6.5 shows the enrollment rates by occupational status groups for *Germany* and the average enrollment rate for all status groups in the respective age cohorts (20-24 years). In 1982 the enrollment rate of children of (tenured) civil servants was five times higher than that of working class children (46.4% versus 8.6%). The relative position of children of manual workers did not change during the decade. In 1990 the enrollment rate of civil servants was still five times higher (59.7% versus 11.8%). Most children of manual workers are still excluded from a university education while families of the civil servants manage to send almost 60% of their offspring to university. The ideological battles of the 1960's and 1970's for "equal opportunity" and the educational programs which were set up to open the university for the lower classes were not successful; in fact, the *relative deprivation* of working class children did not change despite a considerable expansion of the universities. The failure of these programs is one reason why the system of higher education is unlikely to reach the "universalistic stage" (Trow 1979): Manual workers (and the lower service class workers) make up a substantial proportion of the active population. As long as their children are excluded from higher education – for whatever reason – there remains a substantial "pool" for further expansion.

More successful was the campaign against discrimination in favor of women, as we have seen. Women took advantage of the expansion in higher education, and in some countries they were even able to close the gender gap, for instance, in the United States and in Italy. A cross-classification for the variables sex and social class would show that particularly women of the upper classes participated in higher education: a significantly larger proportion of women at German universities come from the upper classes.[15] Educational policies were much more successful in overcoming discrimination against women than in overcoming the relative deprivation of the lower classes. The "gender gap" is easier to close than the "social class gap."

The relative deprivation of the lower classes cannot be explained exclusively by the low income of working class parents. The statistical category of "civil servants" is very heterogeneous and includes mailmen and railway conductors whose average income is lower than that of skilled manual workers. Nevertheless, enrollment rates of the lower civil service employees are substantially higher than that of manual workers.

Table 6.4 presents two types of social background variables of students at universities and colleges in the *United States*: the family income of dependent students and parents' highest educational level.[16] Selection at American universities can be described in terms of three dimensions: the income of the family, the education of the family, and the type of institution. At two-year public institutions 16% of students come from the highest income level; at four-year private universities offering the Ph.D, 37% of parents are in this income class; 62% of students at private Ph.D. universities have parents with a bachelor's degree compared with 28% at two-year public institutions. Economic affluence *and* the cultural and educational background of the family are important, and both resources must be combined to be accepted by one of the selective (private) universities. The process of selection and the structure of social inequality (analyzed in Chap. 4; Table 4.5) are confirmed by these more recent data, and they did not change during the 1980's.

The mechanisms of social reproduction differ in a number of ways between Germany and the United States. In Germany, a university degree is the most important resource for the social reproduction of the higher civil service. The educational and cultural patrimony is transmitted from one generation to the next in a reproductive cycle which children of the lower classes find difficult to emulate because they failed to

Table 6.4: Social Background of Students by Type of Institution, United States 1990

	Public			Private		
	Total	2-year	4-year PhD	Total	2-year	4-year PhD
	%	%	%	%	%	%
Family income						
Low	39	44	32	36	43	29
Middle	42	40	44	36	37	34
Upper	19	16	24	28	20	37
Parents' education						
High school or less	42	48	29	32	44	23
Vocational	5	5	5	5	7	3
Some college	18	19	18	15	15	12
Bachelor's degree	35	28	48	48	34	62
- Advanced degree	15	11	23	26	16	37

Source: See Appendix I.

accumulate the required educational capital. Compared to the income of managers of large companies or the successful self-employed, that of a higher civil servant is modest. However, high income is not important for their social reproduction: German universities do not charge fees, and the aspirations of the civil servants are directed less toward high income than toward prestige, social exclusivity, and political power. Civil servants wield bureaucratic as well as political power, as can be seen from the professional career of members of the German Parliament: 42% of these are former (tenured) civil servants[17] and they return to office if they fail to become reelected.

The importance of the university for the reproduction of social classes can further be illustrated with an example from East Germany. In West Germany 31% of students had parents with a university degree; in East Germany the proportion was 51% (see Table 6.5). In East Germany access to the academic track of secondary schools and to the university depended upon political conformity with the communist regime: those who showed political opposition were excluded from higher education. In addition, during the 1970's the East German *nomenclatura* became more and more "meritocratic" and technocratic: only those applicants with a university degree were accepted for higher positions in the state bureaucracy and in the nationalized enterprises. These heavily biased selection criteria improved the chances of the ruling elite: the *nomenclatura* was successful in monopolizing a large proportion of university places for their children, who then had better chances of being promoted into similar positions as their parents.

During the early 1950's, when the socialist regime in East Germany was established, many sons of manual workers were promoted to high positions in the party and state bureaucracy *without* a university degree. The bourgeois elite were driven out and an "emerging" new elite came to power (circulation of elite). Thirty years later the *nomenclatura* reproduced itself, and the university played an important role in legitimizing this kind of social reproduction (Mayer and Solga 1994). The growing proportion of parents with a university degree (as shown in Table 6.5) suggests processes of social closure and social reproduction in West Germany during the late 1980's – despite the strong expansion of universities. However, East German universities had been even more "exclusive" in the sense that their students were children of the *nomenclatura*. In West Germany the university is an important institution for the social reproduction of the civil servants; in East Germany it served the social reproduction of the *nomenclatura*.

In the *United States* the cycles of social reproduction are more

Table 6.5: Parent's Highest Educational Level, West Germany 1985-1991; East Germany 1991

	West			East
	1985	1988	1991	1991
	%	%	%	%
University / college	27	30	31	51
Apprenticeship	41	38	34	17
Other	32	32	35	32

Source: See Appendix I.

complex. Cultural patrimony is not enough to pay for those universities which are important for a professional career. Table 6.4 clearly shows that at least two resources must be combined to overcome the selective barriers of the elite universities. The "reproductive cycles" are at least as closed as they are in Germany. At an average German university 31% of the parents of students have a university degree; at selective private universities in the United States 62% of parents have a bachelor's degree and 37% have an advanced degree. Although no cross-classification is available, it is very likely that parents in the highest income class are also those with the highest educational level. Affluence and cultural heritage are not alternative routes to the "higher circles," but the two resources must be *combined*. Academic credentials legitimize the economic power, and economic resources are required to buy the prestigious credentials.

Appendix to Chapter 6: Unemployment of Qualified Workers in Germany and the United States

Table 6A shows that unemployment among qualified workers increased continuously after the mid-1970's in Germany and reached a very high level among female university graduates in the mid-1980's. Women seem no longer to be protected from unemployment by a university degree; nevertheless, the enrollment rates of men and women increased in Germany throughout the 1980's. In the United States the unemployment rate of college graduates followed a more cyclical pattern with particularly high unemployment rates in the mid-1980's. However, during the whole period the unemployment rate of college graduates was substantially lower than the average unemployment rate. In the United States it still pays to go to college, whereas in Germany university degrees have been continuously devalued. With these figures in mind the different patterns in Figs. 6.1-6.4 become even more puzzling.

Table 6A: Unemployment Rates by Level of Qualification, West Germany, United States, 1973-1993

	Germany (West)								United States			
	Men				Women				Men		Women	
Year	All	Appr	Coll	Uni	All	Appr	Coll	Uni	All	Coll	All	Coll
	%	%	%	%	%	%	%	%	%	%	%	%
1973	1.4	+	+	+	1.7	+	+	+	4.7	1.8	5.8	2.7
1974	3.4	+	+	+	3.8	+	+	+	4.8	1.8	6.0	2.3
1975	4.0	2.9	3.0	1.5	5.6	3.8	4.8	1.2	9.0	2.5	9.5	3.6
1976	3.3	2.5	3.1	2.0	5.7	4.5	5.4	1.7	7.8	2.4	8.5	3.5
1977	3.1	2.2	2.7	2.1	5.9	4.5	5.1	2.1	7.5	2.8	8.5	4.2
1978	2.9	2.0	1.9	1.7	5.7	4.2	4.0	2.1	6.3	2.2	7.0	3.0
1979	2.3	1.6	1.6	1.7	5.0	3.6	4.2	2.3	5.8	1.9	6.6	3.0
1980	2.7	1.8	1.5	1.9	5.2	3.7	4.5	2.7	6.8	1.8	6.7	2.5
1981	4.4	2.9	2.1	2.5	7.2	5.0	6.2	3.9	8.1	2.1	7.6	3.0
1982	6.9	5.1	3.3	3.3	9.1	6.6	8.7	5.0	10.3	3.2	8.9	3.3
1983	8.0	5.9	3.9	4.0	10.6	7.7	9.3	6.4	11.9	3.6	9.7	4.0
1984	8.1	6.1	3.6	4.3	10.6	7.8	9.3	7.3	6.9	2.7	6.1	2.7
1985	8.0	5.9	3.3	4.2	10.9	7.9	9.4	7.6	6.1	2.4	6.0	2.5
1986	7.3	5.3	2.7	3.9	10.6	7.4	8.8	7.5	6.2	2.3	5.8	2.4
1987	7.6	5.4	2.8	4.2	10.6	7.3	8.3	8.1	6.0	2.5	5.2	2.1
1988	7.4	5.4	3.1	4.4	10.4	7.2	8.4	8.5	5.1	1.6	4.2	1.9
1989	6.5	4.8	2.8	4.0	9.3	6.5	7.7	7.3	4.7	2.3	4.0	2.0
1990	5.8	4.4	2.5	3.5	8.2	5.7	6.6	6.4	4.4	2.1	4.4	2.3
1991	5.5	4.1	2.3	3.1	7.0	4.7	5.5	5.3	5.8	2.8	5.2	2.8
1992	6.1	4.6	2.6	3.2	7.4	5.0	5.3	5.2	+	+	+	+
1993	8.1	6.3	3.6	4.0	9.0	6.3	6.2	5.9	+	+	+	+

Levels of formal qualification:

Appr= German apprenticeship system; Coll = specialized college (Germany); 4-year colleges/universities (USA); Uni=University (Germany).

+ Data not available.   Sources: See Appendix I.

With the time series data in Table 6A the *elasticity* of enrollment rates in relation to unemployment has been computed.[18] For Germany these coefficients are positive, with 0.70 for men and 0.82 for women. These coefficients are to be interpreted as follows: If the unemployment rate for male (female) university graduates increases by 1%, the enrollment rate increases by 0.70% for men and by 0.82% for women. For the United States these coefficients are negative, with -0.36 for men and -0.56 for women. When unemployment among university graduates increases in Germany, the enrollment rates go up; this labor market reaction may be predicted from Boudon's model of "perverse effects." When unemployment among college graduates increases in the United States, the enrollment rates go down; this labor market reaction may be predicted from the human capital theory. However, neither theory explains why labor market behavior in Germany is so different from that in the United States.

7

Cyclical Variations in Higher Education

7.1 Long Cycles[1]

Industrialization, the expansion of capitalism, and regularly recurring economic recessions began as early as the late 19th century to turn the attention of social scientists to the cyclical nature of economic and political processes. Juglar in 1889 published the results of his empirical study into the business cycle in France, the United Kingdom, and the United States. Pareto in his *Trattato di sociologia* postulated periodically alternating eras of faith and skepticism as influencing societal value systems.[2] And Dehio (1948) identified a cyclical structure in the outbreak of major European wars – periods characterized by nations striving for balance alternating with periods dominated by a will to hegemony.

Cycles are more than mere fluctuations. Whereas the latter represent random oscillations lacking any ostensible pattern, cycles consist of fairly regular "waves" resembling those of a pendulum in their to-and-fro movement. Societal processes that are characterized by such cyclical waves follow a certain structural pattern, with a largely unvarying course that can be ascertained and measured. It is the goal of those analyzing economic and political cycles to identify and explain these structures (Wallerstein 1984, p. 559).

The principal model of such regularity in events over the long term is Kondratieff's (1926) concept of "long cycles." This model sees the expansion of the capitalist economic system as interrupted periodically by crises, which have occurred every 50-60 years from the beginning of industrialization until today. These crises are international in scope and grip all capitalist industrial nations more or less simultaneously. Kondratieff's model has inspired the search for empirical evidence of such a hypothesized pattern underlying various economic indicators (Ewijk 1982; Metz 1984) as well as analyses into the periodic alternation between progressivism and conservatism as dominant political ideologies. As regards the latter, Namenwirth (1973) and Weber (1981) uncovered a cycle encompassing conservative, parochial, progressive, and cosmopolitan phases which repeats itself after 50-60 years, and which runs parallel to Kondratieff's long cycles. The possibility of analyzing processes of long-term change on the basis of such long cycles has retained its fascination for social scientists down to the present (for a review, see Goldstein 1988; Spree 1991).

On the other hand, however, the notion that historical processes are determined by long-term cycles has met with rejection from a number of directions. Kondratieff and his successors (Schumpeter 1939; Mandel 1980) have been criticized particularly for their lack of an explanation for the long-term nature of the cycles. While the existence of a business cycle, with alternating periods of recession and prosperity, is universally acknowledged, most economists reject the plausibility of explanations for the specific duration of cycles at 50-60 years (Kuznets 1940; Garvy 1943; Eklund 1980). This duration cannot be explained in terms of processes of technological innovation or of the functional survival time of long-lived capital goods. At the most, long cycles find a basis in descriptive statistics, in some cases merely as a statistical artifact.[3]

Kondratieff's concept of long cycles has also been criticized on methodological grounds. In his critique of historicism, Popper (1972, p. 298) emphasized the dynamic nature of science: we do not know today what the state of tomorrow's knowledge will be. Since our future knowledge will affect the course of history, it is impossible to make long-term predictions. In this view, to claim that wars or crises occur – with lawlike regularity – in cycles of 50-60 years is to deny the influence of politics and rational policy making upon society. Max Weber regarded theories claiming to have discovered objective laws behind historical events as nonsense (Mommsen 1974, p. 258).

With the help of Keynesian economic policies, Western industrial nations were able after World War II to attain stable economic growth. Economic crisis appeared a thing of the past, the concept of long cycles lost relevance, and Kondratieff was forgotten. However, the economic recession of the 1980s and the dramatic rise in unemployment came almost exactly 50 years after the worldwide economic depression of the 1930s. Interest then renewed in the concept of long cycles, and Kondratieff once again became a frequently cited author (Bornschier and Suter 1990).

7.2 Higher Education and the Business Cycle: Independence or Interrelationship?

Over the past century the system of higher education in many countries has undergone periods of expansion and periods of stasis or contraction, and the duration of the cycle across such periods has generally been 20-30 years. This duration may perhaps be explained by the effect of succeeding generations. It has been argued that working-class children who attend university will themselves have children with higher enrollment rates. This increase continues from generation to generation, albeit on a lower level (see Chap. 1.2). For example, Fig. 7.3 shows the effect of the GI bill allowing veterans of World War II to become college students (Jencks and Riesman 1968, p. 94). Between 1950 and 1952 there was a sharp increase in the proportion of an age cohort graduating from college. This effect was repeated 20 years later (around 1972) although at a lower level.

In this chapter the technique of spectral analysis is employed to examine the relationship between cyclical patterns in the educational and those in the economic system. The purpose of the analysis is not to establish the existence of long cycles as described above but to assess whether the cycles that can be identified in either system (a) follow an exclusively system-specific pattern or (b) influence each other reciprocally. Empirically determined cycles of approximately the same duration in the educational and the economic system would suggest a causal relationship between the two systems. The indicator taken here for the state of the economic system is gross national product and that for expansion of the education system are enrollment rates at universities.

However, such evidence of similar duration of the cycles in the two systems and thereby of a relationship between the systems does not in itself indicate the *direction* of the relationship. It is therefore necessary not only to determine the duration of cycles but also to locate them precisely on the time axis and thus to identify a possible phase shift of one vis-à-vis the other. If expansion in universities, for example, is observed some two or three years after growth in the economy, one could conclude that the former results from the latter. In this case a period of "cooling off" in the process of educational expansion following one of accelerated growth in student numbers can be interpreted as a response to the state of the nation's business cycle.

Thus, the two most important parameters in this analysis are the *duration of cycles* in different systems and the *phase shift* between these cycles. Comparison of the duration of cycles in different systems indicates whether the systems are independent of one another or are potentially interrelated. If the cycles do show similar duration and may therefore be interrelated, examination of the phase shift between them may clarify the nature of the relationship.

Analyses of this sort can be made regarding the relationship between systems as long as sufficient data are available for long-term time series. An example is offered by the controversial relationship between labor union organization and the inflation rate, long a subject of debate in the social sciences and in politics. In a study of British labor unions, Bain and Elsheikh (1976) used regression analysis to demonstrate a significant relationship between the level of union organization and the inflation rate over the period 1893-1970. Their explanation of this relationship (p. 62) is as follows: when prices rise, increasing numbers of workers join unions to protect their threatened income, in response to which wages then rise.

However, spectral analysis of these three sets of time series data (union organization, wages, prices) shows the phases of the respective cycles to be shifted vis-à-vis one another in a way that is not consistent with the thesis of Bain and Elsheikh. While the duration of each cycle is shown to be approximately 30 years, which is a basis for the significant regression coefficients obtained by these authors, the variable that emerges as temporally primary (i.e., with a phase lead) is that of union organization, with a subsequent increase in wages and in prices after about three years.[4] This demonstrates that unions are first able to increase their relative influence on the basis of increased worker organization, that they then make use of this increased influence during wage negotiations with management, and that the resulting wage increases lead to an immediate rise in the prices of goods produced. The analysis of phase shifts in these cycles consequently discloses a relationship that is at variance with the conventional view in labor union research.

7.3 Trend, Cycle, and Chance

It has already been pointed out that a time series such as that presented in Figs. 1.1-1.4 (Chap. 1) can be divided into three components: a trend, a cycle, and a (random) chance or "disturbance" (Borchardt 1977). The *trend* refers to a long-term, often secular tendency underlying the observed variations over time. In the present case the trend comprises those factors which over the past century have led to the virtually uninterrupted growth in university enrollment despite substantial "disturbances" and periods of short-term stasis.

The second component, that of the *cycle*, represents a regular, wavelike variation along the trend. Introduction of this component into the analysis takes into account the fact that expansion of educational institutions has not followed a smooth, continuous course but one resembling waves, with times of expansion giving way to those of stasis, which in turn are followed by times of renewed expansion. To speak of cycles in this context is to perceive a regularity in the variations around the trend which show a roughly constant and measurable duration. The curve of educational expansion over time has indeed not been smoothly upward but has included phases characterized by stasis or short- term decline; the question is whether these variations describe a regular, repetitive structure, or whether they represent mere random chance and "disturbance." The third component, *chance*, comprises merely the remaining variation.

The starting point for the computations presented in this chapter are time series for the enrollment rates in different countries covering the period of approximately 120 years (1870 to 1990). For these time series a trend[5] was computed which was then subtracted from the time series, yielding the residuals. These are then used to estimate a harmonic function (see Fig. 7.2). The estimated values for the sinusoidal curve are finally subtracted from the residuals and this gives the "chance" element.

Separating out the trend allows one to focus specifically on the *cyclical* factor that influences the growth in university enrollment. This involves identifying the deviations from the trend that are of a regular, cyclical nature and therefore permit the formulation of more general propositions on the cyclical variations in higher education in different countries. That which remains as unexplained residual variation is regarded as "chance disturbance," explicable only by recourse to concrete historical description.

The past century has seen an almost continuous expansion in both the educational and the economic system. In the time series the trend component provides no evidence as to whether or to what extent the expansion of these systems has been interrelated; it demonstrates only that progressive industrialization and modernization have been accompanied by parallel expansion in universities and in the economy. Rather, it is the cyclical pattern that furnished insight into the dynamic processes of growth. The cycles show the varying rates of growth in the respective systems. The existence of a similar pattern in two systems over a long period of time, with changes in their relative growth rates varying in pace with one another, suggests either that they influence one another, or that both are influenced by a third system which determines the rate of growth in both. The analysis in the following sections therefore focuses specifically on the *cyclical* component of the time series.

7.4 Results of Spectral Analysis

The study of (long-term) cyclical variations is of central concern in research on the business cycle. Econometric analyses concentrate, for instance, on the question of whether variations show a regular, cyclical structure, and, if so, what duration these cycles have. Regarding the duration of cycles one distinguishes between those of the long term (40-60 years, "Kondratieff cycles"), medium term (15-30 years; "Kuznets cycles"), and short term (7-11 years; "Juglar cycles"). Here we ask whether the phases of educational expansion show a cyclical nature, and, if so, what is the duration of a cycle, and what is the relationship between these cycles and those in the economy? This analysis considers the following nations: Germany, the United States, Italy, France, and Japan.

Figure 7.1 (see end of this Chapter presents the variations (residuals) from the sixth-degree polynomial term (trend)[6] for university enrollment and gross national product (all Figures at the end of this Chapter). This shows in the case of Germany an expansion of universities particularly in those periods of below-average GNP. This anticyclical relationship is evident during the depressions of 1878-1890 and 1928/1929-1933; in these periods the university growth curve (residuals) is above the zero point while the economic growth curve is beneath it.

Spectral analysis can be used to *decompose any time series into a set of harmonic waves*. In other words, the method seeks to approximate cyclical processes – as shown in Figs. 7.1-7.6 (residuals) – by a set of harmonic functions (sinusoidal waves) which may have generated the cyclical process. This method can be compared to regression analysis; however, rather than a linear regression approach, a sinusoidal curve is used as the estimation function. For example, the sinusoid function which is fitted to the residuals for educational expansion in Fig. 7.2 has a cyclical duration of 38.5 years (period). This curve (estimation function) accounts for 36% of variance in the residuals; what remains is "chance." That a curve with this duration represents the optimal solution is indicated by results in Fig. 7.7, which presents the spectral density function across the range of possible frequencies.[7] The height of the spectral density function here represents the relative amount of residual variance explained by the corresponding cyclical duration of the sinusoidal function. This reaches its highest value (0.57) at a frequency of 0.16, that is, with a sinusoidal function allowing a cyclical duration of 38.5 years.

Figure 7.7 also reveals that not only the cycle for university expansion but also that for the economic system (GNP) has a duration of 38.5 years. Although of the same duration, the cycles in these two systems show a phase shift relative to one another, with that for educational expansion following that for GNP by 15.1 years (see Table 7.1). Due to the degree of this phase shift the difference cannot be interpreted as a phase lag in the adjustment of university enrollment to the state of the business cycle but suggests, rather, an anticyclical behavior on the part of students.[8]

An additional cycle appears in the time series data on the German economy, having a duration of 8.1 years; there is very little evidence of a corresponding cycle for the educational system. Whereas the major cycle (38.5 years) accounts for 36% of variance in the data on the educational system, it accounts for only 19% in the case of the economic system. Including cycles of both lengths (8.1 and 38.5 years) in the regression analysis increases the proportion of explained variance in the former only from 36% to 37% but that in the latter from 19% to 31%.

In the case of *Germany*, therefore, both systems, the educational and the economic, show expansion that occurs in cycles of some 38 years' duration (Kuznets cycles) but phase- shifted by 15 years (anticyclical behavior). That the second cycle of 8 years (Juglar cycle) is relevant only in the context of the economic system shows, on the other hand, the independence of university enrollment vis-à-vis *short-term* fluctuations in the business cycle.

Results of analyses correspondingly to those for Germany are presented below for Italy, France, the United States, and Japan. This cross-national comparison should determine whether there are differences among countries regarding the relationship between educational and economic expansion that may perhaps be due to characteristics specific to the educational institutions in the respective countries.

The data for *Italy* show cycles in university enrollment and in GNP that have a duration of 27.8 years in each case, with a phase shift in which educational expansion follows that in the economy by 9.5 years. Here, too, there is a further cycle, but one that is of only minor significance, particularly as regards the universities; the duration of this (Juglar) cycle is 14.7 years, with a lag of 4.7 years (see Figs. 7.4 and 7.9).

In *France* the duration of cycles for the two systems is not identical, that for educational expansion being 23.8 years and that for economic expansion 19.2 years. As this difference is relatively small, the phase shift was calculated; the lag was approximately half the duration of the cycles (11 years) and can be interpreted as an instance of anticyclical behavior. As far as can be determined in this analysis, short-term fluctuations in the business cycle are not of relevance for the level of university enrollment (see Figs. 7.5 and 7.10).

In Chap. 1 three competing theories are advanced to explain the expansion in higher education. For instance, the theory of human capital was developed in the context of modernization theories and maintains that universities expand in step with economic growth and technical progress; this view perceives a straightforward relationship between higher education and the economic system: university enrollment expands in times of economic growth and contracts in those of economic recession – notwithstanding short periods of adaptation between the two systems (lag).

As early as the turn of the century, the Prussian statistician Eulenburg cast doubt upon explanations of university expansion based on the business cycle. Eulenburg's skepticism was founded on his observation that, "favorable economic conditions may tend to impede university attendance and unfavorable conditions to encourage it."[9] If Eulenburg's observation is correct we expect to find an "anticyclical" behavior between the educational and the economic system: University enrollment is particularly high during times of the economic depression when unemployment is high and status competition is intense among workers who seek to improve their position by acquiring as many educational certificates as possible.

Results in each of the three European countries considered here seem to contradict the human capital theory: In Germany, Italy, and France the residuals of university enrollment and GNP show almost over the whole observation period a consistently "anticyclical" behavior, i.e., university enrollment increases strongly during economic depressions and declines during periods of the economic boom. This pattern of correspondence between the two systems may point to increased status competition during periods of high unemployment when many job seekers try to improve their position by acquiring more certificates.

In contrast, results for the *United States* can be interpreted better in terms of the theory of human capital. Here there are two cycles in the educational system of approximately equal strength (20 and 11.6 years' duration) as well as two of virtually the same duration in the economic system (21.7 and 12.2 years). The phase shift (lag) of only 2.4 years in the Kuznets cycle indicates a short-term reaction of students to altered conditions in the job market. It seems that enrollment rates in the United States are strongly influenced by the business cycle. Regarding the Juglar cycles, on the other hand, university enrollment shows a phase lead of 4.1 years over the economic conditions. As this phase lead is difficult to interpret we do not follow it up here (see Figs. 7.3 and 7.8).

The relationship between educational and economic expansion in the United States distinguishes itself from that in Europe in two respects. First, the process of educational expansion is more clearly characterized by cycles of medium-term duration (20 years). Secondly, the phase shift in cycles between the two systems is shorter. This shorter lag in adjusting to economic conditions represents a greater sensitivity on the part of American students to an altered job market.

The expansion of universities in *Japan* is influenced by two cycle components of approximately similar strength – one of 35.7 years (Kuznets) and one of 11.1 years (Juglar). The corresponding cycle components for expansion of the economy show a duration of 31.3 years and one of 14.7 years. The Kuznets lag in educational expansion of 6.9 years may still be interpreted as a delayed adjustment to market conditions though the adjustment time is longer than in the United States. The Juglar lag, on the other hand, does not remain stable over time and varies between 6.9 and 1.9 years and therefore eludes interpretation (see Figs. 7.6 and 7.11).

Figure 7.6 shows for Japan that the phase lag between university enrollment and the economic system increases over time, and Fig. 7.11 shows that there is a strong cyclical pattern in the economic time series, but only a weak one in the educational system.[10] Both results suggest that it is difficult to interpret the expansion of higher education in Japan in either of the theories presented above. The pattern changes over time: Between 1890 and 1920 enrollment rates seem to follow closely the business cycle; after 1960 the pattern appears as that of an "anticyclical" behavior.

Cross-national comparisons such as those presented here point up the respective institutional features in the various countries. Regarding the system of higher education a principal difference between institutions in Europe and those in the United States is that, whereas universities in the former are subject to a central public bureaucracy, those in the later depend more closely upon the private economy. Due to the greater private burden of financing higher education in the United States, students there tend to respond more to signals emanating from the general economic condition of the country. As the results of this time series analysis confirm, the greater the proportion of educational costs that is borne by the state, the less the educational system responds to economic conditions.

In this respect the institutional structure of higher education in Japan can be compared to that in the United States. While Japanese universities are more closely regulated by a central bureaucracy, the expansion of student enrollment figures depends almost entirely on private institutions. Since private colleges and universities charge relatively high tuition, students at these institutions probably react more sensitively to economic downturns. However, empirical findings are ambiguous and do not lend themselves easily to an interpretation in terms of the competing theories as outlined above.

7.5 Variation of the Filter

In each of the analyses described in the preceding section the secular trend in the time series data was subtracted by means of a sixth-degree polynomial. Selection of a particular trend term simultaneously limits the possible duration of any cycles that may be identified in the residuals, and no mathematical procedure is available for making the selection. The issue of selecting an appropriate trend to separate long term growth from cyclical variations belongs to the thorniest problems of spectral analysis. This selection is plausible on the basis of certain specific characteristics in the data set. Two considerations guide the choice. On the one hand, the data manipulation should not entail the loss of any observations (as occurs, for instance, in procedures using a moving average). On the other, cycles of longer duration are to be eliminated, as these cannot be analyzed with the existing time series data set (encompassing a period of 104-125 years). Applying the rule of thumb that a cycle should have the chance to repeat itself at least two or three times within the period covered means that cycles with a duration longer than 35-40 years must be filtered out. This is achieved with a sixth-degree polynomial, whereas a polynomial of lower degree often does not eliminate cycles spanning 40 years or more.

This section deals with the influence on the outcomes of spectral analysis that results from *variation* of the filter. Table 7.1 presents the results for three countries obtained by six different filters for the level of university enrollment and GNP. In all, 36 spectral analyses are included here, each instance being considered with a polynomial and with a high-pass filter. Polynomials are conventional filters, for which, however, no transfer function can be calculated. A high-pass filter suppresses low frequencies (stop band) while allowing cycles of higher frequency (pass band). The transfer functions for high- pass filters indicate the frequencies that are filtered out and those that are permitted to pass. For each type of filter three variants are calculated (Gottman 1981; see also Appendix to this chapter).

In the analyses using polynomials, the degree is varied, taking the third-, sixth-, and seventh-degree polynomials. In those using high-pass filters, the end of the stop band and beginning of the pass band are varied so as to filter out cycles of progressively longer duration (lower frequency). The first high-pass filter suppresses cycles lasting longer than 90 years (stop band); cycles of 80-90 years are partially permitted (transition band); and those of less than 80 years are completely permitted (pass band). In the second high-pass filter, the stop band is set at 60 years and the pass band at 55; in the third high- pass filter, the stop band is set at 50 years and the pass band at 45.[11]

For each country the first set of figures refer to results based on the polynomial and the second set to those based on the high-pass filter. The set of figures for each include: duration (in years) of the educational cycles, duration of the economic cycles, and the length of the respective phase shift (of the educational cycles relative to the economic cycles, negative values indicating a lag and positive figures a lead). Figures in parentheses beneath the cyclical durations represent the value of the spectral density function (the higher, the more significant); those beneath the phase shift refer to the coherence (corresponding to a correlation coefficient, varying between 0 and 1 and measuring how closely educational and economic cycles are related to each other). The proportion of explained variance in the residuals ($R2$), calculated on the basis of nonlinear regression, is given for one sinusoidal function (major cycle) and for the combination of two sinusoidal functions (two cycles). Values marked by an asterisk are those combining three sinusoidal functions (variance explained by three cycles).

For example, the results for the United States using the third-degree polynomial reveal the following. The university enrollment rate expanded in a cyclical pattern consisting principally of three harmonic waves (sinusoidal waves) lasting, respectively, 62.5, 20.8, and 12.2 years. The major cycle (62.5 years) accounts for 29% of the variance in the residuals, while the combination of three cycles accounts for 49%. Growth in the GNP also shows a cyclical pattern of three such waves, with durations of 50.0, 21.7, and 11.9 years, respectively. Here the combination of three cycles accounts for 48% of the variance in residuals.

Spectral analysis enables one to evaluate fairly clearly the differential effect of the various filters, demonstrating the cycles in the residuals that are filtered out as opposed to the cycles that remain. As Table 7.1 shows, the higher the degree of the polynomial, the shorter the duration of the cycles that remain in the residuals; the effect of the high-pass filter is similar, with the duration declining from the first to the third such filter.

Table 7.1: Results of Spectral Analysis

type of filter	type of cycle	Germany/FRG polynomials UER	GNP	lag/lead	Germany/FRG high-pass filter UER	GNP	lag/lead	Italy polynomials UER	GNP	lag/lead	Italy high-pass filter UER	GNP	lag/lead	USA polynomials UER	GNP	lag/lead	USA high-pass filter UER	GNP	lag/lead
3rd polynomial/ 1st high-pass filter	Kondrat.	55.6 (.84)	50.0 (.93)	-12.9 (.92)	62.5 (1.1)	62.5 (1.1)	-10.7 (.92)	-	55.6 (.79)	-	-	55.6 (1.0)	-	62.5 (.33)	50.0 (.28)	-	50.0 (.15)	55.6 (.37)	+4.3 (.84)
	Kuznets	-	-	-	-	-	-	27.8 (.56)	-	-	25.0 (.68)	-	-	20.8 (.31)	21.7 (.38)	-2.0 (.82)	20.8 (.43)	20.8 (.34)	-0.4 (.82)
	Juglar	-	-	-	-	-	-	-	9.6 (.05)	-	11.9 (.10)	-	-	12.2 (.09)	11.9 (.13)	+4.1 (.93)	12.8 (.15)	6.2 (.05)	-
	R2: cycle 1	.47	.54	-	.70	.72	-	.26	.50	-	.42	.67	-	.29	.23	-	.25	.24	-
	cyc. 2/3	-	-	-	-	-	-	-	.51	-	.49	-	-	.49*	.48*	-	.44*	.46*	-
6th polynomial/ 2nd high-pass filter	Kondrat.	-	-	-	-	-	-	-	-	-	-	-	-	-	-	-	50.0 (.16)	41.7 (.32)	-
	Kuznets	38.5 (.57)	38.5 (.34)	-15.1 (.95)	41.7 (.59)	38.5 (.80)	-14.3 (.87)	27.8 (.64)	27.8 (.40)	-9.5 (.88)	25.0 (.74)	26.3 (.47)	-12.0 (.93)	20.0 (.30)	21.7 (.41)	-2.4 (.83)	20.8 (.42)	20.8 (.41)	-0.4 (.86)
	Juglar	8.2 (.05)	8.1 (.25)	-3.1 (.93)	21.7 (.34)	-	-	14.7 (.06)	14.7 (.10)	-4.7 (.77)	11.9 (.12)	11.9 (.13)	-5.5 (.96)	11.6 (.23)	12.2 (.14)	+4.1 (.87)	12.8 (.15)	6.2 (.06)	-
	R2: cycle 1	.36	.19	-	.41	.47	-	.37	.19	-	.47	.31	-	.17	.25	-	.25	.23	-
	cyc. 2/3	.37	.31	-	.54	-	-	.38	.25	-	.54	.39	-	.29	.32	-	.45*	.51*	-
7th polynomial/ 3rd high-pass filter	Kondrat.	-	-	-	-	-	-	-	-	-	-	-	-	-	-	-	-	-	-
	Kuznets	20.8 (.46)	35.7 (.25)	-	41.7 (.66)	38.5 (.80)	-14.7 (.81)	26.3 (.63)	27.8 (.43)	-10.5 (.92)	25.0 (.76)	26.3 (.48)	-12.0 (.92)	20.0 (.29)	21.7 (.41)	-2.2 (.84)	20.0 (.46)	20.8 (.48)	-0.4 (.83)
	Juglar	8.1 (.07)	8.1 (.27)	-3.0 (.98)	21.7 (.31)	-	-	13.5 (.09)	14.7 (.12)	-4.2 (.91)	11.9 (.11)	11.9 (.12)	-5.5 (.92)	11.6 (.23)	11.9 (.15)	+4.2 (.88)	12.8 (.17)	6.1 (.07)	-
	R2: cycle 1	.20	.14	-	.46	.48	-	.30	.21	-	.48	.33	-	.16	.23	-	.26	.27	-
	cyc. 2/3	.22	.30	-	.58	-	-	.32	.27	-	.55	.40	-	.29	.32	-	.35	.32	-

Definition of high pass filters:
1st high pass filter: 90/80 years; 2nd high pass filter: 60/55 years; 3rd high pass filter: 50/45 years. First figure gives end of stop band in years; second figure gives beginning of pass band in years.
Number of years (=N) for which data are available for each country: Germany N=125; Italy N=122; USA N=111.
UER: university enrollment rates; GNP=gross national product   * R2 for 3 cycles

Example for Germany, 6th polynomial:
Two cycles were found in the residuals of UER: 38.5 years (Kuznets) and 8.2 years (Juglar). The Kuznets cycle explains 36% of variation in the residuals of UER (R2=0.36). Two cycles were found in the residuals of GNP: 38.5 years (Kuznets) and 8.1 year (Juglar). The first cycle explains 19% of variation; the two cycles together explain 31% of variation in the residuals. The Kuznets cycle for UER lags 15.1 years behind the Kuznets cycle for GNP (lag: 15.1 years). Figures in parentheses give values of spectral density function for each cycle. Figures in parentheses in the column "lag/lead" give the value of coherence.

Example for US, 2nd high-pass filter:
Three cycles were found in the residuals of UER: 50.0 years (Kondratieff); 20.8 years (Kuznets); 12.8 years (Juglar). The first cycle explains 25% of variation in the residuals of UER; the three cycles together explain 45% of variation. Three cycles were found in the residuals of GNP: 41.7 years (Kondratieff); 20.8 years (Kuznets); 6.2 years (Juglar). The first cycle explains 23% of variation in the residuals of GNP; the three cycles together explain 51% of variation. The Kuznets-cycle for UER lags 0.4 years behind the Kuznets cycle for GNP (lag: -0.4 years).
Sources: see Appendix I.

Thus, in either case a *decision* must be made: with the polynomial regarding the degree and with the high-pass filter regarding the beginning of the pass band. In both cases the decision determines the differentiation between what variance is to be assigned to the trend and what variance to cyclical waves. This decision cannot be made on the basis of an objective formula but depends on the features of the given time series and on the purpose of the analysis. The goal of this section is to demonstrate the way in which the choice of filter to be used in the spectral analysis results in a modification of results obtained from it.

The numerous details in Table 7.1 can be assembled into an overall mosaic, providing a more or less complete picture of the set of frequencies that make up the original time series. What is important is not the question of whether varying the filter affects the results of spectral analysis (which is almost always the case), but whether the composite picture provides insights into the relationship between the educational and economic systems, and whether these coincide with what is already known about the institutions of higher education in each country.

As both the duration of cycles and the phase shifts between them vary according to the filter used in the analysis, we therefore select below only the specific results that are replicated by at least a second filter. We can regard such cycles as showing a certain "resistance" to influence by filter specific effects and thus as indicating with greater probability the actual pattern in the time series.

Kuznets Cycles (15-40 years). In this frequency band a typical pattern can be ascertained in each of the three European countries analyzed here: the educational and economic systems expand in cycles of roughly the same duration. Growth in the numbers of university students follows growth in the GNP with a considerable phase lag, sometimes amounting to one-half the length of the cycle. In Germany this pattern is found using the sixth-degree polynomial and the second and third high-pass filters (cycle duration approximately 40 years; lag 14-15 years). In Italy it is obtained with the sixth- and seventh-degree polynomial and with the second and third high-pass filters (cycle duration approximately 26 years; lag 10-12 years). Similar results are yielded by the analysis in the French case[12] using the sixth- and seventh-degree polynomial. These findings support the assumption that growth rates of university enrollment are particularly high during periods of high unemployment and that individuals respond to this situation by acquiring even more credentials (intensified status competition).

The cycles in the United States show a duration of 20 years but a short phase lag between university enrollment and GNP – across all filters. The short phase shift between the economic and the educational cycles is interpreted in the sense that students in the United States are sensitive to labor market conditions and react to poor employment opportunities by reduced enrollment rates; these findings may be understood as a support for the human capital theory.

Results for Japan are inconsistent and difficult to interpret for reasons which have already been discussed; therefore, data for Japan are not followed up here.

Kondratieff Cycles (40-70 years). Spectral analysis shows long cycles in virtually all time series considered here. A similar pattern is also observed in most countries regarding the phase shift, with university expansion showing a lead over growth in GNP of some 2-4 years. However, in cycles of such long duration, such a relatively minor phase shift is of little significance. In France, the United States, and Japan an expansion in both systems is evident over long cycles, and one that are approximately synchronous with one another. Only in Germany does the analysis reveal a considerable phase lag in educational expansion (10-12 years) with respect to the long cycle.

Although one can reliably determine the existence of long cycles by means of the high-pass filter, the time series considered here presents a particular problem for their analysis, as a period of 55-60 years is difficult to confirm in a data set covering only some 110 years. Cyclical waves spanning 60 years can, on the other hand, be regarded as belonging to the overall secular trend and thus not as comprising cyclical variations within the time series. In the present analysis such long waves fall in the transitional stage between "trend" and "cycle" and therefore are not examined further.

Juglar Cycles (7-11 years). Significant Juglar cycles seldom emerge from these spectral analyses. Only in he United States and Japan does the spectral density function reach a higher value for cycles of 10-12 years (e.g., 0.23 for the sixth- and seventh- degree polynomial in the United States). As noted in a previous section, the results demonstrate that European universities (those in Germany, France, and Italy) do not appear to react to short-term fluctuations in the business cycles but are influenced exclusively by longer term cycles in the economic system.

7.6 The Strength of Spectral Analysis

The set of empirical findings presented in Table 7.1 demonstrate the filter-specific variability of results: the period of cycles and the existence of leads or lags between the economic and the educational system change with the type of filter which is used to eliminate the trend. Can spectral analysis be recommended as a reliable method to test assumptions on the interaction between different social systems? If spectral analysis can be used to confirm any hypothesis (presuming that one chooses the "correct" filter), then the findings appear as mere statistical artifacts projected into the residuals by the filter.

However, we know that many statistical techniques produce different results depending on the definition of specific parameters.[13] The advantage of spectral analysis is that it exactly shows how findings vary with different assumptions on the underlying trend. More importantly, spectral analysis is able to decompose any time series into its cyclical components and to show how different time series interact with one another. In Table 7.1 cycles of long duration[14] are successively eliminated and spectral analysis reveals the cyclical structure of the remaining components.

As noted above, there is no definitive answer to the question, which trend is "correct." We have tried to illustrate how findings vary with the trend and, more important, which results do *not* change even if the trend is changed. Most of the findings of Table 7.1 confirm hypotheses which have been discussed in previous chapters – even if some results remain ambiguous or contradictory.

Over the past decade historical date sets have been published in many countries containing long-term time series documentation of numerous social indicators. These data sets offer social scientists an important source for the development of theories and the verification of hypotheses. Many hypotheses which could hitherto be tested only in regard to cross-sectional data can now be reevaluated in terms of variance in indicators over time. The controversy between competing theories of educational expansion, to take the case of the present analysis, cannot be resolved on the basis of data from only a limited period. This is also the case in other areas, such as the relationship between labor union membership and inflation and that between the expansion of social welfare and economic growth.

Spectral analysis can provide important insights into the processes of change in social systems and the relationships among various systems. In particular, three features can be evaluated: (a) the *cyclical* components that make up the pattern of development in a social system over time as, for instance, in the educational system, (b) the *duration* of major cycles and the comparison of cycles in different systems, and (c) the degree of *synchronicity* (lead/lag) between the cycles in different systems. This point is particularly important if one speculates on the causal structure between different social systems.

One must, however, also recognize the limitations of spectral analysis. Any variation in the definition of the trend leads to different results, and only the resulting *set* of relationships is appropriate for interpretation. The technique is not suitable for examining long-term cycles; one can set a filter for virtually any time series that produces "long cycles." Therefore the goal of the present analysis is to ascertain not the duration of cycles in educational expansion but the relationship of these to cycles in the economic system, and whether this relationship remains stable despite variation of the filter.

The findings in Table 7.1 allow to identify a relatively stable "tendency" which can be summarized fairly concisely as follows: In the United States changes in university enrollment react to changes in the business cycle within a relatively short period of time (lag of 2-3 years) and this finding is stable within the domain of the Kuznets cycles regardless of the filter used. University enrollment in the three European countries shows no response to short-term economic fluctuations in the domain of the Juglar cycles. In the domain of Kuznets cycles, enrollment at European universities shows an anticyclical behavior.

Thus, the nature of the relationship between the cycles in the two social systems varies with the *length* of the cycles. In terms of long-term cycles the systems react differently than in terms of short-term cycles, and one may speculate whether these differences may be explained by the differences in the institutional structure which have been analyzed in previous chapters.

Appendix to Chapter 7

Definition of Time Series
UER = university enrollment rate: We used total number of students enrolled in universities divided by age cohorts 20-24 years for Germany, Italy, France (5 cohorts), and Japan (4 cohorts). For the United States we used the number of bachelor's degrees for each year divided by the average of cohorts 20-24 years (=1 cohort).

GNP = gross national product: The time series has been corrected for inflation (constant prices) and divided by the total population (GNP per head of population).

High-Pass Filter

We used the filter program "Nulfil" developed by Metz and Stier (1991). An essential point in modern filter theory is the fact that no ad hoc solutions (such as moving averages) are accepted, but filters are designed in such a way that they accomplish prespecified amplitude and phase functions. For our purpose it is important to note that the phase function of "Nulfil" is zero for all frequencies. We used the following specifications to filter the original time series: FFT = 2048 (number of frequency points for which an estimation is computed); iter=5 (number of iterations). "Nulfil" has been written by Metz and Stier (1991) for the mainframe. We adapted this program to the PC.

Transfer Functions

These show which frequencies (f) are transferred to the filter output (value of transfer function=1) and which frequencies are eliminated (value of transfer function=0). Table 7A only shows the values of the transfer function in the transition band.

Spectral Analysis

The original time series have been extended to 500 data points (=padding). For instance, for Germany 125 data points are available. We added 475 zeros to obtain 500 data points. This technique is applied to identify the peaks more accurately.

We used a Daniell window with 9 weights to smooth the periodogram. There is a trade-off effect between padding (periodogram shows more

Table 7A: Transfer Functions

1st high-pass filter SE=90 years (f=0.0111) PE=80 years (f=0.0125)		2nd high-pass filter SE=70 years (f=0.01429) PE=65 years (f=0.01539)		3rd high-pass filter SE=50 years (f=0.02) PE=45 years (f=0.0222)	
0.0000000	(2048)	0.0000000	(2048)	0.0000000	(2048)
.....		.....		.....	
0.0000000	(93.1)	0.0000000	(70.6)	0.0000000	(50.0)
0.0000000	(89.0)	0.0000000	(68.3)	0.0001906	(48.8)
0.0181426	(85.3)	0.2451930	(66.1)	0.1234305	(47.6)
0.4025243	(81.9)	0.8792673	(64.0)	0.4191267	(46.5)
0.8941895	(78.8)	1.0000000	(62.1)	0.7518603	(45.5)
1.0000000	(75.9)	1.0000000	(60.2)	0.9692501	(44.5)
1.0000000	(73.1)	1.0000000	(58.5)	1.0000000	(43.6)
.....		.....		.....	
1.0000000	(2.0)	1.0000000	(2.0)	1.0000000	(2.0)

SE=end of stop band; PE=end of pass band; f=frequency.

details) and a window with many weights (wide-band estimates for spectral density function smooth out some detail). However, if periodograms are averaged in a wider interval of frequencies to form the estimated spectral density (=many weights), the statistical stability of the estimate is enhanced (power of the test statistic).

Confidence intervals for values of spectral density function given in Table 7.1 may be computed according to the following formula:

$$[EDF/X2(\alpha)]*p(f).$$

EDF=equivalent degrees of freedom; $X2(\alpha)$= value of Chi-square of given level of significance (α) and given EDF; $p(f)$= estimate of spectral density function.

Example: We used a Daniell windows with 9 weights. For this window the EDF are 18. The value of Chi-square for 18 DF and $\alpha \leq 0.05$ =28.87. 18/28.87=0.62. All values of density function given in table 1 have to be multiplied by 0.62 to obtain the lower boundary of confidence interval. The upper boundary may be computed according to the above given formula (factor: 1.92). For more details see Gottman (1981, pp. 216-228).

Test for White Noise
This test statistic shows whether the periodogram could have been produced by a random variable (=white noise; value of periodogram for all frequencies=constant). We used "Fisher's Kappa" to test for white noise. For N=500 (padding!) the minimum values of Fisher's Kappa are as follows:

$\alpha \leq 0.05$: $8.39 \leq$ kappa < 9.96; $\alpha \leq 0.01$: kappa ≥ 9.96. For more details see Fuller (1976, p. 284).

We obtained a significance level of $\alpha \leq 0.05$ for the following spectral analyses: 6th and 7th polynomials France; 5th, 6th and 7th polynomials US. For all other spectral analyses we obtained a significance level of $\alpha \leq 0.01$.

Stationarity
None of our time series met the standards of stationarity accurately.

However, we did not transform our time series (logarithm). We tried to avoid manipulation of the series as much as possible. The logarithm is – in technical terms – a filter for which no transfer function can be computed (no linear filter). Therefore we do not know whether this filter has a phase lag of zero. Only for Italy we used the logarithm transformation because the standards of stationarity are seriously violated for this country.

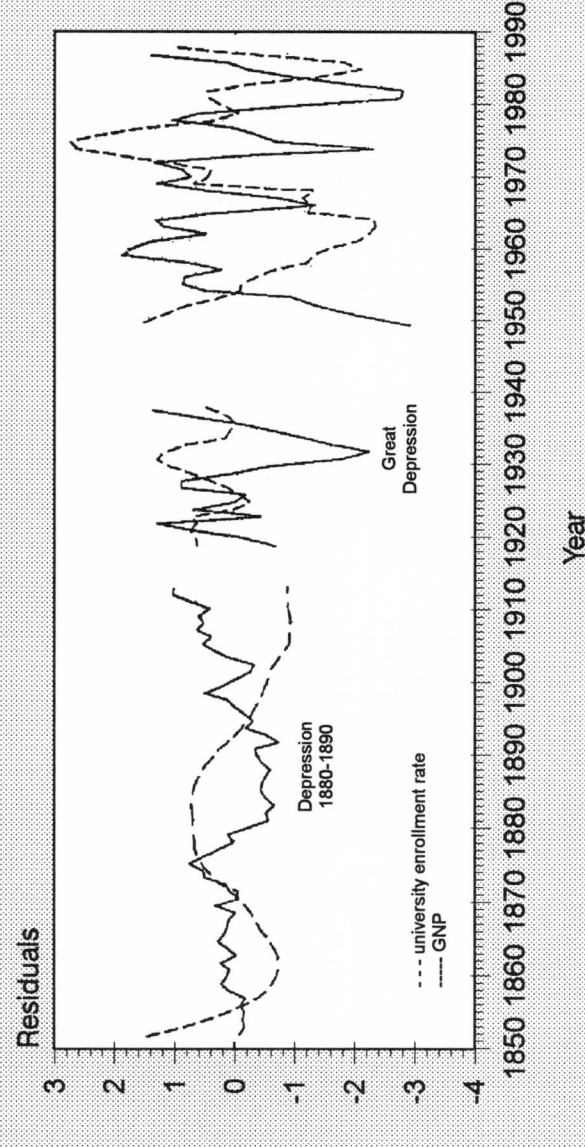

FIGURE 7.1 Residuals, Germany 1850-1989

Trend, 6th-degree polynomial

218

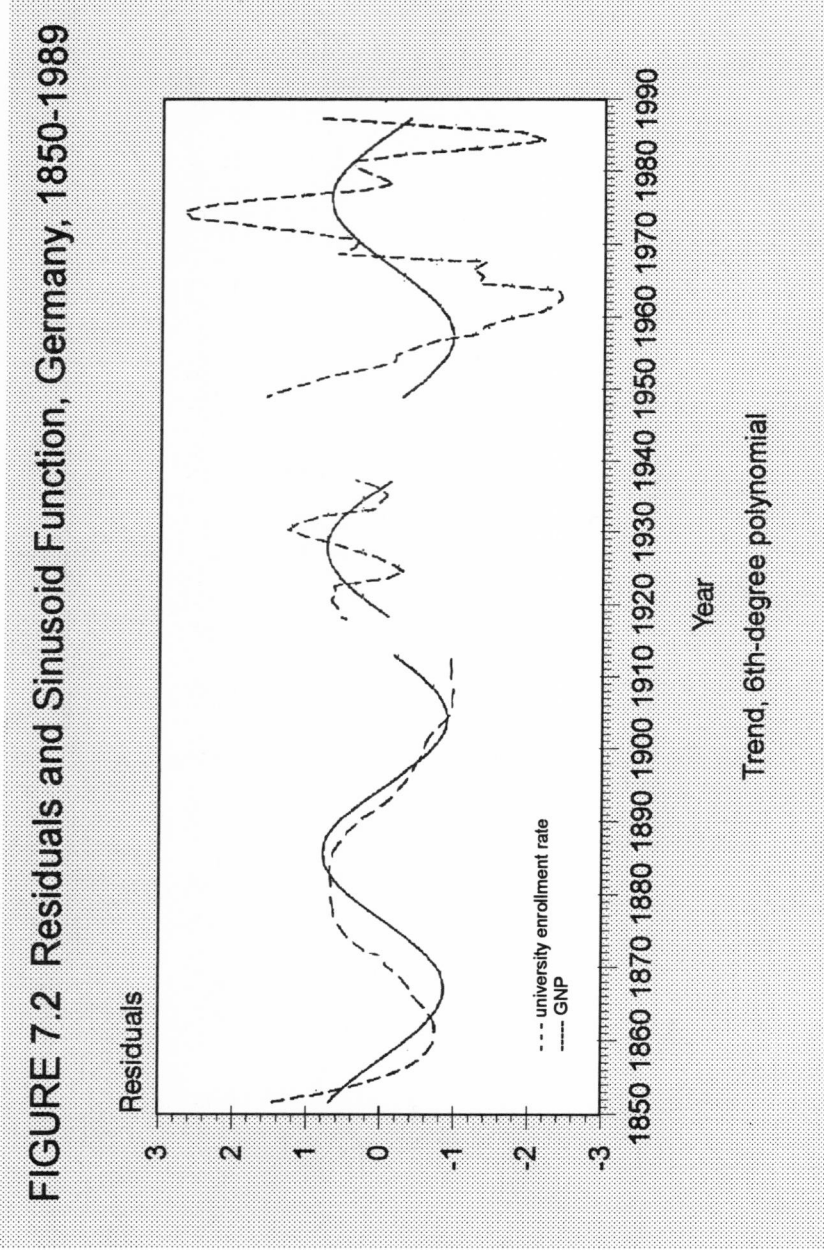

FIGURE 7.2 Residuals and Sinusoid Function, Germany, 1850–1989

Residuals

- - - university enrollment rate
—— GNP

Year

Trend: 6th-degree polynomial

FIGURE 7.3 Residuals, United States, 1870-1988

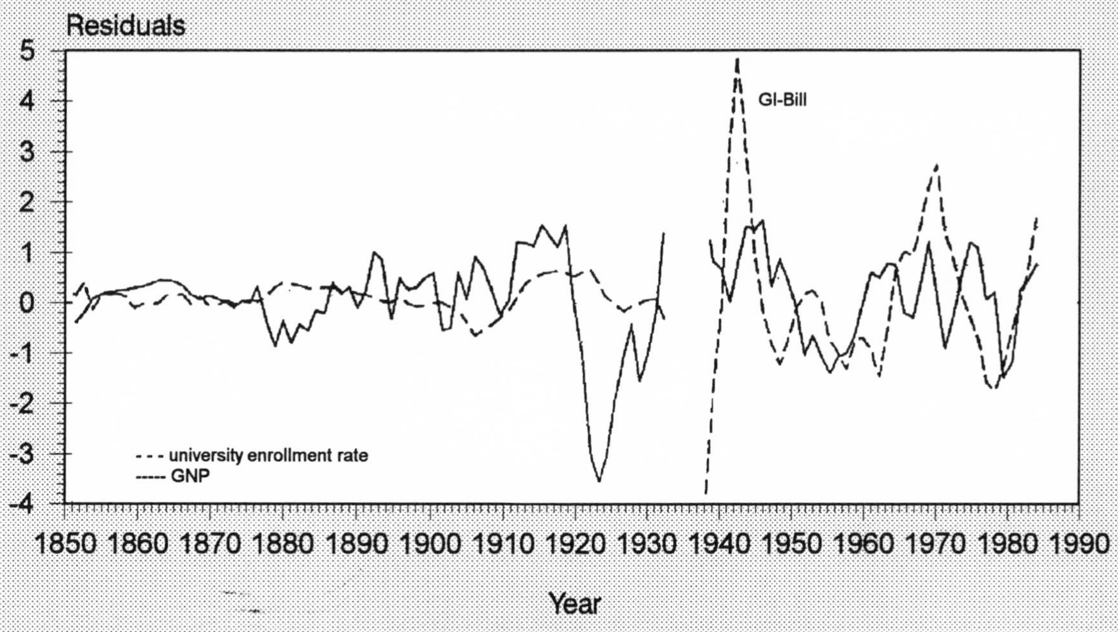

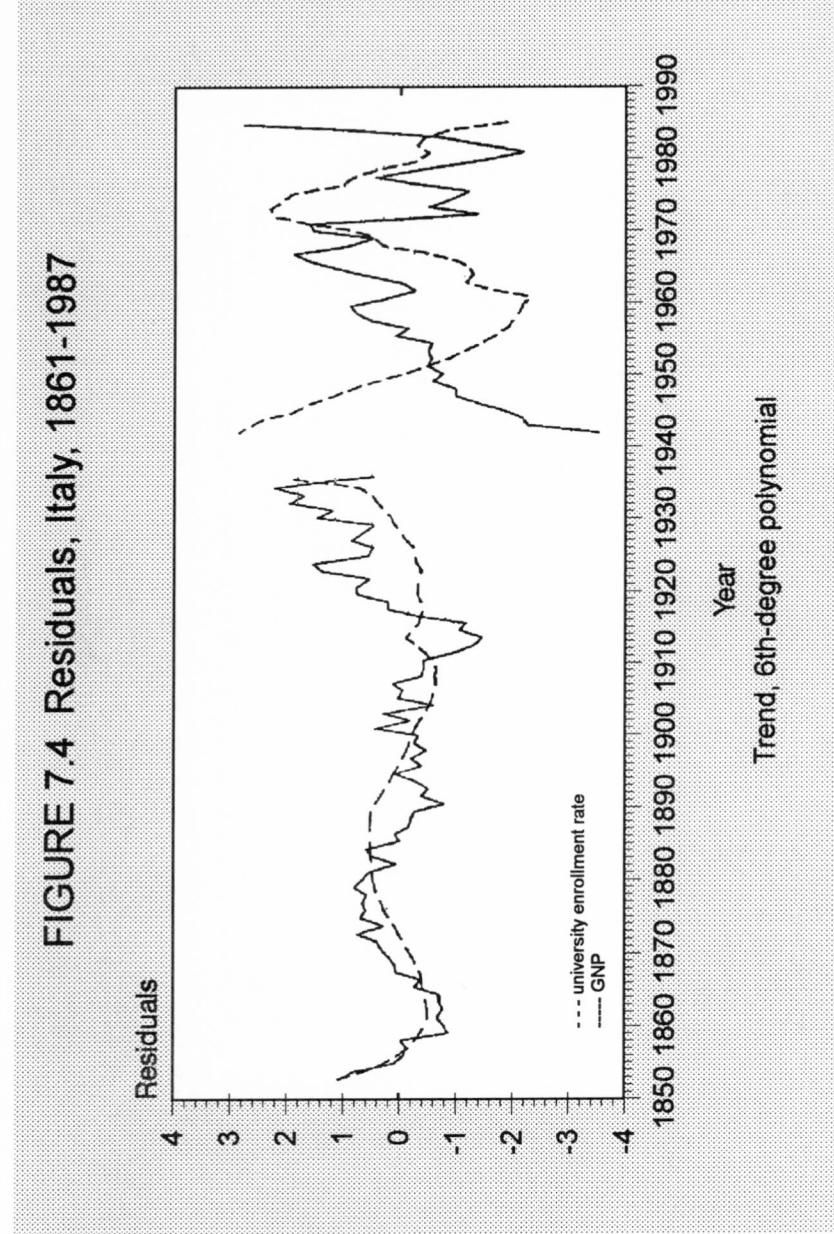

FIGURE 7.4 Residuals, Italy, 1861-1987

Residuals

- - - university enrollment rate
—— GNP

1850 1860 1870 1880 1890 1900 1910 1920 1930 1940 1950 1960 1970 1980 1990

Year

Trend, 6th-degree polynomial

221

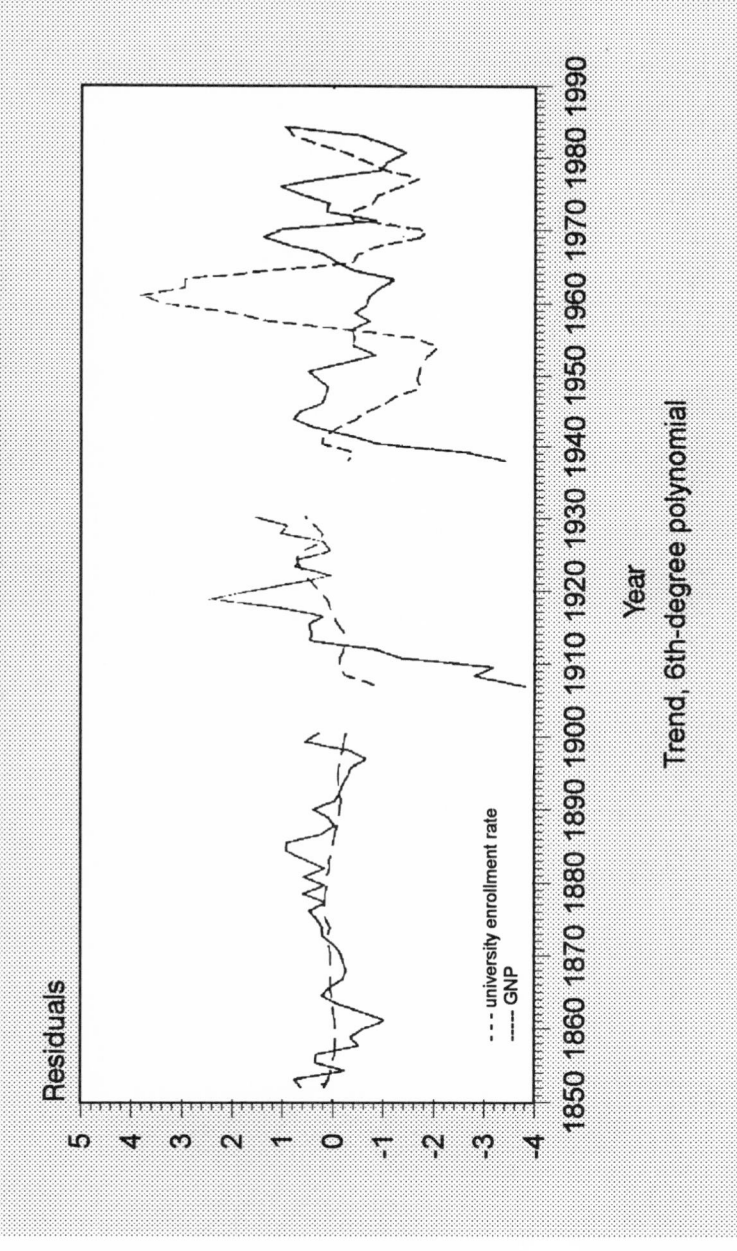

FIGURE 7.5 Residuals, France, 1871-1986

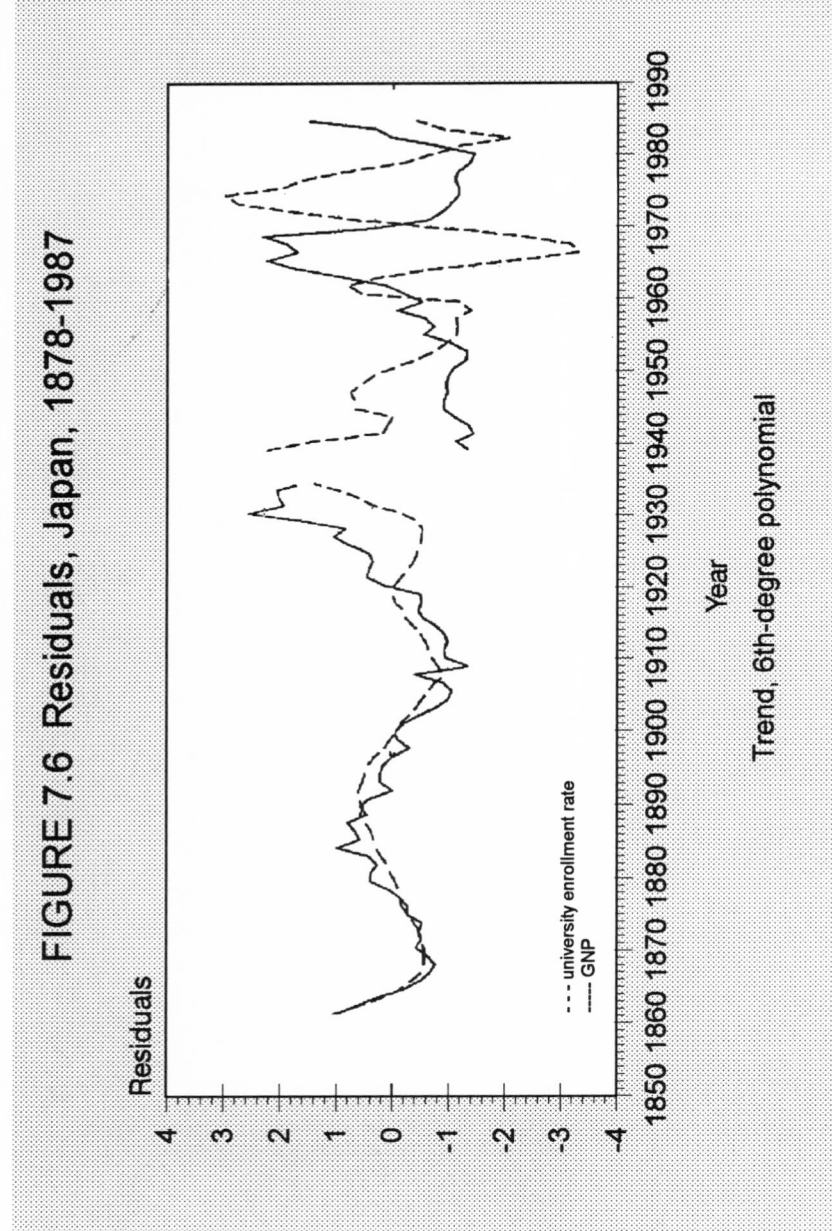

FIGURE 7.6 Residuals, Japan, 1878-1987

223

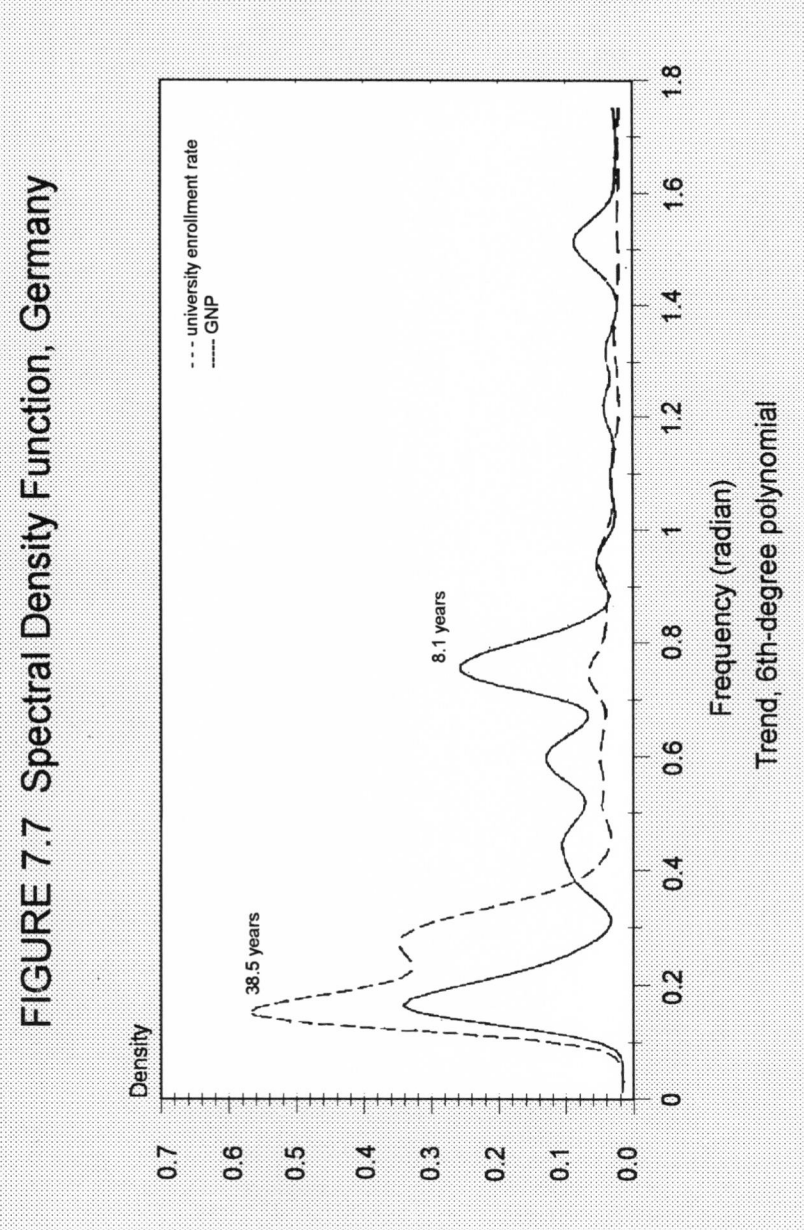

FIGURE 7.7 Spectral Density Function, Germany

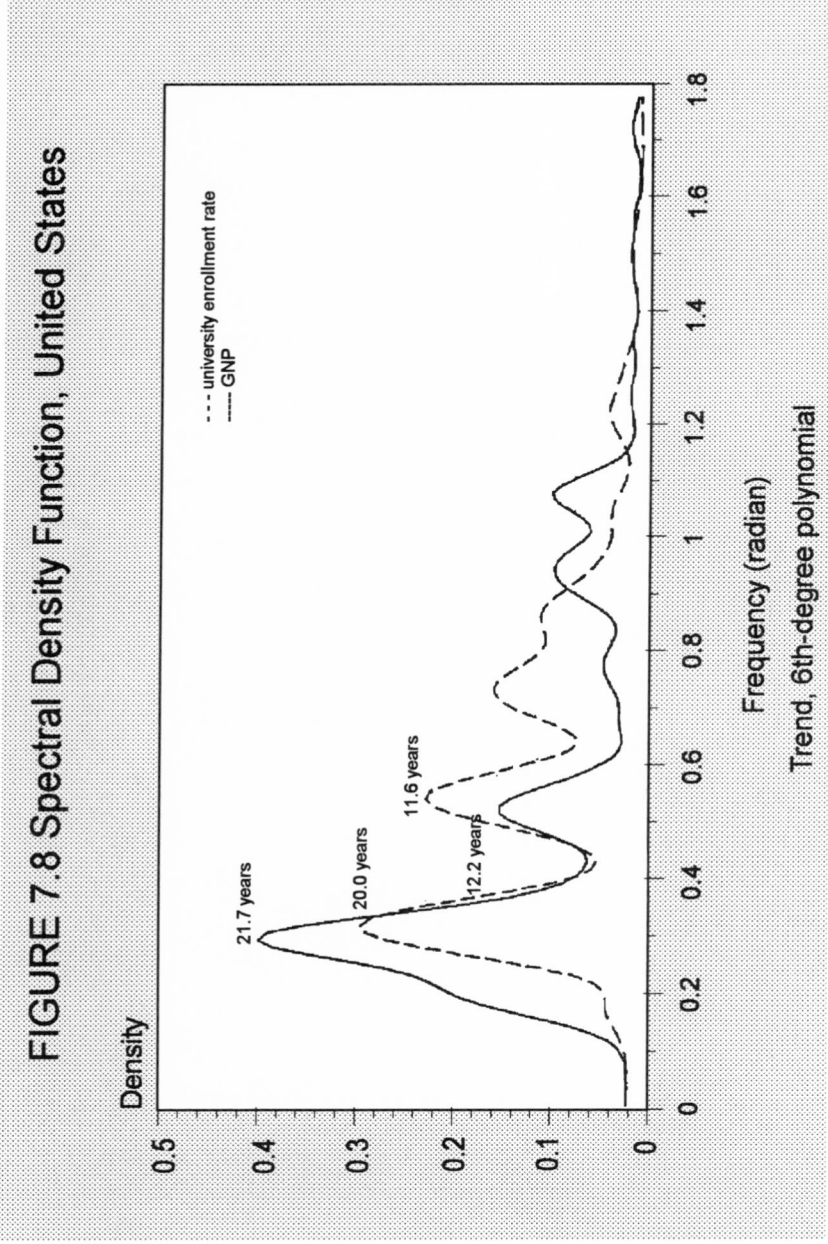

FIGURE 7.8 Spectral Density Function, United States

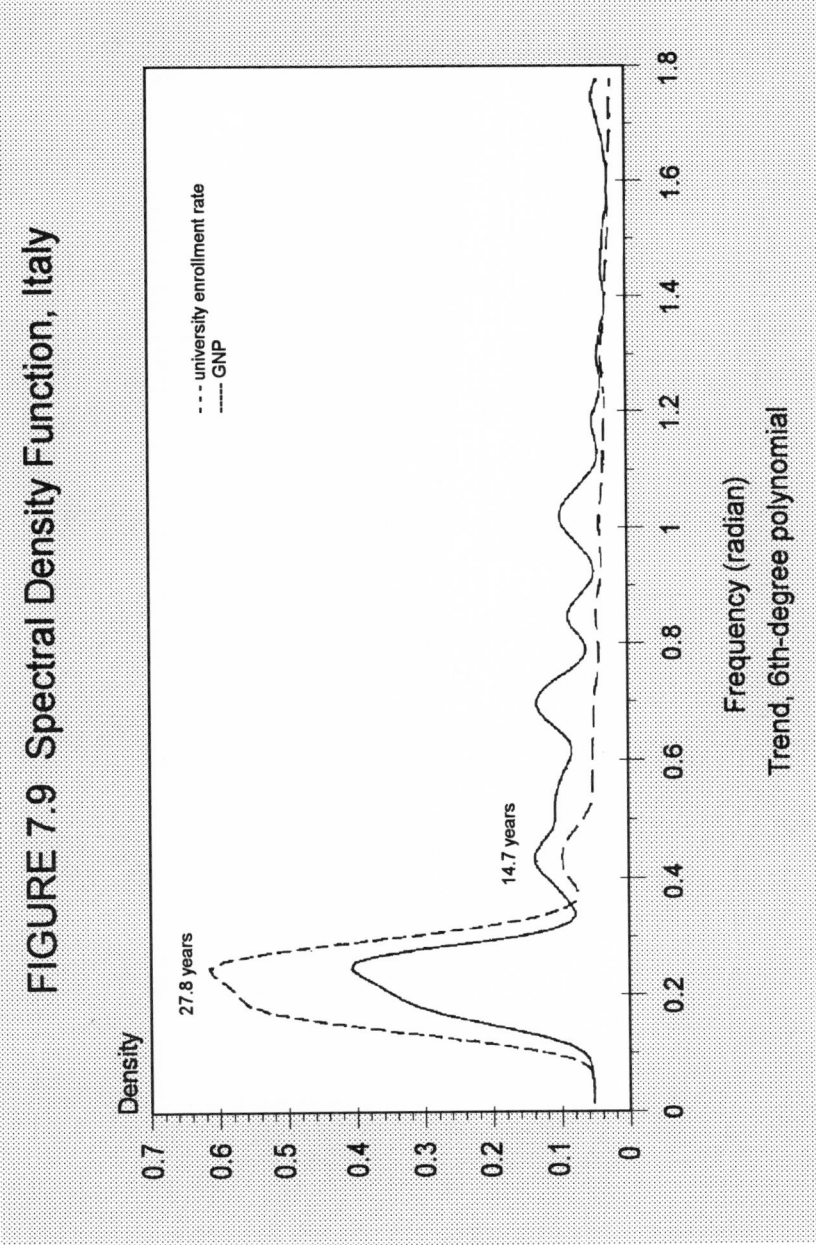

FIGURE 7.9 Spectral Density Function, Italy

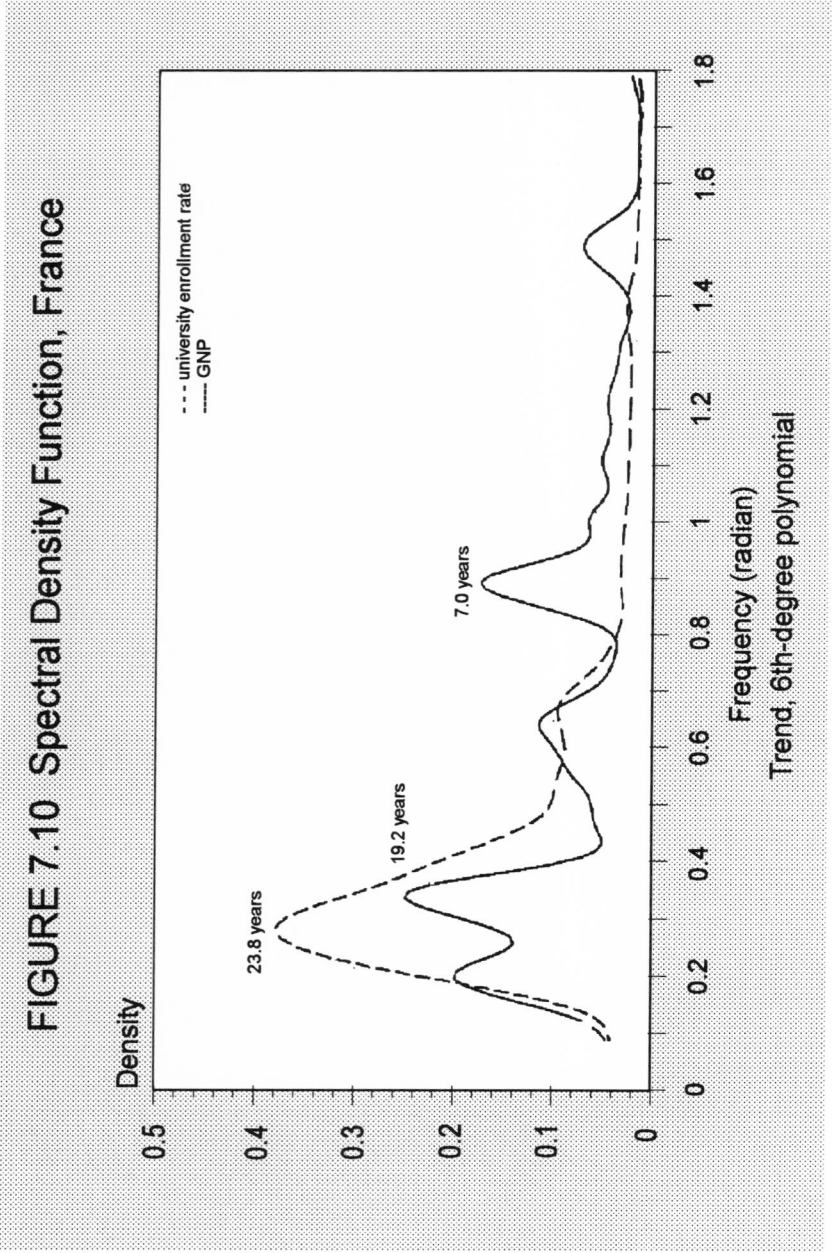

FIGURE 7.10 Spectral Density Function, France

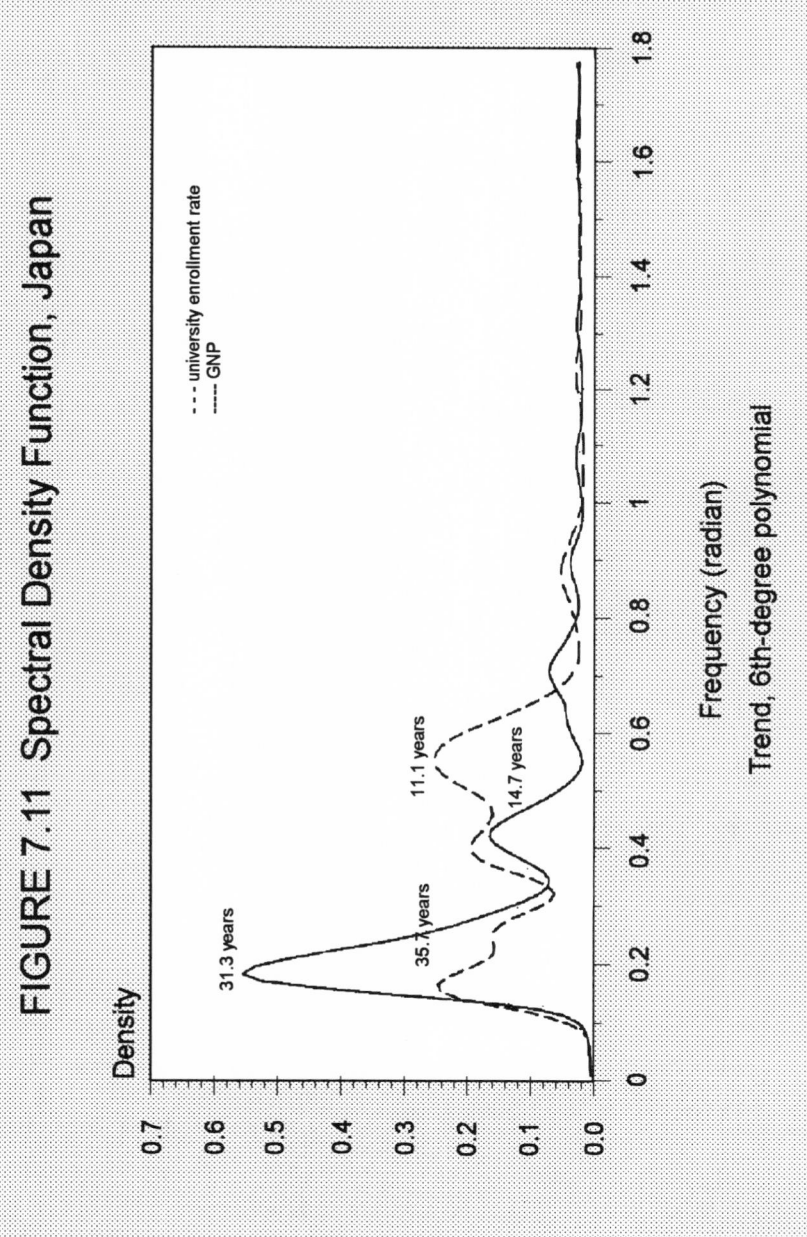

FIGURE 7.11 Spectral Density Function, Japan

8

Conclusions

8.1 Who Benefited by Educational Expansion?

The analysis presented in this volume covers a period of 120 years of educational expansion. At the end of the 19th century fewer than 2% of German school leavers went on to study at university, and female students did not even enjoy the right of university admission. Today in the United States as many as 35% of school leavers obtain university seats, and of these, the majority at all universities are women.

Who have been the beneficiaries of this remarkable process of educational expansion? Which groups in society have been able to take advantage of it? Has it made Western society more open, mobile, and democratic?

Women, without a doubt, count among those benefiting from educational expansion. This is the case in each of the countries examined here, with the exception of Japan. of Lower social strata, on the other hand, have hardly been able use it to improve their relative position. The poor girl from a remote rural area may now enjoy the privilege of attending university, but working class children of all ethnic backgrounds are still largely excluded. Fewer than 1% of German university students at the turn of the last century were children of working class families, and although the corresponding figure 90 years later has risen to 15%, this still lies far below their proportion of the working population.

A central concern of the present study is to portray educational expansion not merely in quantitative terms – presuming the growth to be nothing but "more of the same" – but in terms of the social conflicts that have driven it. The course of modernization involves social conflicts among social groups struggling over economic, political, and cultural rights, and the opening of universities to new groups in society is a crucial precondition for their emancipation. The rising number of middle-class students a century ago reflects the growing political influence that the bourgeoisie was then acquiring, but it also presented them a weapon in their effort to establish its political and cultural hegemony vis-à-vis other social strata. Today's predominance of women at universities and the controversy in the United States over quotas for ethnic minorities are contemporary instances of the same struggle for social mobility that has been waged by various groups since the middle of the 19th century for university access.

While the university represents, strictly, an institution of research, training, and meritocratic competition, it is unable to insulate itself against the contemporary conflicts being fought in its social environment, and these find their reflection in its halls of education. As technical training and formal diplomas take on ever more importance in determining one's income and professional opportunities, the conditions of university access increasingly become a political issue. Parallel to the cyclical course of educational expansion is a comparably cyclical history of conflicts over the right to participate in it. In Germany this history reached its first peak during the interwar years, and a second with the student movement of the 1960s; the conflict over university quotas for the children of immigrants – not only for Germany but for many European countries – may well become the next peak in this history.

Thus, the demand for educational access on the part of an upwardly mobile social group in modern society represents one aspect of its general struggle for equal opportunity and political rights. Access provides it with a weapon to use in breaking the hegemony of hitherto dominant social groups and in forcing a new "circulation of elites" in the economic and political system.

8.2 The Circulation of Elites

Modern society is mobile; there is a constant circulation of individuals who compete within a differentiated occupational structure over income, power, and prestige. A number of institutions have evolved to channel this mobility, including the educational system , in addition to the marketplace and the political arena. Each of these systems is characterized not only by means for achieving upward mobility but also by forms of discrimination and self-deselection which limit or even diminish the actual extent of mobility.

In the marketplace and in politics it is possible to pursue a career without particular educational achievement. The heroes in the marketplace are entrepreneurs, managers, "robber barons," who are able within their own life time to amass enviable wealth and status. To liberal ideologists, the marketplace is the very embodiment of mobility, open and free to all, and where each individual regardless of race, class, and sex determines his or her own fate. This ensures a continuous circulation within the economic elite as the successful rise, and the failures are driven out to make way for the more gifted.

Similarly, in the political system a continuous circulation among the elite is ensured by democratic elections. Neither can money buy success, nor may political power be exploited as an avenue to personal wealth. What counts is only the number of votes which the party or candidate obtains in competition with others. Particularly charismatic persons find in this political competition a tailor-made chance for attaining success, regardless of their economic resources and cultural capital.

The central topic of this volume is the opportunities for mobility that are afforded specifically by the educational system, but also the forms of self-deselection inherent in the nature of the educational expansion that has taken place over recent decades. The educational system is one the most important, if not *the* most important, channels of mobility in modern society, for the educational capital acquired here can be liquidated as well in other social systems. Formal diplomas support the career not only of civil servants but also that of managers, politicians, and journalists.

The overall circulation of elites in modern society is therefore the net result of upward and downward mobility in the marketplace, democratic elections, and meritocratic competition in the educational system. By ensuring a constant turnover it protects society from both rigidity and violent revolution. This constitutes, in fact, a major difference between modern and traditional societies.

8.3 Processes of Social Closure

A realistic analysis of these three channels of mobility, however, shows that each tends to develop a characteristic form of closure, and this applies to the marketplace just as it does to the political and educational systems. This book has examined not only educational expansion, resulting opportunities for upward mobility, and the circulation of elites but also self-deselection in the educational system and the conflicts which this spawns.

Processes of social closure are a reaction of the educational system to its own expansion. The more it expands, the stronger counterforces become that seek to limit further expansion through new forms of differentiation, selection, and self-deselection (drop-outs). The cyclical nature of educational expansion is in part due to the – also cyclical – formation of such counterforces, those wishing to find ways of institutionalizing closure and blockage.

Comparable forms of social closure and blockage can also be found in the marketplace and in politics. The more successful a company becomes at competing against other, the larger is the share of the market which it is able to conquer, until it reaches effective monopoly status and is then in a position to put an end to competition altogether. As Marx noted in the 19th century, monopoly is the natural consequence of capital accumulation, and competition therefore ultimately sows the seeds of its own self-destruction. It is the role of antitrust agencies in Western countries to prevent this self-destruction of competition in the marketplace.

The counterpart to this in the political system is the tendency in political parties commonly referred to as the "iron law of oligarchy." To demonstrate the process of oligarchialization Michels (1910) analyzed a political party in which it would have been least expected, the German Social-Democratic Party. Michels postulated that it is precisely the demands of effective competition against other parties which lead "inevitably" to the demise of internal circulation within the party itself. As in the marketplace and in politics, processes of social closure in the educational system create a block to the circulation of elites and put in its place a tendency to the reproduction of elites.

The more educational institutions expand, the stronger counterforces grow that attempt to brake their expansion. Only the form which the closure takes varies from country to country. In Germany, for instance, the institution of *numerus clausus* (subject-specific enrollment capping) has a long tradition, and it is still the most effective means at the disposal of education ministers to control university growth. In the United States and Japan, on the other hand, the educational system has undergone differentiation in the face of growing enrollment rates, with a fundamental distinction being made between elite and mass universities.

The existence of elite institutions effectively devalues the diploma granted by an institution in the mass sector and thus reproduces social structural differentiation at a higher level. At the end of the 19th century only some 5% enjoyed the privilege of higher education; the rest had to content themselves with being able to read and write. At the end of the 20th century, on the other hand, 5% are permitted admission to an elite university, while the rest can only hope to content themselves with a diploma from a mass university. While the educational system is based upon substantive competence and intellectual integrity, these qualities alone are not sufficient, for the door to an elite university opens only before those able to pay. Passing the entrance examination to an elite university requires, in addition to intelligence, the kind of cultural capital that is obtained only in families of the upper strata. The path to elite universities in France and Japan leads through elite secondary schools and special courses that prepare applicants specifically for the entrance examinations. This continuous educational training can be provided only in families which themselves enjoy substantial educational qualification and (particularly in the United States and Japan) the corresponding economic capital. The result of such educational systems is therefore not a circulation but a reproduction of elites.

A principal cause of the collapse of communist states at the beginning of the 1990s can be seen as the blocking of social mobility in each of the three social systems discussed above. There was neither competition in the marketplace, competition of democratic political parties, nor meritocratic competition over university admission. Comparison of social reproduction in the educational system of the former East Germany with that of elite universities in France, the United States, and Japan shows a surprising result: the level of social reproduction at elite universities is almost as high at the self-reproduction of the communist *nomenklatura* in East Germany – in each one finds 60%-70% of university students coming from the dominant elites.

8.4 What Has Changed?

Educational expansion has undoubtedly underpinned democratic attitudes in society and thereby strengthened democratic constitutional principles. Opinion research has shown that attitudes and behavior are influenced by the respondent's educational background. In a study of the moral conscience of volunteers Kohlberg (1969) found significantly more persons to reach the level of "autonomous morality" among those with higher educational qualification than among those with limited educational background. It is also particularly among the better educated that one finds more contemporary value systems, individualism, and political participation (Inglehart 1990). Communitarianism, with its claim to enhancing the moral awareness of society, is also a project in particular of the educated upper class.

Nevertheless, education per se offers no guarantee for democracy and constitutionality. In the first third of the 20th century Germany boasted a university system that was admired and copied all over the world, but almost overnight the Nazis were able to gain power over it and use it to serve their totalitarian program. There was substantial opposition to Nazis among working class organizations – the Communist Party, the Social-Democratic Party, labor unions – but virtually none at the universities. Similarly in Japan, whose educational system could almost emulate that of the United States during the interwar years, one found the country's great advances in modernization to be no obstacle to the militaristic nationalism which led the nation to disaster.

A school principal in the United States, who himself is the survivor of a Nazi concentration camp, sends a letter to his staff colleagues every year in which he recalls seeing professional engineers constructing gas chambers, medical physicians murdering prisoners, and qualified nurses poisoning the handicapped. He ends his letter by saying, "I mistrust education."

Educational expansion is one aspect of modernization, and it is in its consequences just as equivocal as modernization itself. Modernization entails not only the blessings of technology but the increasing destruction of the environment, not only the security of democratic constitutionality but the bureaucratization of the everyday world, not only equality of opportunity and mobility but disintegration of "civil society." Educational expansion leads to the one just as it does to the other.

Notes

Chapter 1

1. Trow (1988); Dahrendorf (1965); Picht (1964); Eigler et al. (1980); Max-Planck-Institut für Bildungsforschung (1980).

2. See Table 1.1 for average annual growth rates between 1870 and 1940 for the United States, Germany, and France (below).

3. It is difficult to compare enrollment rates between countries with different educational systems. Here, enrollment rates have been calculated as follows: For Germany, the number of students at universities, technical universities and *Fachhochschulen* (= four-year professional colleges) as a percentage of five age cohorts (20-24 years). For Japan: (a) before the Second World War, number of students at universities and two-/four-year colleges as a percentage of four age cohorts (average of the cohorts of 20-24 years); (b) after the Second World War: number of students at four-year institutions (excluding two-year colleges) as a percentage of four age cohorts (average of the cohorts of 20-24 years). For the United States: the number of bachelor's degrees and first professional degrees as a percentage of one age cohort (average of the age cohorts of 20-24 years). Thus, enrollment rates have been computed as a percentage of five age cohorts for Germany, four age cohorts for Japan. For the United States the number of university graduates has been computed as a percentage of one age cohort. This operationalization preserves greater comparability with the corresponding figures from Europe; it accounts, on the one hand, for the higher drop-out rate at universities in the United States and, on the other, for the lower academic level of the early semesters of university study there. The computation for enrollment rates which has been used here probably underestimates enrollment rates for women in Japan and overestimates enrollment rates for both men and women in Germany.

4. Lévy-Garboua (1976); Freeman (1976).

5. Bourdieu (1989); Eigler et al. (1980, pp. 62-63); for East Germany see Mayer and Solga (1994); see also Chapter 6.3.

6. This effect can be illustrated in a simple example. Let us imagine a hypothetical two-class society of 100 persons, with 10 university graduates and 90 workers, in which the university enrollment rate among the former is 80% (i.e., 80% of the children of university graduates attend university themselves) and that among working-class families is 20%. Let us also assume equal fertility rates (e.g., two children per family in each class). In the second

generation there will be 26 university graduates [(10 x 0.8) + (90 x 0.2)] and only 74 workers, and in the third generation 36 university graduates [(26 x 0.8) + (74 x 0.2)] and only 64 workers. From generation to generation, however, the rate of growth in the proportion of university graduates declines, and the proportion eventually reaches an upper threshold of stability.

7. Blaug (1970); Vaizey (1962); Becker (1971).

8. See the various forms of the "cobweb" model in Freeman (1975a, 1975b).

9. Bernstein (1975); Rolff (1980); Lenhardt (1984).

10. Riese (1977); Freeman (1976).

11. Burkhardt (1932); Achner (1931).

12. Barbagli (1974, pp. 135, 146); see also Rosenberg (1967, p. 53).

13. There are gaps in the time-series data available for the United Kingdom before 1920. Greenwood (1935, p. 6) presents data on the expansion of the larger British universities (Cambridge, London, Oxford, etc.) in the period before the First World War.

14. Stone (1974, vol. 1, pp. 67-68) points out that the growth can be traced in part to an influx of foreigners; see also Musgrove (1960).

15. An ironic presentation of this "logic" is found in Young (1959).

16. For Germany see Lundgreen (1977) and Manegold (1970); for France see Shinn (1980).

17. The rising enrollment rate during times of high unemployment has been called a "warehouse effect" (Walters 1984). However, this effect has less explanatory power in countries where students bear a high proportion of educational costs. Staying on at university instead of becoming unemployed is too expensive at (private) institutions of higher education in the United States and Japan whereas in Germany (and France) the status of a "student" is preferred to being unemployed.

18. See Rosenberg (1943). However, Milward (1981) doubts whether the "depression" of 1878-1890 actually involved a serious rupture in the business cycle.

19. A time series analysis (spectral analysis) comparing the cyclical movement of university enrollment rates and economic expansion in different countries over a period of more than 100 years is given in Chap. 7; see also Windolf (1992, 1993).

20. Titze (1984) has demonstrated the cyclical course of educational expansion for Germany. The cyclical course for France between 1950 and 1980 has been presented by Cherkaoui (1982, Fig. 1.2) and that for the United States since 1890 by Hamblin (1973, p. 115).

21. The data for the United Kingdom are available only for the years from 1919 to 1938, during which time the number of male students rose from 36,370 to 49,200 and the number of female students from 12,600 to 14,220. Source: Mitchell and Jones (1971, pp. 219-220).

22. See Deutsche Hochschulstatistik (p. 4), edited by the Hochschulvervaltungen; Struppe and Winckler, Berlin, 1931.

23. Holtfrerich (1980, pp. 256-256); Ringer (1969, pp. 62-63).

24. Italy is the only country with increasing enrollment rates during the war. Whereas university enrollment rates dropped almost to zero during the war in Germany and France because male students were drafted, Italian students continued to attend universities in increasing numbers. This "Italian" growth pattern was repeated during the Second World War.

25. A further factor in the drop in university enrollment was the decline in the proportion of foreign students at French universities in the 1930's: from 12,014 in 1925 (20.5% of all students) and 17,281 in 1930 (22%) to 7,964 in 1937 (10.6%). Source: Annuaire statistique de la France, Résumé rétrospective 1966, INSEE, Paris.

26. For instance, in the five cohorts of those aged 20-24 years there were 2,474,465 men in 1925 and 2,450,747 men in 1933 (Germany); thus the size of this age group had declined by approximately 1% (census data). At the same time the number of students rose from 90,000 to almost 117,000 (+30%).

27. Only graduates from higher secondary schools which are entitled by law to provide the 'Abitur' ('baccalauréat' in France) are allowed to enter university.

28. Trow (1988); Meyer and Hannan (1979).

29. The trend function is defined as : $\ln(y) = a + bt$, where y is the enrollment rate, t is time, and b is the regression coefficient. The regression coefficient here represents the average annual growth in enrollment.

30. A more sophisticated method to calculate the exact period of cycles using spectral analysis is given in Chap. 7.

31. It is difficult to characterize the most recent economic depression in terms of the business cycle. Since the early 1980's the "hard core" of unemployment is rising in Germany every five years by approximately 1 million. The period 1975-1985 resembles more the protracted depression from 1876-1893 (see Rosenberg 1943, 1967).

32. See Johnston (1979, p. 304). The analysis here uses the maximum-likelihood estimation routine of SAS. The Durbin-Watson coefficient measures the degree of autocorrelation; this coefficient can take values between 0 and 4, and at values around 2 autocorrelation is not significant.

33. Cycles of economic growth and of educational expansion may have approximately the same period (= duration measured in years), but shifted forward or backward in time (phase lag/lead). For instance, the correlation coefficient between two cycles with identical periods but shifted in time (phase lag or lead) by a quarter of a period, is zero.

34. In Germany first-year students begin with their "major" subject (e.g., law, medicine, sociology) immediately after enrollment in their first semester. Their are no "liberal arts" courses and no undergraduate study. The terms "subject" and "discipline" are used here interchangeably and refer to the specific university subject a student has chosen at the time of enrollment.

35. I was not able to analyze the cyclical variation of university subjects for the period 1950-1990, since the official classification of subjects has changed in the mid-1970's, thus making it impossible to compare the numbers of students in different subjects between the two periods.

36. If r=0, one subject lags a quarter of a period behind the other one. If r=-1, one subject lags half a period behind the other one.

Chapter 2

1. Jencks and Riesman (1968); Jencks (1973).

2. Berg (1970); Bourdieu and Passeron (1971); Boudon (1977); Meyer (1978); Freeman (1976).

3. Weber (1956, p. 736); see also Hintze (1963, p. 31); Bäumer (1930); Behrend (1929).

4. Sources: on aristocratic background, Jarausch 1978, p. 620; on children of university graduates, Sozialer Auf- und Abstieg des Deutschen Volkes, vol. 117 of Beiträge zur Statistik Bayerns, ed. Bayerisches Statistisches Landesamt, Munich, 1930, p. 32, and Preußische Statistik, vol. 236, p. 136; on theology, Preußische Statistik, vol. 167, p. 69, and vol. 236, pp. 54-55.

5. Shinn (1980, pp. 13, 18); see also Kosciusko-Morizet (1973).

6. Quoted in Rosenberg 1973, p. 129 (translation by the present author); see also Holtfrerich 1980.

7. It is probable that a large proportion of the commercial middle class in the Bavarian statistics was classified among the "entrepreneurs"; compare, for example, the (Prussian) figures from earlier years.

8. Source: Statistisches Bundesamt (1972).

9. Male students from families of small or middle-level farmers made up 4.3% of enrollment and female students from this background 1.7% (1928). The corresponding difference for those of working class background was 2.0% versus 0.6%, and that for children of lower level civil servants was 1.7% versus 0.6% (see Table 3.1)

10. A study of pupils' social class in the schools of Kassel (Germany) has shown that in 1913 almost 100% of the 12-year-old sons of university graduates, directors, manufacturers, and military officers attended Gymnasium, as opposed to only 1.9% of those from working class backgrounds. By 1928 the proportion among the latter had risen to 5.3% (Bäumer 1930, p. 30).

11. Kraul (1984, p. 112); see also Lundgreen et al. (1988).

12. These institutions were the 'Realgymnasium' and the 'Oberrealschule' which emphasized foreign languages (French and English) and/or natural sciences in their curricula – at the expense of classical languages latin and greek.

13. Those of aristocratic birth were something of an exception, as they were often able to find positions in the state bureaucracy even without the otherwise necessary credentials.

14. Churchill and Scrutton quoted in Griffith (1977, p. 173).

15. See Kaupen (1969) and Dahrendorf (1960). Cam (1978) in a study of French judges has described the opposition that codification of industrial law

met in the traditionalist/conservative law schools of that country. In 1935, 61% of all judges in France were from the higher social strata and only 5% from families of blue- or white-collar employees. Only when a number of 'juges rouges' from the working class milieu had managed to join the bench did industrial law find acceptance in France. A court in California which sustained a special rule favoring the admission of nonwhite students to a medical school, argued that the "social experiences" of these students represent a special admission qualification since these physicians are needed to care for the nonwhite population (see the case of "Bakke" in Manning 1977, p. 34).

16. Source: Statistisches Bundesamt 1972, p. 142.

17. See Herzog (1982, p. 1029); Klatt (1980, p. 44). The figure for 1976 is based not only on those with (tenured) civil service positions but includes all employees in the public sector.

18. Including 36% whose fathers were Lutheran ministers, i.e., we find a high proportion of professional inheritance among the Lutheran clergy.

19. In technical terms: In Table 2.4 "inflow" percentages are presented; Tables 2.5 and 2.6 show "outflow" percentages. See Featherman and Hauser (1978, p. 66).

20. Titze (1984, p. 93) has suggested a relationship between the dynamic of educational expansion and the choice of subject by students from lower social strata: "Enrollment in the socially more 'open' subjects is more subject to cyclical variations than is that in the socially more 'exclusive' subjects." In other words, the incentives or disincentives deriving from labor market conditions would play a greater role in the choice of subject among the lower strata than among the higher strata. This hypothesis was tested with the available data from 1866-1934, correlating the proportion of students in a given subject that were from the higher strata with the degree of cyclical variation in that subject. The proportions of higher strata students in the various subjects varied between 3.9% (Catholic theology) and 37.5% (Lutheran theology). The mean of the residuals was taken as indicator of the degree of cyclical variation. The results were as follows: $r = 0.11$ for men 1866-1914; $r = 0.09$ for men 1919-1934; $r = 0.08$ for women 1919-1934. None of the coefficients reached statistical significance, and Titze's hypothesis is therefore not verified.

21. Highest civil servant in a Prussian rural district ('Landrat').

22. Theology, law, medicine, arts/humanities.

Chapter 3

1. See also Achner (1931) and Burkhardt (1932).

2. See the Sozialwissenschaftliche Rundschau, appendix to the 'Ärztliche Mitteilungen' (1931, p. 91).

3. Deutsche Hochschulstatistik, edited by Hochschulverwaltungen, vol. 7,

summer semester 1931; see also Chap. 1.4.

4. Source: Who Are the Job Seekers? United States Department of Labor, Washington, United States Government Printing Office, 1937.

5. In 1930 there were 47,000 physicians in Germany; this meant 7.3 physicians per 10,000 inhabitants (source: Studium und Beruf 1935, p. 77). By comparison, there were 24 physicians per 10,000 inhabitants in West Germany in 1982.

6. See Sect. 5.4 on the 'grandes écoles' and the state bureaucracy in France.

7. Source: Studium und Beruf 1935, p. 137.

8. These positions are quoted from Lüders (1931, p. 292).

9. See Schwarz 1931 and Deutsches Philologen-Blatt 1930, p. 449.

10. These numbers exclude 1600 male and 150 female students admitted specifically for education courses (see Studium und Beruf 1934, p. 20)

11. Source: Studium und Beruf 1934, pp. 19-21.

12. Moraw (1987) describes the ways in which the Gymnasium was subjected to political pressure, taking the example of the Kurfürst-Friedrich Gymnasium (Heidelberg).

13. On the role of the prominent German philosopher Martin Heidegger during the early Nazi period of 1933/1934 see Farías (1987).

14. Der Character der Auslese ("The Nature of the Selection"), in Berliner Börsenzeitung, no. 191, 24 Apr. 1936.

15. Frankfurter Allgemeine Zeitung, 14 Oct. 1983, p. 9.

Chapter 4

1. Titze et al. (1985, p. 121) points out that the controversy over education policy is dependent upon the business cycle: when there is a scarcity of highly qualified personnel, there are calls for greater mobilization of a reserve of personnel, but in times of high unemployment the concept of elite universities enjoys increased popularity. In West Germany the discussion of elite universities began particularly with a speech given by the then Foreign Minister Hans-Dietrich Genscher before the German Employers' Organization, in which he stressed the need for private elite universities in Germany (Handelsblatt, 15 Dec. 1983).

2. See Baltzell (1958, p. 306). For example, Frederick W. Taylor, the father of "scientific management," was one of the most prominent products of Exeter. His family in Philadelphia showed all the features of "Philadelphia gentlemen." His father belonged to the "Quaker aristocracy," was one of the city's wealthiest men, and was fully integrated into its cultural life. See also Nelson (1980, p. 27) and Baltzell (1958, p. 122). Cookson and Persell (1985) describe the organization of elite boarding schools in the 1980's.

3. Source: Historical Statistics of the United States, part 1, p. 379, United States Department of Commerce, Washington, 1975.

4. Coleman et al. (1981, 1982); see also Coleman and Hoffer (1987) and Husén (1983).

5. The proportion of pupils coming from the upper social classes is higher at private schools compared to public high schools. This difference must be controlled for statistically.

6. The report of the National Commission on Excellence in Education, addressed to the American people and the Secretary of Health, Education, and Welfare, entitled 'A Nation at Risk – The Imperative for Educational Reform', Washington, April 1983, p. 5.

7. These institutionalized recruitment channels are called pantouflage in France and are discussed in more detail in Sect. 5.4. See Kosciusko 1973; Shinn 1980.

8. This is discussed in detail in Sect. 4.6; see also Karabel (1972, p. 523) and Litt and Parkinson (1979, p. 84).

9. Levy (1986) has analyzed the educational systems in Brazil and other South American countries and confirms the "three-stage model" proposed here.

10. Many examples can be adduced, a few of which are the following: The Comprehensive School of Waldhäuser-Ost in Tübingen applied for a change back to the traditional school system as the result of the low proportion of its pupils obtaining university accreditation (Frankfurter Rundschau, 3 Nov. 1983). The Robert-Koch Comprehensive School in Kreuzberg (Berlin) is threatened with closure because too many German parents reacted to the high percentage of Turkish pupils there and chose to send their children instead to traditional Gymnasien in other parts of the city (Tagesspiegel, 23 June 1985). Because of the comprehensive system introduced in the state of Hessen, 283 pupils in the County of Odenwald are sent over the state line every day to attend traditional schools in the state of Baden-Württemberg (Frankfurter Allgemeine Zeitung, 28 June 1985). French parents in the suburbs of Paris with large populations from North Africa (Morocco, Algeria) send their children to private schools in the city (L'Express, 18 May 1984).

11. The numbers of students at German institutions of higher education increased by 96% between 1975 and 1991. This increase was distributed unevenly by subject and sex. For example, the number of women in law school rose during these years by 196%, the number of men by only 36%. In the subject of economics the number of men increased by 140%, but that of women by 523%. During the 1960's a high proportion of women were enrolled in teachers' colleges, in the late 1970's they studied law and economics. (Source: Statistisches Bundesband Wiesbaden: Bildung im Zahlenspiegel 1977, 1994; the calculations are those of the present author.)

12. The log-linear analysis showed that mobility rates were accounted for almost entirely by structural mobility and only a small proportion by exchange mobility. The term "structural mobility" refers to mobility resulting from all factors which cause a current occupational distribution to differ from that of the fathers, such as a changing occupational structure (e.g., the new service class, differential fertility and marriage rates). The term "exchange mobility" refers to

the degree of equality of opportunities and the openness of society (McClendon 1977).

13. See Fujita (1978). Sabouret (1985) describes the various forms of resignation and vandalism found among those who lose out in this meritocratic competition.

14. Similar figures are found for French universities (Boltanski 1982, p. 318). The ten grandes écoles (engineering schools) with the highest prestige (e.g., École Centrale, Polytechnique) showed a total enrollment of 3285 students in 1957 and one of 4893 in 1978, an increase of 49%. At the same time there was an almost fourfold growth in enrollment in the mass sector.

15. Source: Digest of Education Statistics 1989, National Center for Education Statistics, Washington, DC, p. 212.

16. 16. For a critical analysis of the IUT and the "perverse effects" of expansion, see Boudon (1977).

17. For a description of the conflict between the French government and the anciens élèves of the École Nationale d'Administration, see Le Monde, 2 Aug. 1983, 14 Oct. 1983, and 11 Feb. 1984.

18. This critical assessment of research and teaching at the elite institutions in France is shared by virtually all observers; see Schwartz (1983, p. 64), Kosciusko (1973, p. 27), and Shinn (1980, p. 131).

19. Since the beginning of the 1980's there has been a sharp rise in the proportion of students enrolled in Numerus clausus subjects. This rise can be expected to continue due to the imposition of Numerus clausus restrictions on the study of management science in 1989.

20. A summary of the most important features of the Italian educational system is presented in Educazione Italia '86 – I sentieri della qualità, published by the Centro studi investimenti sociali, Milan, 1987, ed. Angeli. An analysis of the Italian school system can be found in the collection edited by Gattullo and Visalberghi (1986).

21. Somewhat older descriptions of Italian higher education are provided by Clark (1977) and Giglioli (1979); more recent ones are found in Francesco and Trivellato (1985) and Moscati (1983). The awarding of matriculation entitlement to school certificates from the istituti technici in effect made the Italian school system comprehensive. The analysis by Francesco and Trivellato (1985) details the effects which this structural change has had on Italian universities.

22. In Figure 4.1 the number of beginning students in 1953 is compared with the number of university graduates (laureati) in 1958; beginning students of 1986 are compared with graduates of 1991 (time lead of beginning students: five years).

23. In 1984 the present author interviewed recruitment officers from the University of California at Berkeley and from Stanford University. Those from the latter stressed that Berkeley selected "only" according to academic grades, while Stanford considered **in addition** other features, such as sports, music, and art.

24. Official income statistics for the United States show for 1982 an income above $50,000 in 8.2% of families in which a man aged 45-55 years is the head of the household.

25. In addition to the nondenominational schools there are "parochial" schools, many of them supported by the Catholic Church; these are attended by 12% of school children in the United States. Source: The American Freshman – National Norms for Fall 1984, A. Austin et al. (ed.), Council on Education. (The dataset is available on microfilm, ED 255106, Educational Resources Information, Alexandria, VA.)

26. Due to the seniority system income is strongly correlated with age; the higher income groups are therefore overrepresented in Table 4.6: parents of students are aged over 45 years, but the five income groups in the table are based on all age groups in the population.

27. 27. Source: Cummings and Naoi (1974, p. 255); Cummings (1980: 227, Table 8.4).

28. The representation coefficient is calculated as: the proportion of students from group A divided by the relative size of group A in the active population. The figures presented here are biased due to the unavailability of data for each year regarding those in the population aged 45-55 (the probable age of students' fathers); the data used here are based on averages across all age cohorts.

29. An analysis of social background of students enrolled at three German universities (N=2886) is given in Windolf (1995). In an analysis of the social differentiation of students at the Free University of Berlin and the Technical University of Berlin, Preisser (1989) found a high proportion of students from the upper strata in selective subjects (medicine, some engineering subjects) and a high proportion of those from the lower strata in nonselective subjects (education, sociology). Data from Swedish universities also show the subjects of medicine and law to be increasingly popular among the upper strata (Premfors 1979; Gurgsdies 1981).

30. Similar figures for social origin of students enrolled at French "Grandes Ecoles" between 1950 and 1990 are given in Euriat and Thélot (1995).

Chapter 5

1. These were referred to as the "uprooted" (spostati). See Barbagli (1974, p. 66); on the United Kingdom see Musgrove (1960, p. 99). For a criticism of Musgrove see Perkin (1961) and Hart (1972).

2. This – partially corrupt – means of job distribution is referred to in the Italian context as 'clientelismo'; see Shefter (1977) and Graziano (1984). A noncorrupt version was that of the "entitlement" system in Prussia.

3. Sources: for Germany, Flora (1983), chapter on government employees, p. 263; for the United Kingdom, Mitchell (1975, p. 60); for the United States, Historical Statistics of the United States, part I, pp. 1102-1103, Washington,

1970. The term "civil servant" is used here for all employees in the public sector without regard to nationally specific differences in status grades (e.g., the tenured 'Beamte' versus the nontenured 'Angestellte' in Germany).

4. Weber (1957, p. 260) noted that, "In the modern state the real power rests necessarily and unavoidably in the hands of the civil service."

5. Michels (1957, p. 260) described the organizational structures of the SPD and the labor unions as "promotion machines" for a "worker aristocracy." "Thus the working class movement fulfills for German workers a role similar to that of the Catholic Church for some elements in the petit bourgeoisie and for farmers. Both serve the most intelligent strata as a means for social ascent."

6. Hoogenboom (1960); Legendre (1968); Ryan (1972).

7. In Germany (and also in France) the hierarchy of educational certificates (e.g., college/university degree) corresponds to the hierarchy of higher positions in the state bureaucracy that graduates may attain during their professional career.

8. Bourdieu and Passeron (1970); Bourdieu (1989).

9. The 'grands corps' are the top bureaucratic institutions in France, such as the Conseil d'État, Cour des Comptes, and Inspection des Finances. Up to the present day most top managers of large (state owned) corporations are recruited among the members of the 'grands corps' (Bauer and Bertin-Mourot 1995).

10. Tocqueville (1951); Skowronek (1982); Nelson (1982).

11. Quoted in White (1948, p. 307).

12. Quoted in White (1948, pp. 308-9).

13. Quoted in Key (1962, p. 383).

14. This was Democratic Senator William Marcy's blunt corollary; quoted in Nelson (1982, p. 759).

15. Quoted in Banfield (1969, p. 191), emphasis added.

16. Hays (1964); Hofstadter (1955); Hoogenboom (1960).

17. Skowronek (1982); Schattschneider (1942, p. 139).

18. Quoted in Rosenbloom (1984, p. 5).

19. Source: US Department of Commerce: Historical Statistics of the United States, Washington 1970, Part I, Series Y 308-317, pp. 1102-3. US Department of Commerce: Statistical Abstracts of the United States, Washington DC, Vol. 1973-1988, Chapter "Federal Government Finances and Employment."

20. Wolfinger (1972); Meyerson and Banfield (1969, p. 175).

21. Quoted in Hoogenboom (1959, p. 311).

22. The history of political institutions in France (Sect. 5.4) provides further confirmation of this hypothesis.

23. The testing procedures had become bureaucratic and inflexible. Savas and Ginsburg (1973, p. 75) report the following case. A municipality planned to hire an engineer. According to the Civil Service Act, each applicant for the position was to take a test, and the hiring agency had to chose from among the three candidates with the highest scores. However, the top six scorers were utterly unsuited for the position due to the technical training which the work required. "Only by finally persuading four of the top six to waive their legal

claims to the job, thereby elevating number seven to number three, was the agency able to hire the man with the needed experience." Such a rigid and inflexible bureaucracy was the price that was paid for ending the spoils system. The scores on application tests given by the New York City Police Department vary considerably by ethnic background; only 1.6% of blacks pass the test, 4.4% of hispanics, and 10.6% of whites. "The Guardians' Association, a group of black police officers, called on the Police Department to either reject the results or base promotions to sergeant on the **quota system** instead of on the list of officers who passed the test" (New York Times, 4 Sept. 1984, p. 1; emphasis added).

24. Quoted in Legendre (1968, p. 539), emphasis added.

25. Legendre (1968, pp. 279, 540).

26. The social network from which the patronage system recruited applicants for office was different in France (= the local "people of rank") and in the United States (= the urban immigrants).

27. We find here the historical origin of the 'classes préparatoires'. The social origin of their students is shown in Table 4.7.

28. A similar distinction is made at the College of Social Work (Centre d'Études Supérieures de la Sécurité Sociale), with separate examinations given to students and to employees of the Ministry of Social Affairs. In 1962 there were 30 seats reserved for each group; in 1973 there were 34 for students and 26 for bureaucrats (Sadran 1977, p. 77).

29. Bourdieu (1989); Boudon (1973, p. 115).

30. Quoted in Sadran (1977, p. 89).

31. Kelsall (1974, p. 173) has shown in a study of the civil service in the United Kingdom that students from Oxford or Cambridge tend to score better on the oral than on the written examination.

32. Labov (1966) has shown in linguistic studies that it is the middle class rather than the upper class who tend to show particular attention to correctness of pronunciation. He refers to this phenomenon as middle class hypercorrectness.

33. The "first" path is that for "normal" students (concours étudiant); the "second" is for bureaucrats already employed at lower levels in the administration (concours fonctionnaire); the "third" opens the door to representatives of various organizations such as labor unions and to employees of municipal authorities.

34. Source: Le Monde, 29 July 1986, p. 6; 1 Aug. 1986, p. 1; and 30 Apr. 1986, p. 13.

35. The position of 'Landrat' was crucial in terms of the political control of the Prussian provinces. Many of these county executives were aristocrats (Junker) **and** trained university lawyers; this distinguished them from French or British aristocrats (see Table 2.5 above). Source: Röhl (1967, p. 116); see also Jarausch (1984, p. 31).

36. For details of this training in the court system and the Prussian administration which was copied by the Japanese government, see Sect. 5.6.

37. The Northcote-Trevelyan Report on reform of the civil service was published in 1853, but the practice of giving examinations to applicants was introduced only in 1870/1871; see Hart (1972, p. 65), H. Finer (1927), Rosenbloom (1984), S.E. Finer (1952).

38. Quoted from Hattenhauer (1980, p. 301).

39. Quoted in Hattenhauer (1980, p. 299); emphasis added.

40. The German word 'Ablösung' is translated here in the sense of "being relieved, superseded, replaced"; in legal terms it may also mean "dismissed."

41. Quoted by Hattenhauer (1980, pp. 306-307).

42. Although the bureaucracy in Japan was reorganized in 1945 under pressure from the American occupation authorities, it returned in the 1950's to many of the principles which had originally been adopted at the end of the 19th century; see Kubota (1969).

43. Passin (1966); Cummings (1980). The division of the Japanese education system into elite and mass sectors developed out of these two types of schools. The imperial universities became the (public) elite sector; the numerous private law schools, which accepted any student who could pay the tuition fees, and which did not have a standardized curriculum, expanded into the (private) mass sector (see Sect.. 4.5).

44. From a comparative point of view it can be seen here that states (e.g., Germany) which developed an educational **system**, i.e. standardized curricula for secondary schools and universities, recognize university examinations nationwide and entrance examinations are not important for social mobility. In states with a fragmented educational "system" (e.g., Japan) entrance examinations become a crucial barrier to social mobility.

45. The "big eight" are elite academic schools founded between 1877 and 1908; these are attended particularly by children from the upper social strata and prepare them for university study. The most exclusive of these is the "number one" school in Tokyo. See Passin (1966); Kubota (1969, p. 61-62).

46. Kubota (1969, p. 74, Table 22). Little had changed in this respect in the mid-1970's: among those serving as section head or higher 62.3% had attended Todai University; 88.6% in the Finance Ministry and 76% in the Foreign Office. In addition, approximately one-third of board chairmen of the leading corporations in Japan had attended this university. See Rohlen (1983, pp. 88-89).

47. The feudal aristocracy did, however, retain a crucial position, for example, in the upper house of Parliament (a "House of Peers") and the Privy Council. The latter had an advisory function and consisted of 26 members appointed by the Emperor for life. The House of Peers and the Privy Council were both intended to offset the power of Parliament and political parties.

Chapter 6

1. Only enrollment rates at universities and four-year colleges are shown in Fig. 6.2. Two-year colleges do not offer an academic or professional education and are therefore excluded. In 1960 the enrollment rate of men at four-year institutions was 16.4%, that of women was 1.3%; the absolute difference in 1960 between men and women was 15.1%. In 1991 the enrollment rate of men was 41.6% that of women 8.3%; the absolute difference was 33.3%. In Germany the absolute difference in enrollment rates between men and women was 11.9% in 1991.

2. See Figs. 4.1 and 4.2.

3. See Table 6A at the end of this chapter, which presents unemployment rates between 1973 and 1990 for the skilled work force in the United States and Germany.

4. Given the very low unemployment rates in Japan until the early 1990's it is, nevertheless, difficult to explain the decline of enrollment rates for men in terms of the human capital theory.

5. It must also be considered that Germany still has a multitier secondary educational system; for the majority of children the decision of whether to attend university is made at the age of 12 when parents decide whether their children will attend the academic track of the secondary school system (Gymnasium). Germany was (and still is) the only advanced Western country with a multitier secondary educational system; there are only a few comprehensive secondary schools in Germany. The multitier system in Germany provides an additional reason for why the expansion of higher education in Germany did not react to the economic recession.

6. See Sect. 1.2 (collective conflict theory).

7. It is not to deny that this institution is supported by cultural patterns. However, it is important here to point out that the level of juridification is higher in the United States, i.e., there are more antidiscrimination laws in the United States than in Japan or in Germany.

8. "Biological" factors (IQ) and the distribution of cognitive abilities in the population (bell curve; Herrnstein and Murray, 1994)) can certainly not explain this ceiling. Institutions of higher education are "flexible" and they adjust their curriculum to the cognitive abilities of their clientele.

9. In 1974/1975 students at specialized colleges were added to the tertiary educational sector; see the "jump" in the curve in Fig. 6.1.

10. A more detailed analysis of the cyclical character of expansion was given in Chap. 1.4 (Fig. 1.9); see also Chap. 7.

11. See Lammers and Hickson (1979); Windolf (1988); Paul Windolf: Bildungsexpansion und Arbeitsmarkt, Habilitation thesis, University of Marburg, 1985., p. 314; Maurice et al. (1986); Lutz (1976).

12. There is another difference in the division of labor between the two countries: In Germany nurses are trained in an apprenticeship program in the

hospitals whereas physicians are educated at university. The division of labor between the two professions is more rigid in Germany than in the United States where nurses are trained at colleges and the hierarchical differentiation is less pronounced. The questions arises to what extent the educational system influences different patterns of work tasks and what is "effect" and what is "cause" in the relationship between the educational system and the division of labor.

13. The conclusion that there are even more managers in Japan than in the United States is, however, premature; just the opposite is true. In Japan, there is no strong relationship between training and work task, and the distribution of students over university subjects does not determine their future work task.

14. Pareto (1923, paragraphs 2056 and 2057). See also the last chapter in Mosca (1950) and Meisel (1958).

15. At German universities 29% of women compared to 24% of men come from the upper classes in 1991 (Bundesministerium für Bildung und Wissenschaft 1992: p. 98, Table 2.26).

16. The highest level attained by either parent.

17. Figure for 1995 (12th German Parliament).

18. The equation is: $\ln(y) = \ln(a) + bx$. x = unemployment rates; y = enrollment rates; b = coefficient of elasticity.

Chapter 7

1. An earlier version of this chapter has been published in International Journal of Comparative Sociology 34 (1993) and is coauthored by Joachim Haas, University of Heidelberg. I thank J. Haas for his authorization to publish part of the joint article in this book.

2. "In history a period of faith will be followed by a period of skepticism, which will in turn be followed by another period of faith, this by another period of skepticism, and so on" (Pareto 1983, p. 1692).

3. As early as 1937 Slutzky demonstrated that the application of appropriate filters (e.g., moving average, first differencing) can construe cycles out of "white noise" (i.e., random fluctuation).

4. These preliminary results are derived from a study of cyclical fluctuations in the number of labor union members, carried out at the Department of Sociology, University of Heidelberg in which the present author was involved.

5. Table 7.1 shows the different trends which have been used for these computations.

6. The sixth-degree polynomial uses the following function to estimate the trend: $Y = at + a_2t^2 + a_3t^3 + a_4t4 + a_5t^5 + a_6t^6$ (t=year; y=enrollment rates). The value thereby estimated for the trend is subtracted from the time series, yielding the residuals, an operation referred to as filtering. The time series is filtered to eliminate certain frequency bands, in the present case cycles with a duration

longer than 35-40 years are filtered out. One distinguishes here between the "filter input" (observed data, based on annual observations) and "filter output" (trend = polynomial). Since an additive model is used here, the filter input minus filter output yields the residuals.

7. The frequency is the reciprocal of period. For simplification, details are not presented here in terms of the frequency domain but only in terms of the time domain (years). It should be noted that the "peaks" of the spectral density function are to be interpreted as frequency bands. A spectral density function with a "peak" at, for example, a cycle duration of 38.5 years means a band of variable width around 38.5 years. The longer the time series, the narrower this band is. In Figs. 7.7-7.11 the frequencies are given in terms of radians. The cycle duration (= period) can be calculated by the following formula: 6.28/frequency = cycle duration (in years).

8. The lag/lead is calculated as the average phase shift for the overall time series. Differing lag/lead structures may occur in the various subperiods. Residuals for Japan (Fig. 7.6), for instance, show that the lead/lag between university enrollment and GNP increases over time: Between 1880 and 1890 both residuals almost overlap (lead/lag = 0), but after 1960 we observe an almost "anticyclical" behavior of both systems (large lead/lag between enrollment rates and GNP).

9. Eulenburg (1904, p. 256). For a similar conclusion regarding Italian universities before World War I, see M. Barbagli (1974, pp. 134-136).

10. The values of the spectral density function are considerably higher for GNP (0.56) than for university enrollment (0.25). The variation explained by two cycles is 55% for GNP, but only 34% for university enrollment (see Table 7.1).

11. With a high-pass filter the amplitudes for all frequencies in the domain of the stop band are set to zero. The output consists of a time series containing only the frequencies in the domain of the pass band. Therefore, the output of the high-pass filter corresponds to the residual term obtained by subtraction of the trend. It is important for the present analysis that the filter does not produce a phase shift. The filter program used here is "Nulfil," developed by Metz and Stier (1991). I wish to thank Rainer Metz for making this program available for the present analysis. More details of the statistical procedure are given in the "Appendix" to this chapter.

12. Results for France and Japan are not shown in Table 7.1 but may be obtained upon request from the author.

13. This is the case, for instance, for factor analysis or cluster analysis.

14. A trend is defined as a "cycle" of long duration (period).

Appendix I: Sources

Figures 1.1-1.5 and Figures 1.8-1.11

Germany: *Preußische Statistik* (Statistik der Landesuniversitäten und Hochschulen), edited by Königliches Statistisches Bureau, Berlin, Vol. 125 (1890-92), Vol. 167 (1899/1900), pp. 46-148; Vol. 223 (1908/09), pp. 44-194; Vol. 236 (1911/12), pp. 54-170. *Deutsche Hochschulstatistik*, edited by Hochschulverwaltungen, Berlin:Struppe & Winckler, Vol. 1929 and 1930.

Statistik des Deutschen Reiches, edited by Kaiserliches Statistisches Amt, Berlin 1915, Vol. 240 (census 1910), pp. 79-85.

Statistische Jahrbücher für das Deutsche Reich, edited by Statistisches Reichsamt Berlin, Vol. 1930 -1938, chapters "population" and "education"

Statistische Jahrbücher der Bundesrepublik Deutschland, edited by Statistisches Bundesamt Wiesbaden, Vol. 1955 - 1994, chapters "population" and "education".

F. Eulenburg: *Die Frequenz der deutschen Universitäten*. Leipzig 1904: Teubner.

United States: *Historical Statistics of the United States*, edited by US Department of Commerce, Washington DC 1970, Part I, pp. 385-390.

Digest of Education Statistics, edited by National Center for Education Statistics, Washington DC, Vol. 1970 - 1994, chapter on "Higher Education".

Statistical Abstract of the United States, edited by the U.S. Department of Commerce, Bureau of the Census, Vol. 1960-1994, chapters on "education" and "population".

Japan: *Japan's Growth and Education - Educational Development in Relation to Socio-economic Growth* (The 1962 White Paper on Education), edited by the Ministry of Education, Government of Japan, Tokyo 1963, MEJ 6557.

Japan Statistical Yearbook, edited by Statistics Bureau (Office of the Prime Minister), Management and Coordination Agency, Tokyo, Vol. 1955 - 1994, chapters on "Population" und "Education, Culture and Religion" and "School Education, Science and Technology".

France: *Annuaire statistique de la France*, edited by Institut National de la Statistique et des Études Économiques (L'INSEE), Paris 1966, Résumé rétrospectif, pp. 148-180.

Figure 1.6

M. Barbagli: Discoccupazione intellettuale e sistema scolastico in Italia. Bologna 1974: Il Mulino, p. 135, Graf. 4.2.

Annuario Statistico Italiana, edited by Istituto Centrale di Statistica, Roma, Vol. 1897, pp. 63-65.

Tables 1.1 and 1.4
Germany: See sources for Figures 1.1-1.5 and additional sources:
W.G. Hoffmann: *Das Wachstum der Deutschen Wirtschaft seit der Mitte des 19. Jahrhunderts.* Berlin 1965: Springer (Appendix). B.R. Mitchell: *European Historical Statistics 1750-1970,* London 1975: Macmillan.
Labour Force Statistics, edited by OECD, Department of Economics and Statistics, Paris, Vol. 1961 bis 1990.
Main Economic Indicators, edited by OECD, Department of Economics and Statistics, Paris 1989.
P. Flora: *State, Economy, and Society in Western Europe 1815 - 1975, Vo. I - The Growth of Mass Democracies and Welfare States.* Frankfurt 1983: Campus.
A. Maddison: Phases of Capitalist Development. *Banca Nazionale del Lavoro Quarterly Review* 121 (1977), pp. 103-137.
J.Kuczynski: *Die Geschichte der Lage der Arbeiter unter dem Kapitalismus.* Berlin 1962: Akademie-Verlag, Vol. 3, p. 266; Vol. 4, p. 315; Vol. 5, p. 197.
Sachverständigenrat: *Arbeitsplätze im Wettbewerb, Jahresgutachten 1988/89.* Stuttgart and Mainz 1988: Kohlhammer, Appendix pp. 231-240.
Statistics of National Accounts 1950 - 1961 und 1960 - 1990, edited by OECD, Department of Economics and Statistics, Paris. 1964 und 1987.
USA: *Historical Statistics of the United States,* edited by US Department of Commerce, Washington 1970, Part I, pp. 385-390. *Digest of Education Statistics,* edited by National Center for Education Statistics, Washington DC, Vol. 1978-1990. J.W. Kendrick: *Productivity Trends in the US.* Princeton 1961: Princeton University Press, Appendix A, pp. 291-295.
Yearbook of National Accounts Statistics, edited by Statistical Office of the United Nations, Department of Economic and Social Affairs, New York, Vol. 1958, pp. 235-240.
Italy: *Statistiche storiche dell'Italia,* edited by Istituto Centrale di Statistica, Roma 1964, pp. 78-85.
Annuario Statistico dell'Istruzione Italiana, edited by Istituto Centrale di Statistica, Roma, Vol. XIX, 1967.
France: *Annuaire statistique de la France,* edited by Institut National de la Statistique et des Études Économiques (L'INSEE), Paris 1966, Résumé rétrospectif, pp. 148-156.
Évolution de la population active en France depuis cent ans d'après les dénombrements quinquennaux, in: Études et Conjoncture 3/1953, pp. 230-288, série rouge - Économie française.
Japan: See sources for Figures 1.1-1.5 and additional sources: *Education in 1956 - 1975, Annual Report,* edited by Ministry of Education, Tokyo 1958-1977.
Japan Statistical Yearbook, edited by Statistics Bureau (Office of the Prime Minister), Management and Coordination Agency, Tokyo, Vol. 1955 - 1990, chapter on "Government Employees and Election".
K. Ohkawa: *The Growth Rate of the Japanese Economy since 1878.* Tokyo 1957: Kinokuniya Bookstore (Appendix).
K. Ohkawa und H. Rosovsky: *Postwar Japanese Growth in Historical Perspective -*

A Second Look, in: L. Klein und K. Ohkawa (eds.), Economic Growth - The Japanese Experience since the Meiji Era, Homewood 1968: Irwin.
E. Schulze: *Japan als Welt- und Industriemacht,* Vol. 2. Stuttgart 1935: Kohlhammer, pp. 320-330.
Japanese Trade and Industry, edited by Mitsubishi Economic Research Bureau, London 1936: Macmillan, pp. 12-15.

Tables 2.1 - 2.2 and 2.4 - 2.6
Prussia: *Preußische Statistik,* Vol. 167 (1899/1900), pp. 46-148; Vol. 223 (1908/09), pp. 44-194; Vol.. 236 (1911/12), pp. 54-170.
Bavaria: E. Jansen: Die soziale Herkunft der Studenten an den bayerischen Universitäten. *Zeitschrift des Bayrischen Statistischen Landesamtes,* 1927, pp. 449-479.
Sozialer Auf- und Abstieg des Deutschen Volkes, Heft 117 der Beiträge zur Statistik Bayerns, edited by Bayrisches Statistisches Landesamt, München 1930.
Germany (Deutsches Reich): *Deutsche Hochschulstatistik,* edited by Hochschulverwaltungen, Berlin: Struppe & Winckler, Vol. 1928- 1934.
J. Conrad: Einige Ergebnisse der deutschen Universitätsstatistik. *Jahrbücher für Nationalökonomie und Statistik* 32 (1906), pp. 433- 492.

Table 2.3
K. Keller: Die soziale Herkunft der Schüler der höheren Lehranstalten. *Zeitschrift des Preußischen Statistischen Landesamtes* 65 (1926), pp. 392-405.

Figure 4.1
Annuario Statistico Italiana, edited by Istituto Centrale di Statistica, Roma, Vol. 1960 -1994, chapter on "istruzione superiore" and "populazione".
Annuario Statistico dell'Istruzione Italiana, edited by Istituto Centrale di Statistica, Roma, Vol. XIX 1967.

Table 4.1
Fact Book for Academic Administràtors 1981/82, edited by American Council on Education, Washington DC: 1983.
Fall Enrollment in Higher Education, edited by National Center for Education Statistics, Washington DC, Vol. 1960 - 1983. *Digest of Education Statistics,* edited by National Center for Education Statistics, Washington, DC, Vol. 1971-1994, chapter on
"Higher Education".

Table 4.2
Annuaire statistique de la France, edited by Institut National de a Statistique et des Études Économiques (L'INSEE), Paris, Vol. 1960 - 1994, chapter on "l'enseignement".
Statistique de l'enseignement, edited by Ministère de l'Education, Paris, Vol. 1960-1983, chapter on "l'enseignement supérieur".

Table 4.3
Japan Statistical Yearbook, edited by Statistics Bureau (Office of the Prime Minister), Management and Coordination Agency, Tokyo, Vol. 1955-1994, chapter on "Education, Culture and Religion" and "School Education, Science and Technology"

Table 4.4
Statistische Jahrbücher der Bundesrepublik Deutschland, edited by Statistisches Bundesamt Wiesbaden, Vol. 1960-1994, chapter on "Bildung und Kultur".
Bildung im Zahlenspiegel, edited by Bundesministerium für Bildung und Wissenschaft, Bonn/Statistisches Bundesamt, Wiesbaden, Vol. 1975-1994.
Grund und Strukturdaten, edited by Bundesminister für Bildung und Wissenschaft, Bonn, Vol. 1973/74 - 1988/89.

Table 4.5
American Council on Education: The American Freshman - National Norms for Fall 1982 und 1984, edited by A. Astin et al., available on microfilm ED 228 906 (1982) und ED 255 106 (1984), Computer Microfilm International, 3900 Wheeler Ave., Alexandria, Virginia 22304, USA.
Stanford: Research department of Stanford University; own survey of the author.

Table 4.6
Cummings 1980: 227.

Table 4.7
Data for the different types of "*Grandes Ecoles*" are given in the following publications: Le Bras (1983); Bodiguel (1974); Sadran (1977); Bourdieu (1981).
Un bagne bienheureux, in: Le Monde de l'Education, juillet-aout 1982, pp. 26-30.

Table 4.8
Annuaire statistique de la France, edited by Institut National de la Statistique et des Etudes Economiques (L'INSEE), Paris, Vol. 1962-1989, chapter on "l'enseignement" and "population".
Bilan Formation-Emploi 1977, edited by l'INSEE, serie 78 D, démographie et emploi, Paris 1981.
Recensement général de la population de 1982, formation, edited by l'INSEE, Paris.

Tables 4.9 and 4.10
Das soziale Bild der Studentenschaft in der Bundesrepublik Deutschland - 11. Sozialerhebung des Deutschen Studentenwerks, edited by Bundesminister für Bildung und Wissenschaft, Bonn 1986: Bock, pp. 99-115.
Peisert et al. (1988); Kazemzadeh and Schaeper (1983).

Table 6.1
Bildung im Zahlenspiegel, edited by Bundesministerium für Bildung und

Wissenschaft, Bonn/Statistischen Bundesamt, Wiesbaden, Vol. 1975-1994.
Grund und Strukturdaten, edited by Bundesminister für Bildung und Wissenschaft, Bonn, Vol. 1973/74 - 1988/89.
Statistische Jahrbücher der Bundesrepublik Deutschland, edited by Statistisches Bundesamt Wiesbaden, Vol. 1955 - 1994, chapter on "education".

Table 6.2
Digest of Education Statistics, edited by National Center for Education Statistics, Washington DC, Vol. 1970 - 1994, chapter on "Higher Education".
Statistical Abstract of the United States, edited by the U.S. Department of Commerce, Bureau of the Census, Vol. 1960-1994, chapters on "education".

Table 6.3
Japan Statistical Yearbook, edited by Statistics Bureau (Office of the Prime Minister), Management and Coordination Agency, Tokyo, Vol. 1960 - 1994, chapters on "Education, Culture and Religion" and "School Education, Science and Technology".

Table 6.4
The Condition of Education 1994, edited by the National Center for Education Statistics, U.S. Department of Education. Washington 1994, NCES 94-149, p. 321, Table 51-1.

Table 6.5
Das soziale Bild der Studentenschaft in der Bundesrepublik Deutschland - 13. Sozialerhebung des Deutschen Studentenwerkes, edited by Bundesminister für Bildung und Wissenschaft, Bonn 1992: Bock, pp. 93-98.

Table 6A (Appendix Chapter 6)
Germany: *Amtliche Nachrichten der Bundesanstalt für Arbeit*, edited by Bundesanstalt für Arbeit, Nürnberg, Vol. 1973-1994, issues March, September/October of each year (special survey on unemployment by level of qualification).
Beruf, Ausbildung und Arbeitsbedingungen der Erwerbstätigen, Reihe 4.1.2, Fachserie 1 (Bevölkerung und Erwerbstätigkeit), Ergebnisse des Mikrozensus, edited by Statistisches Bundesamt Wiesbaden, Stuttgart: Kohlhammer, surveys for the years 1976, 1978, 1980, 1982, 1985, 1986, 1988, 1990, 1992.
Sachverständigenrat: *Jahresgutachten, Vol. 1988/89-1993/94*. Stuttgart and Mainz: Kohlhammer (Appendix).
United States: *Handbook of Labor Statistics*, edited by US Bureau of Labor, Washington DC: 1985, p. 164.
Statistical Abstracts of the United States, edited by US-Department of Commerce, Washington DC, Vol. 1985-1994, chapter on "Labor Force Status".

Figures 6.1 - 6.3
See sources for Figures 1.2 and 1.4 (Germany, United States, Japan).

Figure 6.4
Annuario Statistico Italiana, edited by Istituto Centrale di Statistica, Roma, Vol. 1960 -1993, chapter "populazione" and "istruzione".

Figure 6.5
Das soziale Bild der Studentenschaft in der Bundesrepublik Deutschland - 13. Sozialerhebung des Deutschen Studentenwerkes, edited by Bundesminister für Bildung und Wissenschaft, Bonn 1992: Bock, pp. 57-58, Fig. 2.5.

Table 7.1 and Figures 7.1 - 7.11
Germany: *Preußische Statistik (Statistik der Landesuniversitäten und Hochschulen)*, edited by Königlichen Statistischen Bureau, Berlin, Vol. 125 (1890-92), Vol. 167 (1899/1900), pp. 46-148; Vol. 223 (1908/ 09), pp. 44-194; Vol. 236 (1911/12), pp. 54-170.
Deutsche Hochschulstatistik, edited by Hochschulverwaltungen, Berlin:Struppe & Winckler, Vol. 1925-1930.
J. Conrad: Einige Ergebnisse der deutschen Universitätsstatistik. *Jahrbücher für Nationalökonomie und Statistik* 32 (1906), pp. 433-492.
Statistik des Deutschen Reiches, edited by Kaiserlichen Statistischen Amte, Berlin 1915, Vol. 240 (Cenus 1910), pp. 79-85.
Statistische Jahrbücher für das Deutsche Reich, edited by Statistischen Reichsamt Berlin, Vol. 1930 -1938, chapter "Gebietseinteilung und Bevölkerung" and "Unterrichtswesen".
Statistische Jahrbücher der Bundesrepublik Deutschland, edited by Statistischen Bundesamt Wiesbaden, Vol. 1955 - 1993, chapter on "Gebiet und Bevölkerung" and "Unterricht und Bildung", "Bildung und Kultur".
Bildung im Zahlenspiegel, edited by Bundesministerium für Bildung und Wissenschaft, Bonn und vom Statistischen Bundesamt, Wiesbaden, Vol. 1975 - 1993.
W. Albert and C. Oehler: *Materialen zur Entwicklung der Hochschulen 1950-1967*, Vol. 1, Hannover 1970: Hiss.

Italy: *Statistiche storiche dell'Italia*, edited by Istituto Centrale di Statistica, Roma 1964.
Annuario Statistico dell'Istruzione Italiana, edited by Istituto Centrale di Statistica, Roma, Vol. XIX, 1967.
Annuario Statistico Italiana, edited by Istituto Centrale di Statistica, Roma, Vol. 1897, pp. 63-65.
Annuario Statistico Italiana, edited by Istituto Centrale di Statistica, Roma, Vol. 1960 -1993, chapter on "populazione" and "istruzione".
France: *Annuaire statistique de la France*, edited by Institut National de la Statistique et des Études Économiques (L'INSEE), Paris 1966, Résumé rétrospectif,

pp. 148-160 and Vol. 1960-1993, chapter on "effectifs de l'enseignement supérieur" and "population".
Statistique de l'enseignement, edited by Ministere de l'Education, Paris, Vol. 1960 - 1993, chapter on "l'enseignement supérieur".
United States: *Historical Statistics of the United States*, edited by US Department of Commerce, Washington DC 1970.
Digest of Education Statistics, edited by National Center for Education Statistics, Washington DC, Vol. 1970 - 1993, chapter on "higher education".
Fact Book for Academic Administrators 1981/82, edited by American Council on Education, Washington DC: 1983.
Fall Enrollment in Higher Education, edited by National Center for Education Statistics, Washington DC, Vol. 1960 - 1983.
Statistical Abstracts of the United States, edited by US-Department of Commerce, Washington DC, Vol. 1950-1993, chapter on "population by age".
Japan: *Japan's Growth and Education - Educational Development in Relation to Socio-economic Growth (The 1962 White Paper on Education)*, edited by Ministry of Education, Government of Japan, Tokyo 1963, MEJ 6557.
Japan Statistical Yearbook, edited by Statistics Bureau (Office of the Prime Minister), Management and Coordination Agency, Tokyo, Vol. 1955 - 1993, chapter "Population" and "Education, Culture and Religion", "School Education, Science and Technology".

For Gross National Product (GNP) the following sources were used:
W.G. Hoffmann: *Das Wachstum der Deutschen Wirtschaft seit der Mitte des 19. Jahrhunderts*. Berlin 1965: Springer, Appendix.
Sachverständigenrat: *Jahresgutachten*, Vol. 1988/89 - 199/94, Stuttgart and Mainz:Kohlhammer (Appendix).
J.W. Kendrick: *Productivity Trends in the US*. Princeton 1961: Princeton University Press, Appendix A, pp. 291-305.
K. Ohkawa: *The Growth Rate of the Japanese Economy since 1878*. Tokyo 1957: Kinokuniya Bookstore (time series in Appendix).
K. Ohkawa und H. Rosovsky: Postwar Japanese Growth in Historical Perspective, in: L. Klein und K. Ohkawa (eds.), *Economic Growth - The Japanese Experience since the Meiji Era*. Homewood 1968:Irwin.
Japanese Trade and Industry, edited by Mitsubishi Economic Research Bureau. London 1936: Macmillan, pp. 12-15.
B.R. Mitchell: *European Historical Statistics 1750-1970*. London 1975: Macmillan.
P. Flora: *State, Economy, and Society in Western Europe 1815 - 1975, Vo. I - The Growth of Mass Democracies and Welfare States*. Frankfurt 1983: Campus.
A. Maddison: Phases of Capitalist Development. *Banca Nazionale del Lavoro Quarterly Review* 121 (1977), pp. 103-137.
Yearbook of National Accounts Statistics, edited by Statistical Office of the United Nations, Department of Economic and Social Affairs, New York, Vol. 1958, pp. 235-243.
Labour Force Statistics, edited by OECD, Department of Economics and Statistics,

Paris, Vol. 1961 bis 1987.
Main Economic Indicators, edited by der OECD, Department of Economics and Statistics, Paris 1989.
Statistics of National Accounts 1950 - 1961, 1953-1982, 1960 - 1985, edited by OECD, Department of Economics and Statistics, Paris 1964, 1984 und 1987.

Appendix II: Enrollment Rates in Higher Education 1850-1992

Year	Germany	Italy	France	USA	Japan1	Japan2
1850	0.58	*	*	*	*	*
1851	0.56	*	*	*	*	*
1852	0.54	*	*	*	*	*
1853	0.53	*	*	*	*	*
1854	0.51	*	*	*	*	*
1855	0.50	*	*	*	*	*
1856	0.49	*	*	*	*	*
1857	0.49	*	*	*	*	*
1858	0.48	*	*	*	*	*
1859	0.48	*	*	*	*	*
1860	0.48	*	*	*	*	*
1861	0.47	0.35	*	*	*	*
1862	0.48	0.31	*	*	*	*
1863	0.49	0.33	*	*	*	*
1864	0.50	0.37	*	*	*	*
1865	0.51	0.41	*	*	*	*
1866	0.48	0.45	*	*	*	*
1867	0.48	0.50	*	*	*	*
1868	0.48	0.49	*	*	*	*
1869	0.52	0.49	*	*	*	*
1870	0.45	0.53	*	1.25	*	*
1871	0.59	0.53	0.28	1.59	*	*
1872	0.62	0.52	0.29	.98	*	*
1873	0.64	0.52	0.29	1.30	*	*
1874	0.66	0.48	0.29	1.34	*	*
1875	0.68	0.44	0.29	1.35	*	*
1876	0.69	0.44	0.30	1.32	*	*
1877	0.68	0.45	0.30	1.08	*	*
1878	0.69	0.47	0.30	1.20	0.24	0.24
1879	0.69	0.48	0.32	1.22	0.27	0.27
1880	0.70	0.50	0.33	1.27	0.26	0.26
1881	0.73	0.51	0.35	1.43	0.30	0.30
1882	0.75	0.57	0.37	1.41	0.31	0.31

Year	Germany	Italy	France	USA	Japan1	Japan2
1883	0.78	0.61	0.39	1.39	0.31	0.31
1884	0.80	0.63	0.39	1.15	0.35	0.35
1885	0.82	0.68	0.40	1.31	0.40	0.40
1886	0.83	0.72	0.41	1.14	0.41	0.41
1887	0.84	0.73	0.43	1.14	0.48	0.48
1888	0.85	0.75	0.46	1.28	0.45	0.45
1889	0.84	0.76	0.52	1.23	0.48	0.48
1890	0.84	0.79	0.50	1.25	0.50	0.50
1891	0.82	0.82	0.60	1.34	0.55	0.55
1892	0.81	0.87	0.68	1.31	0.52	0.52
1893	0.82	0.93	0.70	1.43	0.47	0.47
1894	0.83	0.99	0.75	1.65	0.48	0.48
1895	0.85	1.04	0.75	1.79	0.51	0.51
1896	0.88	1.10	0.81	1.81	0.51	0.51
1897	0.91	1.08	0.81	1.84	0.58	0.58
1898	0.94	1.04	0.87	1.79	0.64	0.64
1899	0.98	1.02	0.87	1.81	0.68	0.68
1900	1.02	1.02	0.91	1.87	0.74	0.74
1901	1.07	1.01	0.94	1.91	0.84	0.84
1902	1.08	0.99	0.95	1.89	0.96	0.96
1903	1.08	0.99	0.98	1.91	0.96	0.96
1904	1.08	1.00	1.02	1.90	1.12	1.12
1905	1.08	1.03	1.06	1.93	1.17	1.17
1906	1.12	1.09	1.13	1.92	1.20	1.20
1907	1.16	1.06	1.21	1.89	1.26	1.26
1908	1.18	1.04	1.27	1.94	1.31	1.31
1909	1.22	0.99	1.30	2.13	1.31	1.31
1910	1.26	0.95	1.32	2.05	1.28	1.28
1911	1.27	0.95	1.33	2.07	1.32	1.32
1912	1.30	0.94	1.33	2.17	1.33	1.33
1913	1.30	0.98	1.33	2.34	1.42	1.42
1914	1.08	1.04	1.36	2.44	1.40	1.40
1915	*	1.02	*	2.42	1.43	1.43
1916	*	1.17	*	2.48	1.48	1.48
1917	*	1.33	*	2.29	1.51	1.51
1918	*	1.53	*	2.10	1.54	1.54
1919	2.19	1.78	1.02	2.36	1.52	1.52
1920	2.17	1.65	1.51	2.62	1.74	1.74
1921	2.19	1.48	1.64	2.94	1.94	1.94
1922	2.11	1.41	1.63	3.25	2.11	2.11
1923	2.12	1.32	1.58	3.76	2.26	2.26
1924	1.66	1.34	1.57	4.26	2.44	2.44
1925	1.45	1.40	1.60	4.58	2.65	2.65
1926	1.52	1.33	1.74	4.84	2.85	2.85

Year	Germany	Italy	France	USA	Japan1	Japan2
1927	1.61	1.27	1.81	5.08	2.95	2.95
1928	1.76	1.17	1.91	5.32	3.16	3.16
1929	1.91	1.26	1.98	5.48	3.26	3.26
1930	2.11	1.25	2.18	5.63	3.29	3.29
1931	2.22	1.25	2.32	5.97	3.23	3.23
1932	2.11	1.40	2.50	6.30	3.16	3.16
1933	1.90	1.48	2.63	6.23	3.11	3.11
1934	1.47	1.59	2.78	6.16	3.10	3.10
1935	1.41	1.66	2.70	6.29	3.08	3.08
1936	1.36	1.82	2.49	6.39	3.10	3.10
1937	1.44	1.99	2.56	6.82	3.13	3.13
1938	1.63	2.15	2.81	7.24	3.24	3.24
1939	*	2.50	3.10	7.65	3.54	3.54
1940	*	3.90	*	8.05	4.04	4.04
1941	*	*	*	7.93	*	*
1942	*	*	*	7.82	*	*
1943	*	*	*	6.49	*	*
1944	*	*	*	5.20	*	*
1945	*	*	*	5.35	*	*
1946	*	6.36	3.76	5.73	*	*
1947	*	6.21	3.97	8.79	6.42	8.03
1948	*	6.20	4.87	11.29	5.89	7.36
1949	*	5.74	5.17	15.38	5.01	6.26
1950	3.93	5.78	5.30	18.16	5.18	6.48
1951	4.02	5.62	5.38	16.46	5.36	6.70
1952	4.13	5.55	5.61	14.39	6.27	7.84
1953	4.26	5.44	5.73	13.47	6.59	8.24
1954	4.26	5.26	5.98	13.24	7.03	8.79
1955	4.40	5.23	6.07	13.28	7.26	9.07
1956	4.78	5.29	6.70	14.45	7.51	9.39
1957	5.03	5.49	7.23	15.74	7.67	9.59
1958	5.30	5.73	7.82	16.64	7.82	9.78
1959	5.42	6.07	8.33	17.31	8.12	10.15
1960	5.85	6.48	8.83	17.60	8.53	10.66
1961	6.19	7.07	9.97	17.25	9.02	11.27
1962	6.45	7.72	12.00	17.45	9.69	12.11
1963	6.91	8.39	14.18	17.64	10.45	13.06
1964	7.45	9.05	15.66	18.85	10.99	13.74
1965	8.10	10.75	17.66	19.49	11.97	14.96
1966	9.44	12.22	18.92	19.72	14.35	17.94
1967	10.07	12.95	18.91	19.60	15.47	19.34
1968	10.87	13.87	19.74	21.33	15.91	19.89
1969	11.47	15.15	19.04	23.18	15.98	19.98
1970	13.45	16.70	18.29	24.06	15.66	19.58

Year	Germany	Italy	France	USA	Japan1	Japan2
1971	14.06	18.56	19.06	24.42	15.56	19.45
1972	14.81	19.60	19.50	25.54	16.67	20.84
1973	16.03	20.94	19.55	26.86	18.49	23.11
1974	17.33	22.81	20.35	27.74	20.74	25.92
1975	18.60	24.34	22.42	26.41	23.02	28.78
1976	19.49	25.17	23.28	26.02	24.95	31.19
1977	20.01	25.51	23.55	25.34	26.77	33.46
1978	20.32	25.91	24.15	24.99	27.85	34.81
1979	20.45	25.25	24.36	24.48	27.75	34.69
1980	20.99	25.49	24.58	23.45	28.14	35.17
1981	21.93	25.18	25.76	23.17	28.09	35.11
1982	22.84	24.53	26.52	23.60	27.81	34.76
1983	23.62	24.26	27.26	24.24	27.81	34.76
1984	23.92	24.42	27.99	24.61	27.71	34.64
1985	23.87	24.00	28.57	24.92	27.07	33.84
1986	24.05	22.96	28.69	25.63	28.11	35.14
1987	24.81	20.76	28.80	26.62	28.31	35.39
1988	26.20	21.88	29.76	27.50	28.98	36.23
1989	27.53	22.40	34.77	28.04	29.34	36.67
1990	28.43	23.96	37.64	28.27	29.70	37.13
1991	30.42	26.35	39.76	28.98	28.99	36.24
1992	32.49	26.99	42.83	31.25	29.43	36.79

* Data unknown/not available (e.g. First and Second World War).

For Germany, Italy, France, and Japan *enrollment rates* are listed. The total number of students enrolled at universities and colleges (man and women) was divided by five age cohorts (20-24year old).

For the United States *graduation rates* are listed: bachelor's degrees + first-professional degrees divided by the average of the 20-24year old (1 cohort). For Germany, and particularly for Italy and France, enrollment rates are overestimated because drop-out rates have not been taken into account. Enrollment rates for Japan and graduation rates for the United States are more comparable because of the very low drop-out rate in Japan. After 1989 enrollment rates for Germany are those for West-Germany only. *Japan1:* Total number of students divided by five age cohorts; *Japan2:* After the Second World War the total number of students was divided by four age cohorts. The unusual increase in enrollment rates in France after 1988 is due to a change in classification categories and to the increase of high school graduates. During the Mitterand era the French government announced to increase the proportion of high school graduates to 80% of an age cohort.

References

Achner, L. 1931: Der Arbeitsmarkt der geistigen Berufe. *Allgemeines Statistisches Archiv* 21: 481-495.

Archer, M. 1979: *The Social Origins of Educational Systems*. London: Sage.

Bäumer, G. 1930: *Schulaufbau, Berufsauslese, Berechtigungswesen*. Berlin: Heymanns.

Bain, G. and Elsheikh, F. 1976: *Union Growth and the Business Cycle. An Econometric Analysis*. Oxford: Blackwell.

Baltzell, E. D. 1958: *Philadelphia Gentlemen - The Making of a National Upper Class*. Glencoe Ill.: Free Press.

Banfield, E.C. 1969: *Urban Government*. New York: Free Press.

Barbagli, M. 1974: *Disoccupazione intellettuale e sistema scolastico in Italia*. Bologna: Il Mulino engl.: *Educating for Unemployment*. New York 1982: Columbia University Press).

Bartholomew, J.R. 1978: Japanese Modernization and the Imperial Universities 1876-1920. *Journal of Asian Studies* 37: 251-271.

Bauer, M. and Berin-Mourot, B. 1995: *L'acces au sommet des grandes entreprises françaises 1985-1994*. Paris: C.N.R.S/ Boyden.

Behrend, F. 1929: *Vom Sinn und Unsinn des Berechtigungswesens*. Leibzig: Quelle & Meyer.

Benda, J. 1927: *La trahison des clercs*. Paris: Grasset.

Berg, I. 1970: *Education and Jobs - The Great Training Robbery*. New York: Praeger.

Bernstein, B. 1975: *Class, Codes and Control - Towards a Theory of Educational Transmissions*, Vol. 3. London: Routledge & Kegan.

Blaug, M. 1970: *Economics of Education*. Harmondsworth: Penguin.

Bodiguel, J.L. 1974: Sociologie des élèves de l'Ecole Nationale d'Administration. *Revue internationale des sciences administratives* 60: 230-244.

_____. 1978: *Les anciens élèves de l'ENA*. Paris: Presses de la fondation nationale des sciences polititques.

Bofinger, J. 1977: *Schullaufbahnen im gegliederten Schulwesen und ihre Bedingungen*. München: Ehrenwirth.

Boltanski, L. 1982: *Les cadres - La formation d'un groupe social*. Paris: Minuit.

Borchardt, K. 1977: Trend, Zyklus, Strukturbrüche, Zufälle. *Vierteljahrschrift für Sozial- und Wirtschaftsgeschichte* 64: 145-178.

_____. 1982: Zwangslagen und Handlungsspielräume in der großen Wirtschaftskrise der frühen dreißiger Jahre, in: K. Borchardt (ed.), *Wachstum, Krisen,*

Handlungsspielräume der Wirtschaftspolitik. Göttingen: Vandenhoeck & Ruprecht.

Bornschier, V. and Suter, C. 1990: Lange Wellen im Weltsystem, in: V. Rittberger (ed.), *Theorien der Internationalen Beziehungen.* Opladen: Westdeutscher Verlag (Politische Vierteljahresschrift, special issue no. 21), pp. 174-197.

Boudon, R. 1973: *L'inégalité des chances - La mobilité dans les sociétés industrielles.* Paris: Colin.

_____. 1977: *Effets pervers et ordre social.* Paris: PUF.

Bourdieu, P. 1979: *La distinction - Critique sociale du jugement.* Paris: Minuit.

_____. 1981: Épreuve scolaire et consécration sociale. *Actes de la recherche en sciences sociales* 39: 3-70.

_____. 1989: *La noblesse d'état - Grandes Écoles et esprit de corps.* Paris: Minuit.

Bourdieu, P. and Passeron, J.C. 1964: *Les héritiers – Les étudiants et la culture.* Paris: Minuit.

Bourdieu, P. and Passeron, J.C. 1970: *Fondements d'une théorie de la violence symbolique.* Paris: Minuit.

Bowles, S. and Gintis, H. 1976: *Schooling in Capitalist America.* London: Routledge & Kegan.

Brubacher, J.S. and Rudy, W. 1968: *Higher Education in Transition - A History of American Colleges and Universities.* New York: Harper & Row.

Bundesministerium für Bildung und Wissenschaft 1992: *Das soziale Bild der Studentenschaft in der Bundesrepublik Deutschland – 13. Sozialerhebung des Deutschen Studentenwerks.* Bonn/Bad Honnef: Bock.

Burchardt, F. 1932: Statistik der Berufsüberfüllung, mit besonderer Berücksichtigung der geistigen Berufe. *Allgemeines Statistisches Archiv* 22: 481-491.

Cam, P. 1978: Juges rouges et droit du travail. *Actes de la recherche en sciences sociales* 19: 3-27.

Carr-Saunders, A.M. and Wilson, P.A. 1933: *The Professions.* Oxford: Clarendon.

Castles, F. and Marceau, J. 1989: The Transformation in Gender Inequality in Tertiary Education. *Journal of Public Policy* 9: 493-507.

Cherkaoui, M. 1982: *Les changements du système éducatif en France 1950-1980.* Paris: PUF.

Clark, B.R. 1977: *Academic Power in Italy.* Chicago: University of Chicago Press.

_____. 1983: *The Higher Education System.* Berkeley: University of California Press.

Coleman, J.S. et al. 1981: Questions and Answers. *Harvard Educational Review* 51: 526-545.

_____. 1982: *High School Achievement - Public, Catholic, and Private Schools Compared.* New York: Basic Books.

Coleman, J. and Hoffer, T. 1987: *Public and Private High Schools.* New York: Basic Books.

Collins, R. 1971: Functional and Conflict Theories of Educational Stratification. *American Sociological Review* 36: 1002-1018.

_____. 1979: *The Credential Society.* New York: Academic Press.

Cookson, P. and Persell, C. H. 1985: *Preparing for Power - America's Elite Boarding Schools*. New York: Basis Book.

Cummings, W.K. 1980: *Education and Equality in Japan*. Princeton: Princeton University Press.

Cummings, W.K. and Naoi, A. 1974: Social Background, Education, and Personal Advancement in a Dualistic Employment System. *The Developing Economies* 12: 245-273.

Dahrendorf, R. 1960: Bemerkungen zur sozialen Herkunft und Stellung der Richter an Oberlandesgerichten. *Hamburger Jahrbuch für Wirtschafts- und Gesellschaftspolitik* 5: 260-275.

_____. 1965: *Arbeiterkinder an deutschen Universitäten*. Tübingen: Mohr.

Darbel, A. and Schnapper, D. 1969: *Les agents du système administratif, Vol. I and II*. Paris: Cahiers du centre de sociologie Européenne.

Dehio, L. 1948: *Gleichgewicht oder Hegemonie*. Krefeld: Scherpe.

Dibelius, W. 1930: Die Überfüllung der Universität. *Deutsches Philologen Blatt* 38: 265-272.

Domhoff, G.W. 1983: *Who Rules America Now?* Englewood Cliffs: Prentice Hall.

Eigler, H. et al. 1980: Quantitative Entwicklungen - Wem hat die Bildungs-expansion genutzt?, in: H.G. Rolff et al. (eds.), Jahrbuch der Schulentwicklung, Band I. Weinheim und Basel: Beltz.

Eklund, K. 1980: Long Waves in the Development of Capitalism? *Kyklos* 33: 383-419.

Epstein, C.F. 1983: *Women in Law*. New York: Anchor.

Epstein, L.D. 1967: *Political Parties in Western Democracies*. New Brunswick N.J.: Praeger.

Eschenburg, Th. 1961: *Ämterpatronage*. Stuttgart: Schwab.

Eulenburg, F. 1904: *Die Frequenz der deutschen Universitäten*. Leibzig: Teubner.

Euriat, M. and Thélot, C. 1995: Le recrutement social de l'élite scolaire en France – Evolution des inégalités de 1950 à 1990. *Revue françaises de sociologie* 36: 403-438.

Ewijk, C. 1982: A Spectral Analysis of the Kondratieff-Cycle. *Kyklos* 35: 468-499.

Farías, Victor 1987: *Heidegger et le nazisme*. Paris: Editions Verdier.

Featherman, D.L. and Hauser, R.M. 1978: *Opportunity and Change*. New York: Academic Press.

Finer, H. 1927: *The British Civil Service*. London: The Fabian Society.

Finer, S.E. 1952: Patronage and the Public Service - Jeffersonian Bureaucracy and the British Tradition. *Public Administration* (London) 30: 329-360.

Flanders, A. 1975: *Management and Unions*. London: Faber.

Flexner, A. 1930: *Universities - American, English, German*. New York: Oxford University Press.

Flora, P. 1983: *State, Economy, and Society in Western Europe 1815-1975*, Vol. I. Frankfurt: Campus.

Francesco, C. and Trivellato, P. 1985: *L'Università incontrollata - Alcune cose da sapere prima di inscriversi*. Milano: Angeli.

Freeman, R.B. 1975a: Overinvestment in College Training? *The Journal of Human*

Resources 10: 286-311.

_____. 1975b: Legal "Cobwebs" - A Recursive Model of the Market for New Lawyers. *The Review of Economics and Statistics* 57: 171-179.

_____. 1976: *The Overeducated American*. New York: Academic Press.

Fujita, H. 1978: *Education and Status Attainment in Modern Japan*. Stanford University: School of Education (Dissertation).

Fuller, W. 1976: *Introduction to Statistical Time Series*. New York: Wiley.

Garvy, G. 1943: Kondratieff's Theory of Long Cycles. *The Review of Economic Statistics* 25: 203-220.

Gattullo, M. and Visalberghi, A. 1986: *La scuola italiana dal 1945 al 1983*. Firenze: Scandicci.

Giglioli, P. 1979: *Baroni e burocrati*. Bologna: Mulino.

Giles, G.J. 1985: *Students and National Socialism in Germany*. Princeton: Princeton University Press.

Goldstein, J. 1988: *Long Cycles – Prosperity and War in the Modern Age*. New Haven/London: Yale University Press.

Gottman, J. 1981: *Time-Series Analysis*. Cambridge: Cambridge University Press.

Graziano, L. 1984: *Clientelismo e sistema politico*. Milano: Angeli.

Greenwood, M. 1935: University Education - Its Recent History and Function. *Journal of the Royal Statistical Society*, Part I, Vol. XCVII: 1-33.

Griffith, J.A.G. 1977: *The Politics of the Judiciary*. Glasgow: Fontana-Collins.

Grusky, D.B. and Hauser, R.M. 1984: Comparative Social Mobility Revisited: Models of Convergence and Divergence in 16 Countries. *American Sociological Review* 49: 19-38.

Gunst, R.F. and Mason, R.L. 1980: *Regression Analysis and Its Application*. New York: Marcel Dekker.

Gurgsdies, E. 1981: Chancen und Probleme der Öffnung des Hochschulbereichs - Eine Untersuchung über Hochschulreform und Hochschulexpansion in Schweden. *Zeitschrift für Sozialisationsforschung und Erziehungssoziologie* 1: 187-204.

Hadrich 1931: Der Hartmannbund im Kampf gegen die Überfüllung der Hochschulen. *Sozialwissenschaftliche Rundschau* 32: 484-487.

Halsey, A.H. et al. 1980: *Origins and Destinations - Family, Class, and Education in Modern Britain*. Oxford: Clarendon Press.

Hamblin, R.I. et al. 1973: *A Mathematical Theory of Social Change*. New York: Wiley.

Hart, J. 1972: The Genesis of the Northcote-Trevelyan Report, in: G. Sutherland (ed.), *Studies in the Growth of Nineteenth-Century Government*. London: Routledge & Kegan Paul.

Hartnacke, W. 1931: *Naturgrenzen geistiger Bildung*. Leibzig: Quelle & Meyer.

_____. 1932: *Bildungswahn - Volkstod*. München: Lehmanns.

Hartshorne, E. Y. 1937: *The German Universities and National Socialism*. London: Allen & Unwin.

Hattenhauer, H. 1980: *Geschichte des Beamtentums*. Köln: Heymanns.

Hays, S.P. 1964: The Politics of Reform in Municipal Government in the

Progressive Era. *Pacific Northwest Quarterly* 55: 157-169.

Hays, S.W. and Kearney, R.C. 1984: Examinations in the Public Service, in: D.H. Rosenbloom (ed.), *Centenary Issues of the Pendleton Act of 1883*. New York: Dekker.

Herrlitz, H.G. and Titze, H. 1977: Überfüllung als bildungspolitische Strategie - Zur administrativen Steuerung der Lehrerarbeitslosigkeit in Preußen 1870-1914, in: U. Herrmann (ed.), *Schule und Gesellschaft im 19. Jahrhundert*. Weinheim and Basel: Beltz.

Herrnstein, R. and Murray, C. 1994: *The Bell Curve – Intelligence and Class Structure in American Life*. New York: Free Press.

Herzog, D. 1982: *Politische Führungsgruppen*. Darmstadt: Wissenschaftliche Buchgesellschaft.

Hintze, O. 1963 [1911]: *Der Beamtenstand*. Darmstadt: Wissenschaftliche Buchgesellschaft.

Hofstadter, R. 1955: *The Age of Reform*. New York: Vintage Books.

Holtfrerich, C.L. 1980: *Die deutsche Inflation 1914-1923*. Berlin: de Gruyter.

Hoogenboom, A. 1959: The Pendleton Act and the Civil Service. *American Historical Review* 64: 301-318.

_____. 1960: An Analysis of Civil Service Reformers. *The Historian* 23: 54-78.

_____. 1968: Outlawing the Spoils. Urbana: University of Illinois Press.

Husén, T. 1983: Are Standards in US Schools Really Lagging Behind those in Other Countries? *Phi Delta Kappan*: 455-461.

Ichikawa, S. 1979: Finance of Higher Education, in: W.K. Cummings et al. (eds.), *Changes in the Japanese University*. New York: Praeger.

Ingenkamp, K. 1974: *Die Fragwürdigkeit der Zensurengebung*. Weinheim: Beltz.

Inglehart, R. 1990: *Culture Shift in Advanced Industrial Society*. Princeton: Princeton University Press.

Jacobs, J. 1995: Gender and Academic Specialitites: Trends Among Recipients of College Degrees in the 1980s. *Sociology of Education* 68: 81-98.

Jarausch, K.H. 1978: The Social Transformation of the University - The Case of Prussia 1865-1914. *Journal of Social History* 12: 609-636.

_____. 1984: *Deutsche Studenten 1800-1970*. Frankfurt: Suhrkamp.

Jarousse, J.P. 1984: Les contradictions de l'université de masse dix ans après (1973-1983. *Revue française de sociologie* 25: 191-210.

Jencks, C. 1972: *Inequality*. New York: Basic Books.

Jencks, C. and Riesman, D. 1968: *The Academic Revolution*, Chicago: The University of Chicago Press.

Johnston, J. 1978: *Econometric Methods*. London: McGraw-Hill.

Juglar, C. 1889: *Des crises commerciales et de leur retour périodique en France, en Angleterre et aux États-Unis*. Paris: Guillaumin.

Karabel, J. 1972: Community Colleges and Social Stratifiction. *Harvard Educational Review* 42: 521-562.

_____. 1984: Status-Group Struggle, Organizational Interests, and the Limits of Institutional Autonomy - The Transformation of Harvard, Yale, and Princeton 1918-194O. *Theory and Society* 13: 1-39.

Katz, M.B. 1971: From Voluntarism to Bureaucracy in American Education. *Sociology of Education* 44: 297-332.

Kaupen, W. 1969: *Die Hüter von Recht und Ordnung - Die soziale Herkunft, Erziehung und Ausbildung der deutschen Juristen.* Neuwied: Luchterhand.

Kazemzadeh, F. and Schaeper, H. 1983: *Fachspezifische Studentenprofile.* Hannover: HIS.

Keiser, G. 1930: Das Hochschulstudium in Deutschland im SS 1930. *Sozialwissenschaftliche Rundschau* 31: 1028-1030.

Keller, K. 1926: Die soziale Herkunft der Schüler der höheren Lehranstalten. *Zeitschrift des Preubischen Statistischen Landesamtes* 65: 392-405.

Kelsall, R.K. 1974: Recruitment to the Higher Civil Service, in: P. Stanworth and A. Giddens (eds.), *Elites and Power in British Society.* Cambridge: Cambridge University Press.

Kessler, M.C. 1978: *La politique de la haute fonction publique.* Paris: Presses de la fondation nationale des sciences politiques.

Key, V.O. 1962: *Politics, Parties, and Pressure Group.* New York: Crowell.

Klatt, H. 1980: Die Verbeamtung der Parlamente. *Aus Politik und Zeitgeschichte* 44: 25-47.

Kohlberg, L. 1969: Stage and Sequence - The Cognitive-Developmental Approach to Socialization, in: D.A. Goslin (ed.), *Handbook of Socialization Theory and Research.* Chicago: Rand McNally, pp. 347-480.

Kondratieff, N.D. 1926: Die langen Wellen der Konjunktur. *Archiv für Sozialwissenschaft und Sozialpolitik* 56: 573-609.

Kosciusko-Morizet, J.A. 1973: *La 'mafia' polytechnicienne.* Paris: Seuil.

Kotschnig, W.M. 1937: *Unemployment in the Learned Professions - An International Study of Occupational and Educational Planning.* London: Oxford University Press.

Kraul, M. 1984: *Das deutsche Gymnasium 1780-1980.* Frankfurt: Suhrkamp.

Kubota, A. 1969: *Higher Civil Servants in Postwar Japan.* Princeton: Princeton University Press.

Kuznets, S. 1940: Schumpeter's Business Cycles. *American Eco nomic Review* 30: 257-271.

Labaree, D.F. 1984: Academic Exellence in an Early U.S. High School. *Social Problems* 31: 558-567.

Labov, W. 1966: Hypercorrection by the Lower Middle Class as a Factor in Linguistic Change, in: W. Bright (ed.), *Sociolinguistics.* Den Haag: Mouton.

Lammers, C.J. and Hickson, D.J. 1979: *Organizations Alike and Unlike.* London:Routledge & Kegan Paul.

Le Bras, H. 1983: Les origines d'une promotion de polytechniciens. *Population* 38: 491-501.

Legendre, P. 1968: *Histoire de l'administration de 1750 à nos jours.* Paris: PUF.

Lenhardt, G. 1984: *Schule und bürokratische Rationalität.* Frankfurt: Suhrkamp.

Levin, H.M. 1979: Privatschulen im Gesellschaftsgefüge der USA, in: D. Goldschmidt and P.M. Roeder (eds.), *Alternative Schulen.* Stuttgart: Klett-Cotta.

Levine, S.B. 1980: The Rise of American Boarding Schools. *Social Problems* 28:

63-93.

Levy, D. 1986: *Higher Education and the State in Latin America*. Chicago: University of Chicago Press.

Lévy-Garboua, L. 1976: Les demandes de l'étudiant ou les contradictions de l'université de masse. *Revue française de sociologie* 17: 53-80.

Lipset, S.M. 1963: *The First New Nation*. New York: Basic Books.

Litt, E. and Parkinson, M. 1979: *US and UK Educational Policy*. New York: Praeger.

Löwe, A. 1932: Das gegenwärtige Bildungsproblem der deutschen Universität. *Die Erziehung* 7: 1-19.

Lüders, M.E. 1931: Der Druck der Frauen auf den Arbeitsmarkt. *Soziale Praxis* 40: 290-294.

Lundgreen, P. 1977: Wissenschaft und Wirtschaft. *Technikgeschichte* 44: 302-314.

Lundgreen, P. et al. 1988: *Bildungschancen und soziale Mobilität in der städtischen Gesellschaft des 19. Jahrhunderts*. Göttingen: Vandenhoeck.

Lutz, B. 1976: Bildungssystem und Beschäftigungsstruktur in Deutschland und Frankreich, in: H.G. Mendius u.a. (eds.), *Betrieb - Arbeitsmarkt - Qualifikation*. Frankfurt: Aspekte.

_____. 1979: Die Interdependenz von Bildung und Beschäftigung und das Problem der Erklärung der Bildungsexpansion, in: J. Matthes (ed.), *Sozialer Wandel in Westeuropa - Verhandlungen des 19. Deutschen Soziologentages*. Frankfurt: Campus.

Maier, Ch. 1970: Between Taylorism and Technocracy: European Ideologies and the Vision of Industrial Productivity in the 1920s. *Journal of Contemporary History* 5: 27-60.

Mandel, E. 1980: *Long Waves of Capitalist Development*. Cambridge: Cambridge University Press.

Manegold, K.H. 1970: *Universität, Technische Hochschule und Industrie - Ein Beitrag zur Emanzipation der Technik im 19. Jahrhundert*. Berlin: Duncker & Humblot.

Manning, W.H., Hg., 1977: *Selective Admissions in Higher Education*. San Francisco: Jossey-Bass.

Maurice, M. et al. 1986: *The Social Foundations of Industrial Power: A Comparison of France and Germany*. Cambridge: MIT.

Max-Planck-Institut für Bildungsforschung 1980: *Bildung in der Bundesrepublik Deutschland*. Reinbek: Rowohlt.

Mayer, K.U. and Solga, H. 1994: Mobilität und Legitimität. *Kölner Zeitschrift für Soziologie und Sozialpsychologie* 46: 193-208.

McClendon, M. 1977: Structural and Exchange Components of Vertical Mobility. *American Sociological Review* 42: 56-74.

Meisel, J.H. 1958: *The Myth of the Ruling Class*. Ann Arbor: University of Michigan Press.

Metz, R. 1984: Zur empirischen Evidenz "langer Wellen". *Kyklos* 37: 266-290.

Metz, R. and Stier, W. 1991: Filter Design in the Frequency Domain, in: A. Kleinknecht, E. Mandel and I. Wallerstein (eds.), *New Findings in Long Wave*

Research. London.

Meyer, J.W. 1978: The Effects of Education as an Institution. *American Journal of Sociology* 87: 55-77.

Meyer, J.W. and Hannan, M.T. 1979: *National Development and the World System - Educational, Economic and Political Change 1950-1970*. Chicago: University of Chicago Press.

Meyerson, M. and Banfield, E.C. 1969: A Machine at Work, in: E.C. Banfield (ed.), *Urban Government*. New York: Free Press.

Michels, R. 1957 [1910]: *Zur Soziologie des Parteienwesens in der modernen Demokratie*. Stuttgart: Kröner.

Milward, A.S. 1981: Cyclical Fluctuations and Economic Growth in Developed Europe 1870-1913, in: D. Petzina and G. van Roon (eds.), *Konjunktur, Krise, Gesellschaft*. Stuttgart: Klett-Cotta.

Mingle, J.R. 1981: *Challenges of Retrenchment*. San Francisco: Jossey Bass.

Mitchell, B.R. 1975: *European Historical Statistics 1750-1970*. London: Macmillan.

Mitchell, B.R. and Jones, H.G. 1971: *Second Abstract of British Historical Statistics*. Cambridge: Cambridge University Press.

Mommsen, W. 1974: Max Weber als Kritiker des Marxismus. *Zeitschrift für Soziologie* 3: 256-278.

Moraw, F. 1987: *Das Gymnasium zwischen Anpassung und Selbstbehauptung - Zur Geschichte des Heidelberger Kurfürst-Friedrich-Gymnasiums 1932-1946*. Heidelberg: Carl Winter.

Mosca, G. 1950: *The Ruling Class*. London: Greenwood Press.

Moscati, R. 1983: *Università - Fine o trasformazione del mito?* Bologna: Il Mulino.

Müller, D.K. 1977: *Sozialstruktur und Schulsystem - Aspekte zum Strukturwandel des Schulwesens im 19. Jahrhundert*. Göttingen: Vandenhoeck & Ruprecht.

Müller, J. 1931: Allgemeine psychische Grundlagen des Geburtenrückganges und Möglichkeiten seiner Bekämpfung. *Jahrbücher für Nationalökonomie und Statistik* 134: 622-642.

Müller, M. 1931: *Das Berechtigungswesen und seine Bedeutung für den Arbeitsmarkt*. Jena: Böttner.

Musgrove, F. 1960: Middle-Class Education and Employment in the 19th Century. *The Economic History Review* 12: 99-111.

Namenwirth, Z. 1973: Wheels of Time and the Interdependence of Value Change in America. *Journal of Interdisciplinary History* 3: 649-683.

Nelson, D. 1980: *Frederick W. Taylor and the Rise of Scientific Management*. Madison: University of Wisconsin Press.

Nelson, M. 1982: A Short, Ironic History of American National Bureaucracy. *The Journal of Politics* 44: 747-778.

Pareto, V. 1983: *The Mind and Society. A Treatise on General Sociology*. New York: Harcourt, Brace & Co.

Parkin, F. 1974: Strategies of Social Closure in Class Formation, in: F. Parkin, *The Social Analysis of Class Structure*. London: Tavistock.

Passin, H. 1966: *Society and Education in Japan*. New York: Teachers' College,

Columbia University.

Peisert, H. et al. 1988: *Studiensituation und studentische Orientierungen an Universitäten und Fachhochschulen*. Bonn: Bock.

Perkin, H.J. 1961: Middle-Class Education and Employment in the 19th century. *The Economic History Review* 14: 122-130.

Picht, G. 1964: *Die deutsche Bildungskatastrophe*. Freiburg: Olten.

Preisser, R. 1989: *Soziale Herkunft und Studienfachwahl*. Berlin: Humboldt University.

Popper, K. 1972: *Objective Knowledge – An Evolutionary Approach*. Oxford: Clarendon.

Preller, L. 1949: *Sozialpolitik in der Weimarer Republik*. Stuttgart: Mittelbach.

Premfors, R.I. 1979: The Politics of Higher Education in Sweden - Recent Developments 1976-78. *European Journal of Education* 14: 81-106.

Riese, R. 1977: *Die Hochschule auf dem Wege zum wissenschaftlichen Grobbetrieb*. Stuttgart: Klett.

Riesman, D. 1979: *On Higher Education*. San Francisco: Jossey Bass.

Ringer, F.K. 1969: *The Decline of the German Mandarins - The German Academic Community 1890-1933*. Cambridge: Harvard University Press.

Röhl, J. 1967: Higher Civil Servants in Germany 1890-1900. *Contemporary History* 2: 101-128.

Rohlen, R.P. 1983: *Japan's High Schools*. Berkeley: University of California Press.

Rolff, H.G. 1980: *Sozialisation und Auslese durch die Schule*. Heidelberg: Quelle & Meyer.

Rosenberg, H. 1943: Political and Social Consequences of the Great Depression of 1873-1896 in Central Europe. *The Economic History Review* 13: 58-73.

_____. 1958: *Bureaucracy, Aristocracy, and Autocracy - The Prussian Experience 1660-1815*. Cambridge: Harvard University Press.

_____. 1967: *Grobe Depression und Bismarckzeit*. Berlin: de Gruyter.

Rosenbloom, D.H. 1984: Politics and Public Personnel Administration, in: D.H. Rosenbloom (ed.), Centenary Issues of the Pendleton Act of 1883. New York: Dekker.

Rosier, A. 1936: Contribution à l'étude du chômage intellectuel. *Journal de la société de statistique de Paris* 77: 267-325.

Ryan, A. 1972: Utilitarianism and Bureaucracy - The Views of J.S. Mill, in: G. Sutherland (ed.), *Studies in the Growth of 19th Century Government*. London: Routledge & Kegan Paul.

Sabouret, J.F. 1985: *L'Empire du concours - Lycéens et enseignants au Japon*. Paris: Autrement.

Sacks, H.S. (Hg.) 1978: *Hurdles - The Admissions Dilemma in American Higher Education*. New York: Atheneum.

Sadran, P. 1977: Recrutement et sélection par concours dans l'administration française. *Revue française d'administration publique* 1: 53-107.

Savas, E.S. and Ginsburg, S.G. 1973: The Civil Service - A Meritless System? *Public Interest* 32: 70-85.

Schairer, R. 1932: *Die akademische Berufsnot*. Jena: Diederichs.

Schattschneider, E.E. 1942: *Party Government*. New York: Rinehart.

Schelsky, H. 1959: *Schule und Erziehung in der industriellen Gesellschaft*. Würzburg: Werkbund.

Schluchter, W. 1979: *Rationalism, Religion and Domination – A Weberian Perspective*. Berkeley: University of California Press.

Schudson, M.S. 1972: Organizing the 'Meritocracy' - A History of the College Entrance Examination Board. *Harvard Educational Review* 42: 34-69.

Schumpeter, J. 1939: *Business Cycles, Vol. I-II*. New York: Mc Graw-Hill.

Schwartz, L. 1983: *Pour sauver l'université*. Paris: Seuil.

Schwarz, S. 1931: Die doppelte Reifeprüfung. *Erziehung* 6: 679-695

Shefter, M. 1977: Party and Patronage - Germany, England, and Italy. *Politics & Society* 7: 403-451.

Shinn, T. 1980: *L'école Polytechnique 1794-1914*. Paris: Presses de la fondation nationale des sciences politiques.

Skowronek, S. 1982: *Building a New American State - The Expansion of National Administrative Capacities 1877-1920*. Cambridge: Cambridge University Press.

Slutzky, E. 1937: The Summation of Random Causes as the Source of Cyclic Processes. *Econometrica* 5: 105-146.

Spaulding, R.M. 1967: *Imperial Japan's Higher Civil Service Examinations*. Princeton: Princeton University Press.

Spree, R. 1991: Lange Wellen wirtschaftlicher Entwicklung in der Neuzeit. *Historical Social Research* 4: 1-138.

Starr, P. 1982: *The Social Transformation of American Medicine*. New York: Basic Books.

Statistisches Bundesamt 1972: *Bevölkerung und Wirtschaft 1872-1972*. Stuttgart: Kohlhammer.

Stein, L. 1876: *Handbuch der Verwaltungslehre*. Stuttgart: Cotta.

Stone, L., Hg., 1974: *The University in Society, Vol. I*. Princeton: Princeton University Press.

Suleiman, E.N. 1978: *Elites in French Society*. Princeton: Princeton University Press.

Takashi, I. and Ikuo, K. 1984: The Status Quo Student Elite. *Japan Echo* 11: 27-34.

Takayoshi, M. 1966: Development of Democracy in Japan – Taisho Democracy, Its Flowering and Breakdown. *Developing Economies* 4: 610-645.

Teichler, U. 1974: Struktur des Hochschulwesens und 'Bedarf' an sozialer Ungleichheit. *Mitteilungen aus der Arbeitsmarkt- und Berufsforschung* 7: 197-209.

Titze, H. 1981: Überfüllungskrisen in akademischen Karrieren - Eine Zyklustheorie. *Zeitschrift für Pädagogik* 27: 187-261.

_____ . 1984: Die zyklische Überproduktion von Akademikern im 19. und 20. Jahrhundert. *Geschichte und Gesellschaft* 10: 92-121.

Titze, H. et al. 1985: Der Lehrerzyklus - Zur Wiederkehr von Überfüllung und Mangel im höheren Lehramt in Preußen. *Zeitschrift für Pädagogik* 31: 97-126.

Tocqueville, A. de 1951: *De la démocratie en Amérique*. Paris: Gallimard.

Trow, M. 1974: Problems in the Transition From Elite to Mass Higher Education, in: *Policies for Higher Education, General Report of the Conference on the Future Structure of Post-Secondary Education*. Paris: OECD.

_____ . 1979: Elite and Mass Higher Education, in: *Research Into Higher Education, Report From a Conference in June 1978*. Stockholm: National Board of Universities and Colleges.

_____ . 1988: American Higher Education - Past, Present, and Future. *Educational Research* 17: 13-23.

Turner, R. 1960: Sponsored and Contest Mobility and the School System. *American Sociological Review* 25: 855-867.

Tyack, D.B. 1974: *The One Best System - A History of American Urban Education*. Cambridge: Harvard University Press.

US-Department of Labor 1937: *Who Are the Job Seekers?* Washington: US-Government Printing Office.

Vaizey, J. 1962: *The Economics of Education*. London: Faber.

Voit, H. 1989: Allgemeinbildende Schulen 1987/88. *Wirtschaft und Statistik*, no. 3: 171-175.

Wallerstein, I. 1974: *The Modern World-System*. New York: Academic Press.

_____ . 1984: Long Waves as Capitalist Process. *Review* 7: 559-575.

Walters, P.B. 1984: Occupational and Labor Market Effects on Secondary and Postsecondary Educational Expansion in the United States 1922 to 1979. *American Sociological Review* 49: 659-671.

Weber, M. 1956: *Wirtschaft und Gesellschaft*. Tübingen: Mohr.

Weber, R. 1981: Society and Economy in the Western World. *Social Forces* 59: 1130-1148.

White, L.D. 1948: *Introduction to the Study of Public Administration*. New York 1948: Macmillan.

Windolf, P. 1988: Education as a Screening Device, in: P. Windolf et al., *Recruitment and Selection in the Labour Market*. Aldershot: Avebury, pp. 163-198.

_____ . 1992: Cycles of Expansion in Higher Education 1870-1985 – An International Comparison. *Higher Education* 23: 3-19.

_____ . 1995: Selection and Self-Selection at German Mass Universities. *Oxford Review of Eduction* 21: 207-231.

Windolf, P. and J. Haas 1993: Higher Education and the Business Cycle 1870-1990. *International Journal of Comparative Sociology* 34: 167-191.

Wolfinger, R.E. 1972: Why Political Machines Have not Withered Away and Other Revisionist Thoughts. *The Journal of Politics* 34: 363-398.

Wolfinger, R.E. and Field, J.O. 1966: Political Ethos and the Structure of City Government. *American Political Science Review* 60: 306-326.

Young, M. 1959: *The Rise of the Meritocracy 1870-2033*. New York: Random House.

Index

About the Book and Author

As a central institution that ensures equality of opportunity and social justice, the university is the most important channel of social mobility in modern societies. Over the past century, universities have assumed an important role in the political and cultural emancipation of women, minorities, and the lower socioeconomic classes. This expansion in educational institutions was not an isolated event in the years after World War II but rather a phase in a longer, secular process of modernization that started in the late nineteenth century and continues up to the present day.

Expansion and Structural Change explores this development, focusing on the social background of students and the institutional transformation of higher education in several countries. Who have been the beneficiaries of this remarkable process of educational expansion? Has it made Western society more open, mobile, and democratic? These questions are analyzed from a historical perspective that takes into account the institutional change of universities during this century.

Based on archival data for the United States, Germany, Japan, France, and Italy, this study combines both comparative and historical perspectives. It documents the political struggle of different social groups for access to universities as well as the meritocratic selection for higher status positions. This work will be an indispensable reference for anyone searching for a comparative analysis of higher education in the most advanced countries.

Paul Windolf is professor in the Department of Social Sciences at the University of Trier, Germany.